THANK YOU,
MR. PRESIDENT

THANK YOU, MR. PRESIDENT

A White House Notebook

By A. MERRIMAN SMITH

United Press White House Correspondent

HARPER & BROTHERS PUBLISHERS

NEW YORK AND LONDON

9–6

FIRST EDITION

H-V

Dedicated

to

THE WIDOW SMITH

TABLE OF CONTENTS

INTRODUCTION

I got the idea for this book in the pouring rain, in the Bronx and in the rear seat of an open car. President Roosevelt was in another car a bumper length away. And I was gripping a slippery Tommy gun, holding it for a Secret Service agent who was buttoning the top of his raincoat.

I heard him mutter to himself in a mocking voice:

"Oh, you men have such wonderful jobs. All you have to do is follow the President around, live in the best hotels and ride in the finest trains."

He reached for the gun and resumed his post in the center of the rear part of the car. He stared upward at open windows in search of potential villains who might harm the President.

The agent blew angrily at rain running down his nose and spoke again:

"To hell with it."

I thought to myself: Smith, some day you ought to tell the customers—those characters jumping up and down out there in the rain and screaming "Yea, Roosevelt"— just what a rat race this job can be. You spend half the year—war in, war out—away from your family. You miss meals and you see more of your Pullman porter than you do of your wife.

Most people do not realize how many men and women it takes to keep the President of the United States fed, clothed, housed, safe and operating. It takes Secret Service men who can shoot out your eye at fifty yards. It takes men who can write Old English script with the ease that I write a note to the milkman. It takes reporters, railroad men, doctors, lawyers, merchants and more secretaries than Ringling Brothers has clowns.

So, as a young, but rapidly aging White House correspondent, I thought someone might like to know what goes on around a President in the White House, in Poughkeepsie, Independence, Berlin, Hawaii and the seventh floor of the Utah Hotel in Salt Lake City.

THANK YOU,
MR. PRESIDENT

CHAPTER ONE

On Being a White House

Correspondent

THE most direct channel of communication, the most frequently used line between the President of the United States and the public is the White House correspondent.

Our Chief Executives do not always like the idea, but the American citizen has a direct property right in the Presidency. And it is the reporter assigned to the White House who keeps the people up to date on what and how their property is doing.

White House reporters know about as well as White House physicians what a man-killing job the Presidency can be. We saw Franklin D. Roosevelt die over a period of about a year. I saw him take a deep breath and fight successfully for a fourth term when he should have been sitting quietly on the banks of the Hudson River dawdling over his stamp collection and hoarding his last few months of life.

The newspaper and radio men who cover the White House see lots of things. This book is to tell some of the things that were overlooked in the big news of the day.

There are two varieties of White House reporters. The group I am writing about is small—no more than a dozen. They are assigned to the White House as a day-long, full-time job. They spend eight to ten hours a day in their own White House quarters and are classed practically as members of the White House family, although they are employed and paid by their individual news organizations.

The other group consists of the remaining bulk of the Washington news corps—the men and women who come to the White House usually on Presidential press conference days only, or when there is news breaking at 1600 Pennsylvania Avenue of world-shaking importance.

One never knows in this business, but at this writing I am the White House correspondent for the United Press, one of the three major press associations.

The United Press, the Associated Press and International News Service keep men at the White House each moment the President is working. Between these three organizations they serve directly or indirectly every daily newspaper and radio station on earth.

I was assigned to the White House in the fall of 1941 and was there through President Roosevelt's last term and on into the Truman administration. My boss, U.P. Washington bureau chief Lyle C. Wilson, thinks highly of my work, describing me this way: "Smith is the only man who has made a career of going on another man's vacations."

This has entailed land, air and sea travel of more than 125,000 miles since late 1941. Many's the time I've been tired, wet, hungry, sick or completely exhausted. But I wouldn't trade the experience for anything. There just is no other way to get a front seat at the making of history except to be President, and my mother didn't raise me to be one.

The White House reporters have an inner clique described as "the regulars." These are the men whose full-time job is reporting the activities of the President and they are on the job in close proximity to the Chief Executive regardless of whether he is in the White House or in Honolulu. They travel with him and serve as the eyes of the world, staring coldly at everything he does and telling all about it a few minutes later.

The "regulars" in normal times before the war consisted of the three press association reporters, and representatives of the New York, Chicago, Philadelphia and Washington papers. The reason more papers don't keep men on the White House at all times is money.

It takes a lot of it to keep a man on the White House assignment, completely aside from his salary. The expense of a full-time White House correspondent will run close to $10,000 over his salary during the course of a normal year.

My work day starts about nine in the morning when, normally missing breakfast at home and nearly missing the eight-thirty bus, I join two other wire service reporters in the press room of the White House and complain about the night before. We send out for coffee and bemoan our fate. The reporters who work for single newspapers rarely show up until shortly before the regular ten-thirty conference with the President's press secretary.

I hate coffee, but saddled with two coffee-drinking colleagues, I have little choice. About nine-thirty the Presi-

dent starts doing business, after his nine o'clock conference with his staff. A pretty redhead from the press secretary's office comes out and pins to our battered press
room bulletin board the schedule of the President's en-
gagements for the day.

Mr. Roosevelt used to have only five or six callers in
a morning, but from fifteen to twenty is average for Mr.
Truman.

(Incidentally, no other human being in the world is
called "Mr." on the wires of the press associations except
the President.)

We pick up our private line telephones which connect
us directly with our three offices and ask for dictation.
A young thing on the other end of my wire puts on head-
phones and sits down to a typewriter. I say, "Dateline,
please." She taps out "Washington, July 20.—(UP)—"
and then I hear a click in my receiver which signals me
that she is keeping up with my rate of dictation.

"Nine-thirty dash Senator Blank paragraph."

Then I hear her click again and continue dictating
until I have finished the entire list which on a run-of-the-
mine day will include a couple of ambassadors, a Cabinet
member, several members of Congress and assorted hand-
shakers and people with a cause.

Then I hustle out of the press room into the huge
lobby of the White House executive offices to nab the
President's callers as they leave him.

The Senator, the first caller, is in with "the old man"
as all presidents are referred to around the White House,
and we know pretty well that the Senator is not going to
talk. From our own reporters on Capitol Hill we have
been tipped that the Senator is striving for the appoint-

ment of one of his constituents as a Federal judge, but has been making little progress.

The Senator comes out and Jackson, the Negro door-man who has been handing hats to Presidential callers for many Presidents, steps up with a smile and hands the Senator his Stetson. We—the three wire service men have by this time been joined by several other reporters —catch the Senator as he nears the exit of the lobby.

"Well, Senator, what's on your mind today—what did you take up with the President?"

"Oh, nothing important," the Senator says, looking intently at his hatband as though it needed repairing.

"What about that judgeship?"

"Oh, I don't know. It may have come up in passing, but that is not what brought me to the White House. I came on another matter. Just routine."

A late arrival, a reporter who has a paper in the Senator's state, comes up.

"Say, Senator, what about that judgeship—think you'll get it?"

The Senator then goes through his routine again, about coming to the White House on a different "routine matter" and the judgeship was mentioned only "in passing."

"Did you talk any politics?"

"Me?" says the Senator in mock amazement. "I'm much too busy to think about politics. You boys know that."

The reporters grin and one says, "Well, thank you just the same."

"Thanks, boys, maybe I'll have something next time," and the Senator goes to the door of the lobby where a White House policeman calls to his chauffeur, "Senator

Blank's car." And the Senator goes back to Capitol Hill and telephones his friends that the President still is keeping his mind open about the judgeship, but maybe a little more pressure on the White House from the governor would help.

One reporter says, "That's normal for him—zero."

The next caller is an ambassador who claims he came to the White House "just to pay my respects."

The White House reporters have three classifications for callers who produce only a paragraph or two of news —"PR's, CC's and OF's." These mean "pay respects, courtesy call and old friend."

So it goes through the day. The press secretary sees reporters and gives them the documents the President has signed overnight—bills passed by Congress, executive orders and some of his correspondence. Then the reporters go back to the callers. Occasionally during the day, a caller will make news. A labor leader will come out and lambaste the Administration's wage policy. A Republican will say something nice about a Democrat. And generals and admirals just back from far-off lands will report on their experiences.

During the war, one White House reporter—William H. Lawrence of the New York *Times*, and later a war correspondent—found a delightful way to pinion White House visitors who tried to give the correspondents a polite brush-off. It was not long after Pearl Harbor and President Roosevelt was anxious to avoid anything that showed his part in patently political activity. He wanted the public to see him solely as the leader of a united war effort.

A prominent Democratic Senator came to the White

House to talk over a knotty party problem, and on leaving told reporters, "Fellows, it was just a social call."

"Do you mean, Senator," Lawrence asked him, "that with the world going to hell and the President devoting all of his time to running the war, you came in here and took up forty-five minutes of his time just for a social call?"

The Senator spluttered, smiled wanly and walked out. The next time he came to see the President on politics, he described his visit as "routine business."

The President finishes seeing his callers usually by one o'clock when he goes to lunch, walking from his west wing office to eat with his family or guests in the dining room of the White House. He devotes most of the afternoon to paper work. On Friday the Cabinet meets in the long, narrow room overlooking the White House rose gardens.

During the afternoon the White House may release for publication any number of developments which reached the announceable stage during the morning's business. These are brought to the reporters in the press room who have spent the hour after lunch jockeying for the room's only couch—and a nap. The losers try to act like they did not want a nap anyway and studiously read their newspapers.

Probably in no press room in the world do reporters read as many papers as in the White House. By lunch time every day, I usually have read, some sketchily, some in detail, at least the Washington *Post*, the Washington *Times-Herald*, the New York *Times*, the New York *Herald Tribune* and the Baltimore *Sun*. Most of my colleagues have done the same. And after lunch they read the Washington *Star*, the afternoon edition of the *Times-Herald* and the Washington *Daily News*, plus what other papers have come into the press room during the day.

On an average day, the White House closes shop by 6 P.M. or a little after. Negro messengers pass the word from office to office, "He's gone over." Which means the President has left his office and gone to his residential quarters in the White House proper. This word is the signal for most everybody to start for home. The final word to the reporters comes when a press attaché advises "the lid is on."

There is, however, nothing tight about the "lid" at the White House. It can pop off at the most inopportune moments. At two or three in the morning. Or fifteen minutes after you have assured your office that everything is locked up, so it is quite safe for you to go to a cocktail party. When there is hot news, the White House usually puts it out right away. That is, within fifteen or twenty minutes after the news agency and other major radio and newspaper offices have been advised that something big is on its way.

Being a White House correspondent for a wire service is rather like being a doctor when it comes to telephone calls in the middle of the night or hurried trips to town.

Newspaper editors the world over seemingly cherish the idea that when information is unavailable on any given subject at any other source, that puts it up to the White House. These inquiries teletyped from various parts of the nation into our Washington office are telephoned to me and I'm supposed to do something about it.

I only wish some night telegraph editor in Metropolis, U.S.A., who suddenly wonders whether his town is going to get a new sewage disposal plant, could suffer the pleasure of rousing a White House press secretary out of bed at two in the morning with such an inquiry.

Steve Early, Mr. Roosevelt's press secretary, had the early morning or midnight temper of a mountain lion freshly trapped by only one leg. Charlie Ross, Mr. Truman's press officer, hasn't had the job as long as Early held his post, so he still is rather mild about these things. I, however, have great hopes for Charlie and expect him any night to tell me take my query and you know what.

The press secretary usually is protected by an unlisted telephone and can be contacted after hours only through the motherly White House switchboard, the operators of which have no more yen for a bawling out than I do. This means that the press secretary's chief assistant catches most of the midnight hell. Their telephones are always listed.

William D. Hassett was assistant to Early, but under Mr. Truman he is a full-fledged secretary and doesn't bother with such things as night calls from reporters. I called Hassett, when he was doing the press job, one morning about two o'clock. The temperature was in the high twenties.

Hassett answered with a very sharp hello.

"Bill, this is Smitty and I hate like everything to get you out of bed, but the office wants to know . . ."

"Smith," roared Hassett, "I have no slippers on and my feet are cold and you can . . ."

"Wait a minute, Bill, I don't have on any slippers either."

"Well, that doesn't warm me any. I hope you freeze.

Give me your damned query so I can say no and go back to bed."

"The New York *Times* is carrying a piece saying the President and Mrs. Roosevelt are going to Paris . . ."

"Well, if they are," barked Hassett, who, incidentally, is one of the most lovable guys I've ever met on any assignment, "they have not taken me into their confidence and I have no intention of calling the President at this hour and being as unkind as you are to me. GOOD NIGHT."

The net result of this conversation was a message to our New York office from the Washington bureau: WHU (White House) UNCOMMENTING TIMES PARIS ROOSEVELT. SMITH PERSONALLY THINKS TRIP UNLIKELY.

The White House itself is a wonderful thing. It has everything in it from a movie theater to a massage parlor.

The press room, where I spend most of my waking hours, is a large room with ceiling-high windows on two sides. The first thing that impresses a newcomer is the incredible number of telephones. I think there were forty at the last count in a room about eighteen by forty feet. There are about ten desks jammed against each other around the room, and a line of private telephone booths for the wire services.

When all the telephones ring at the same time it sounds like a concert by a swarm of drunken Swiss bell ringers. Each telephone has a different tone and the telephone installation men say they are at the end of their rope in this different-tone business. They say the only new twist will be blinking lights and they already have those over two of the booths.

The White House staff leaves us pretty much alone and the press room is an unsacred oasis in a desert of formality. The reporters for several years have chipped in to have a Man Friday around the place. His name is William Davis. We got him from Western Union, and while he hated getting out of uniform, I believe Davis is a completely happy man. He takes three hours off for lunch which we suspect he eats in some faraway flossy joint like the Wardman Park Hotel.

Davis' principal duty is to haul copies of White House statements and documents to our respective offices. But he has other sidelines. He is our direct contact with the grog shops. If there is some festive occasion—and it is remarkably easy to proclaim most any dull afternoon a festive occasion—Davis is dispatched in search of a bottle. Although he drinks himself in off hours, he is not what one would call an excellent judge of whisky.

The nearest Davis ever came to actual physical harm was one afternoon after a particularly tough Presidential press conference. The gang was pooped out and decided something liquid was in order. It was so hot that whisky was ruled out and Davis was told to go get some Ballantine ale. One of the boys flipped a ten-dollar bill at him, saying we could square up when Davis got back with the ale.

Davis was gone a long time, but finally walked in with a beaming light of pride in his eyes. Under his arm was a comparatively small bundle which he reverently placed before the owner of the ten spot. He handed the reporter sixty-three cents in change.

"My God, Davis," the man exclaimed, "how much ale did you buy to cost nine dollars and thirty-seven cents. And where is it?"

Davis smirked and handed the package over. It was a bottle of eighteen-year-old Ballantine Scotch.

Lawrence of the *Times*, however, came up the next afternoon with a bright idea. He said he would remake the Scotch investment, and literally drink for nothing.

Lawrence bought a gallon thermos jug, a large carton of finely shaved ice, club soda, very small paper cups and a bottle of cheap Scotch. He mixed the liquor, soda and ice together in the jug and put up a sign before it: ALL THE SCOTCH AND SODA YOU CAN DRINK FOR 50 CENTS.

The mixture was so cold that it was almost impossible to drink it. But the unbelieving press rallied around and tried to beat Lawrence's game. The temperature outside was about 98. Two cups of Lawrence's mixture and a walk of about a block in the sun made the imbiber feel like he'd polished off a bottle alone. Everybody was highly satisfied and the word spread. Before long, most of the correspondents from the State Department had joined the party and by late afternoon Lawrence had made back his investment, still had some dregs in the jug and about three dollars to boot.

The White House, however, took a rather conservatively dim view of our business enterprise and it died aborning. We still have the jug in a file cabinet, but it is getting a little rusty around the top.

I'm probably cutting my throat telling tales like these because my office will get the idea that I am a pot and the White House will think I'm trying to give the political opposition ammunition for the next election. But after all, it is our business and the customer doesn't suffer.

Other things about which the public hears little, purely because they don't figure in the news, are the theater, the swimming pool and the doctor's office. The theater is on the ground floor of the east wing of the White House and can seat better than a hundred, although only a fraction of that number usually attends.

Mr. Roosevelt liked movies and they were shown several times a week at the White House. Mr. Truman, however, isn't as much of a movie fan and prefers to spend his evening hours talking with friends or reading history books. The theater is fitted with comfortable armchairs that would do honor to anyone's living room. The screen slides in and out of a huge room-high panel.

Mr. Roosevelt had two favorite spots in the White House—his large, book-lined study where he spent many evening hours over his stamp collection, ship models and navy prints, and the swimming pool.

The pool was a gift to the President from the school children of the nation. It is a long, narrow pool and the water is kept at a temperature which permits year-round swimming. Mr. Roosevelt made up for his inability to walk when he was swimming. He loved to cavort in the pool with his husky sons and had no hesitation in ducking unsuspecting friends. He had the arms, shoulders and chest of a weight lifter.

(Once in Warm Springs, the President was sitting on the side of his bed joking with two of his boys, Elliott and James. Each must have weighed at that time about 175 pounds. They were arguing in loud voices and to still the dispute, the President grabbed each by his belt and rolled back on the bed. With one son in each hand, he flipped them clear across the bed and onto the floor on the other side. And this by a man whose legs were about as thick as the average man's wrist.)

Mr. Truman also uses the swimming pool a great deal.

The current President is an active man and, being President, he can't take the long walks through the city and parks that he enjoyed as a Senator. So he works out in the pool almost every night.

The medical offices are quite elaborate with a rubbing table, dental chair, and radio therapy machine and a sun-lamp that is so elaborate and forceful that you can get a noticeable tan in twenty seconds.

President Roosevelt used to stop by frequently for a quick checkup—almost daily during the sinus season. But Mr. Truman, hardy as a mule from his home state of Missouri, has had little opportunity to use this minia-ture hospital which is at his disposal twenty-four hours a day.

The White House clinic is available to White House employees for such minor aids as nose drops and cough syrup. They have a dandy cough syrup made by the Navy that tastes for all the world like Cointreau and if taken in sufficient quantities, probably would have the same effect.

CHAPTER TWO

Questions and Sometimes Answers

ONE of the most singularly American events at the White House each week is the President's press conference. These meetings between reporters and the Chief Executive have all the qualities of a high school track meet, bear baiting and the third degree administered by heavy-handed plain-clothes men.

Mr. Roosevelt lectured the reporters. He called them liars and used the mighty weight of his high office in pile-driving fashion against the press. Mr. Truman tries to keep everybody happy. His conferences are fast, produce a lot of news and make the reporters wish they had studied shorthand.

Mr. Truman uses virtually the same press conference mechanics as employed by his late predecessor. So, a general description of how they operate will cover both administrations.

The conferences are held in the President's circular office, the reporters standing and filling the room wall to wall. There are no holds barred as far as questions are concerned. The President's answers may not be quoted directly without specific permission from the President. And this permission is given only infrequently for part of a sentence, or just a few words.

When the President speaks for "background only," what he says may be printed or broadcast, but not attributed to him. This is a troublesome classification and few ever understand it clearly. Consequently, it is rarely employed.

"Off the record" means that the President is speaking confidentially and his words must not be publicized in any way. For the most part, what the President says off-record isn't very important. Usually he is explaining why he can't answer a certain question, or he is telling about advance plans which for some reason he wants withheld from publication for the present.

Reporters gather in the White House lobby fifteen to thirty minutes before the conference to discuss the news probabilities of the day. At the appointed time, they file into the President's office, showing their passes to watchful Secret Service men and White House police as they enter.

The front row along the President's desk usually is occupied by the working regulars—the men who will do most of the questioning—and most of the writing. They represent the wire services, metropolitan newspapers and the radio networks. There are no assigned places, but rather an understanding by the correspondents that the men who will have to do most of the work should have the best working space.

The conference begins when either Harold Beckley of the Senate press gallery, or Bill Donaldson of the House gallery, shouts "all in" from the rear of the room.

The President makes what formal announcements he has prepared, then says, "That's about all I have today." Then comes the most heard-about part of the conference —the questioning.

Some Presidents in the past, notably Hoover, required written questions to be submitted in advance. There was no questioning from the floor. And in this manner, if a President wished to dodge an embarrassing question, he just ignored it.

But such was not the case with Mr. Roosevelt who really built the press conference into the popular government instrument that it is today. Nor is it the case with Mr. Truman who'll field any ball thrown at him, curve or otherwise.

The reporters can question the President as long as they please. It is their decision when the conference shall end. The questioning actually closes and the meeting is over when the senior wire service man on the White House assignment decides that the reporters have exhausted the news possibilities for that day and says, "Thank you, Mr. President."

The wire service men and some of the radio representatives then break into a mad, scrambling dash to get out of the President's office, through the office of his appointment secretary, then the big lobby and into the press room where wait the hungry telephones.

Newcomers find this reckless race hard to justify. New men assigned to the White House invariably say, "Why can't we take just a little more time to look over our notes and get our facts straight?"

Truth of the matter is that a reporter who has to handle a Presidential news conference on a spot, immediate basis has to keep his notes straight in his mind and get his facts straight in the twenty or thirty seconds he spends getting to his telephone.

When there is a red-hot story in the conference, the

wire service men usually are dictating to their offices well within thirty seconds after the "thank you."

Their haste to reach telephones often produces tragic, painful results.

The day that Mr. Roosevelt ordered the doors of his office locked while he told reporters he would run for a fourth term, there was in the conference a public relations man for the Civil Aeronautics Board.

The man was standing to the back and to the right of me. I noticed that he was in a direct line between the wire service reporters and the door out of which we would burst. As the conference progressed—the President was reading a letter which we would get in mimeographed form—I leaned back and whispered to the C.A.B. man to get out of the way. He was crippled and walked on two canes and I didn't want to see him hurt.

The President finished reading.

"You've got your news, now go on and get out," he barked.

"Thank you, Mr. President," I shouted, pivoting at the same time and heading for the door.

The crowd was massed around us. Since I was first in line, I lowered my head and drove, fullback style, until I reached the door. I passed the C.A.B. man all right, but heard a commotion back of me as Doug Cornell of the A.P. and Bob Nixon of I.N.S. followed through the crowd. Other reporters were starting for exits.

I finally rammed my way to the door, threw it open and started running. The sprint from the President's office to the press room entails a wide swing in the lobby around a huge, circular Philippine mahogany table. Reporters with leather heels sometimes lose traction

going around this table, and smash into the columns at
the end of the lobby. I once saw a reporter skid on out
into the White House driveway when he failed to make
the turn into the press room.

As I swung around the table that July day, I was pray-
ing that I would not slip as I turned into the press room.
I made it, however, with about an inch to spare and hit
my telephone booth squarely in the middle.

The story itself was simple to handle. It was just the
plain fact that Mr. Roosevelt would run again—if asked
—and he knew darned well he would be asked.

When we finished our dictation, the men stood around
in front of their booths and joked about the scrimmage
in getting out of the President's office.

While we were talking, Bill Simmons, the towering
receptionist for the President's office, stalked into the
press room to inform us that the centrifugal force of
our departure from the President's room had spun the
poor C.A.B. man like a celluloid windmill in a strong
wind.

As he started to spin, he groped for support with his
canes. As about the third wave sped by him, the struggle
was too much for him and he crashed to the floor.

Mr. Roosevelt was popeyed with amazement when the
crowd cleared. Flat on the floor in front of the gadget-
littered Presidential desk was a figure looking for all the
world like a corpse. Staff members quickly helped the
public relations man to his feet. We never saw him around
a conference after that.

When Mr. Truman took office there followed a series
of explosively important press conferences. He was setting up a new administration and each conference had

several new, big-name appointments. The war was not over, the U.N. was in the uncertain stages of establishment and there was a Big Three meeting coming up.

At one conference when the President announced several Cabinet appointments, Harold Oliver of A.P. suffered a painful ankle injury in the stampede to get out of the President's office. Harold is small of stature, and some beefy individual telephone-bound didn't let a small thing like an ankle impede his progress.

Then came VE-Day and I got mine.

As we ripped out of the President's office with the first official news of Germany's surrender, a photographer on a ladder at the door began to fall. Rather than fall onto several reporters he gave the ladder a kick and hopped into an empty chair.

The ladder skidded in front of me and I tripped, bouncing several feet into the air and landing on my left shoulder. I heard it pop when I hit the floor, but scrambled to my feet and made it to the telephone booth.

I dictated for about an hour and then told the U.P. desk I thought I had a broken arm or something vitally wrong. I could not hold anything in my left hand. I hurt plenty.

When I walked out of the booth I toppled over on the press room couch and was later hauled away to the hospital where I spent several days having a shoulder relocated.

The hospital was crowded. They put me in a room with someone else. When I came out of the anesthesia sufficiently to sample some of the whisky which understanding, or rather misunderstanding, friends in the press room sent me to ease my pain, I offered a drink to my roommate.

He was a trifle shy, particularly since most of his ribs were broken. I introduced myself and he said bashfully, "My name is Harry L. Hopkins."

I put down the bottle and called the nurse.

"Look," I said to her. "I've gone completely goofball or else that shot you gave me is lingering too long. The guy over there is trying to tell me he's Harry Hopkins. I know Hopkins and I know the man in that bed just is not . . ."

"Lie down, Mr. Smith," she said snippily. "That *is* Mr. Hopkins. After all, can't there be more than one?"

The boys in the press room rallied round my bed during the first afternoon in the hospital and as each new addition to the group came in, I gravely introduced Harry L. Hopkins.

Jack Doherty of the New York *News* came in with a funeral wreath of some slightly dead and colorless leaves. I presented him to Hopkins.

"Oh, sure," said Doherty, "and I'm Sidney Hillman —Where the hell is Frankfurter?"

This sort of thing went on for two days and Mr. Hopkins left the hospital quite hacked and considering changing his name to Poindexter.

Bob Nixon of I.N.S. was the next press room casualty. During the hectic days leading up to VJ-Day, he was pushed from behind coming out of a doorway, ripped the knees out of some new trousers and broke his glasses.

And there was the girl reporter who carelessly let her shapely instep get in the way of the Chicago *Sun's* 240-pound Tom Reynolds. Running fast, he did not know he had stepped on her foot until she came back to work two days later.

No President was ever feared so much in a press conference as Mr. Roosevelt. He could be as rough and tough as a Third Avenue blackjack artist. And he could be utterly charming, disarming and thoroughly likeable. It just depended on the question, who asked it and how Mr. Roosevelt felt when he got up that morning.

The fear was understandable. It plainly is not a pleasant experience to be taken to task, publicly and face-to-face, by any President of the country.

A reporter cannot argue back unless he is a columnist or editorial writer, and even then it cannot be done in the President's office, but only in print.

There were repeated attempts to argue with Mr. Roosevelt in a press conference, but there never was a clear-cut victory for the reporter.

Jim Wright, the veteran correspondent for the Buffalo *Evening News,* once won a draw with Mr. Roosevelt who had been hypercritical of some people—mostly newspaper bosses—who were attempting, as he put it, to hamstring the Administration's conduct of the war.

Wright—not one of those in the President's mind—interjected that he wanted to know who these people were.

"Oh, Jim," said the President rather disgustedly, "of course you know who they are."

"No, I don't, Mr. President," Wright answered firmly.

"Sure you do," Mr. Roosevelt came back.

"No sir, I honestly don't know and I'd like to know," Wright persisted.

The President's face colored and his half-smile faded into a set, stern expression.

"You know, and everybody in this room knows whom I'm talking about," the President said sharply.

And that ended the matter. There was no mistaking the finality in the President's tone.

The quarrelsome manner in which Mr. Roosevelt dealt with many newspapermen and broadcasters in his latter days should not necessarily outweigh the manner in which he championed reporters during his early days in the White House.

The honeymoon, of course, prevailed during the first part of the New Deal. The newspapers loved him. They began to change their minds—some of them—in 1936. More of them changed in 1940, and there weren't many more to change over in 1944.

Publicly, Mr. Roosevelt forgave the working reporters because they knew not what they did. He claimed repeatedly that the reporters "slanted" stories only on orders from their rich, greedy bosses. To hazard a percentage, Mr. Roosevelt was wrong more than 90 per cent about story slanting.

He once accused me of asking a question on orders from some mystic power above me. In fact he told a press conference he *knew* that I did not want to ask the question. I liked Mr. Roosevelt very much. I think he was a great man. But in this particular instance he manufactured a false story purely to suit his purposes, to dodge an issue.

It happened during an aboard-train press conference coming back from the west coast in 1944. The President had just come from Hawaii and there had been considerable editorial speculation that, just after accepting his fourth term nomination, he had flown to Pearl Harbor to see General MacArthur and Admiral Nimitz purely to emphasize his role as wartime Commander-in-Chief—for the benefit of the voters.

Near the end of the conference, I said:

"Mr. President, are you aware of the fact that a number of newspapers—and some politicians, too—are inferring that this trip had political motives?"

The President laughed and shrugged his shoulders.

"Then they know more about it than I do. There was no politics in it. You were there. You saw what I did."

I forgot about it except to include a brief paragraph far down in my story of the conference.

The first full dress conference he held after the trip, the question was raised with him again, but by another reporter.

I don't have his exact words, but the sense was this:

"A young man whom we all know (and he nodded toward me) asked me that same thing the other day. Now, he knew better. He knew the answer. But he had to ask the question. He had received orders from his big bosses to ask such a question. He's a fine young man and I respect him. I know he did not want to ask such a question, So I don't blame him. He was on the same spot with a lot of other reporters. Very often they have to take orders and do things they know are not right."

I started to speak up, but realization of the futility of an argument stopped me. If the President had done what he had admonished so many other people to do—to think things through—he never would have said what he did.

Certainly, the President must have known that I had not been in direct contact with any of my superiors for over five weeks—even since before he accepted the nomination. The President was the person who ordered us blacked out on communications.

And not to my knowledge have I ever been "ordered" to ask a question or slant a story by any newspaper boss in my life, from the United Press on down to the Athens (Georgia) *Daily Times*. The first time a boss says, "Here, let's do a job on this guy regardless of the facts," then I go back to my old job as night clerk of the Pulaski House in Savannah, Georgia.

As soon as that particular press conference was over, I went to Early.

"Steve," I said, "I didn't want to argue with the President, but will you please tell him he was wrong—that no wire service man is given orders on how to slant questions or stories."

Steve agreed a bit woefully and suggested I tell it to the President myself at the next opportunity. And I did that, on the next trip to Hyde Park.

But all that bluff old Mr. Roosevelt did was chuckle and say he understood.

The longer Mr. Roosevelt lived, the less productive became his news conferences. He became listless and poor of voice. He reached the point when he lost enthusiasm for denouncing certain irritant correspondents as liars. He, however, became increasingly quarrelsome about petty things. Reporters in the back of his office began to have difficulty in hearing his once rich and powerful voice.

He began canceling press conferences for one minor reason or another, remaining sometimes in Hyde Park during his fixed conference days on Friday (morning conference) and Tuesday (afternoon). At the time he died he had not had a full-fledged press conference in more than a month.

When Mr. Truman took over at the broad desk in the

circular office with green-tinted walls, it was like a breath
of fresh air. Coming after a series of nonproductive conferences held by a weakening and war-worried President,
Mr. Truman created an immediately and highly favor-
able impression.

For one thing, he had a lot of new domestic news which
Mr. Roosevelt did not have in his latter days. Mr. Roosevelt could not talk freely about the war, naturally, and
his administration was relatively set.

Mr. Truman, however, came in with a big broom and
began sweeping. The war news, as far as the White House
reporters were concerned, paled temporarily in the light
of new Cabinet members, new policies and in the final
analysis, a new personality.

Where battlewise Mr. Roosevelt had said, "No comment" or "I don't have anything on that today," Mr.
Truman came up with yes-or-no answers. And this was
something Mr. Truman later regretted. He changed his
press conference policy and has now learned how to say
"No comment."

Snap judgment is a wonderful thing when right. But
when it is wrong, it is like the little girl with the curl
in the middle of her forehead—"horrid."

Mr. Truman speaks at press conferences at terrific
speed. The wire service reporters who allegedly catch
every question and every answer—all in longhand, written in stiff-backed notebooks filched from the White
House supply room—come out of his conferences sweating and worried that they may have missed something.

Working, as their saying goes, under the gun, the press
association men have over their heads the constant sword
of misquotation, misinterpretation. Misquoting the

President can boom or depress the stock market during a morning conference.

To get an idea of how difficult the job can be, get a notebook and sit down with five friends during an animated conversation. Try to get on paper every word they say, then leap to a telephone and dictate a sensible account of the conversation.

Tony Vacarro of A.P., an old friend of Mr. Truman's, has made one effort after another to get the President to slow down in his press conference diction.

"Gonna take it slow today?" is Tony's invariable greeting to the President on press conference day. And to date, he has gotten nowhere. Mr. Truman just likes to talk fast, and this speed has tripped him on occasion, making it necessary for the press secretary's office to announce later that the President "misunderstood" a question.

A lot of us have talked with Mr. Truman about taking it just a little easier at press conferences. And he always promises.

But then he gets enthusiastic about a subject thrown at him from the back of the room, and off we go to the races.

My notes after a Truman press conference read like this (my translation is included free of charge):

NOTES: T bg 3 unin imd psct alwys gld c nybdy wa.

TRANSLATION: President Truman told a news conference that no meeting of the Big Three is in immediate prospect, asserting that when another meeting is held it will be in Washington.

QUESTION: Mr. President, have you recalled General Marshall from China?

NOTES: M askt hmwrd rpt but gg bck.

TRANSLATION: President Truman announced today that he requested General George C. Marshall, his special envoy to China, to return to Washington for a report on his mission.

The President emphasized, however, that Marshall would return to China in his same capacity—personal representative of the President with the personal rank of ambassador.

It was possible to make more complete notes with President Roosevelt. He spoke slower than Mr. Truman and his enunciation at most times was much better.

Because I'm a rather sloppy penman, my notes grow cold in a hurry. I couldn't for the life of me read notes on a Truman conference a year later. But before me now is a Roosevelt notebook dated March 17, 1944.

NOTES: tnk be gud tng sy smtg re ILO NA 20 Apl—34 cntrs—vry impt mtg bcs undbtly whn we cme to devise (mind you, a word spelled out) UNs org, ILO will be ind but afltd cum new org of UNs.

That wasn't the lead story of the day, but the notes rough out this way:

I think it would be a good thing to say something today about the meeting of the International Labor Organization in Philadelphia on the twentieth of April. Thirty-four countries will be represented. It will be a very important meeting because when we come to devise the United Nations Organization, the I.L.O. will be independent, but affiliated with the new organization of the United Nations.

Wire service reporters are constantly asked why they don't take up shorthand since they are supposed to record each question and answer. The answer is: Have you ever seen a stenographer who could dictate rapidly from her shorthand book? Shorthand is a continuous process. One line depends on another. But longhand notes are independent. Most reporters of a vintage earlier than the thirties make liberal use of a rather bastard version of the Phillips code—the old Morse operator's system of reducing words to little more than the consonants.

The next President—the Republicans and Democrats have different ideas about who he will be or when he will come along—will find it extremely difficult to discard the press conference system. There's no parliament in this country, and the Congress never has an opportunity to question the head of state publicly.

Thus the job is left up to a lot of reporters who take their job seriously—much too seriously on occasion.

Mr. Roosevelt really made the Presidential press conference what it is today—a third degree in white-hot light.

(Uniformly, the White House reporters exercise good taste. They have innumerable chances to trap a President in the political morass of incongruity. But they never do it to his face.)

Mr. Truman wisely elected to go along with the Roosevelt plan. The reading public, the editors and the reporters like the idea.

But should there come some day to the White House a President who thinks he can drop press conferences—well, he's President and he can do pretty much what he wants. But what a skull beating he's in for! His honeymoon will last exactly up to the time he says "No press conference," or "Please submit written questions."

CHAPTER THREE

Road Work

THE average White House correspondent, after a few years or even months on the job, gets spoiled when it comes to travel. He reaches the point where he will ride in nothing but a drawing room. And a hotel without air conditioning is horrible privation.

At least that was the case until Mr. Truman came along. He seems to make a speciality of visiting small towns where the hotels have no elevators and the bellhops can remember four wars.

Even so, the most luxurious newspaper life today is that lived by a working reporter on the road with a President. It is expensive, but necessarily so, as far as the reporters are concerned. As far as physical accommodations are concerned, they live pretty much on the same level with the President.

This is necessary because the reporters are members of the President's party. They usually live in the same hotel with him, ride the same train and move in the same automobile processions.

Reporters, however, do not share the President's special plane, *The Sacred Cow*, because of obvious space limitations. They travel in a separate plane provided by the Army or chartered from a commercial airline. Even when flying with the Army the White House correspondents pay the equivalent of commercial airline rates.

Traveling with Mr. Roosevelt was an experience in leisurely luxury. He was rarely in a hurry to get anywhere and made his trips—except during campaign years —by easy stages.

Traveling with Mr. Truman is like being on the road with a high school basketball team and a coach who lets the players have their fun.

Mr. Roosevelt loved the splendid. Mr. Truman likes little towns and small talk in the lobby of a small hotel which, if not cleared out by Secret Service agents, would be populated by shoe salesmen and hardware drummers.

The three basic modes of Presidential travel are train, plane and ship. Mr. Roosevelt used the plane only on out-of-country trips. Mr. Truman uses it for most everything, relishing the idea of fast movement.

The Train

The special Presidential train usually consists of from eight to eleven cars. The most important one on the train is the President's private car, custom-built job and always the last on the train.

This car was completed early in the war for President Roosevelt by the American Association of Railroads. The under part of the car is heavily shielded with steel to make it bottom-heavy in the event an assassin tries to bomb the train. The heavy weight would make the car sit down, rather than turn over.

The windows are three inches thick and can stop a .50 caliber machine-gun slug at point-blank range. The windows, because of their thickness, are tinted a slight green which has the same effect as a color filter on a camera. The countryside can be seen through the windows in true color values regardless of glare or reflection.

Extra heavy doors with complicated double locks are at each end of the car. Included in the equipment of "the private," as the car is called, are double galleys for the preparation of food, a dining room large enough for twelve, five staterooms and a comfortable living room. The President's stateroom has a bathroom complete with shower, lavatory and toilet.

The car is not rampantly luxurious, but furnished in subdued taste. The walls are paneled in limed oak and there is dull green carpeting on the floor. The living room has a large sofa and several overstuffed chairs.

Next to the President's car is a compartment car for ranking staff members, and then next in line is the diner. The President has all his meals in "the private." His galleys are used only to fix coffee and late night snacks, most of his food coming from the diner kitchen.

The remainder of the train consists of compartment cars for Secret Service agents and clerical workers, and the cars provided for the newspaper, radio and photographic corps usually are what the railroad people call "six and threes"—six compartments and three drawing rooms. The drawing rooms are assigned on a basis of seniority on the White House assignment.

A wartime innovation on the Presidential train, and now a fixed piece of equipment, is the miraculous radio car developed by the Army Signal Corps under the immediate direction of Lieutenant Colonel Dewitt Greer, who is in charge of the special Signal Corps White House unit.

Whether rolling or not, the radio car maintains constant communication with the White House through short wave and radio teletype. Thus the President always has at his command instantaneous communication facilities with every other world capital.

With the exception of "the private" and the radio car, the rolling stock usually is in regular commercial service when not being used by the President. The railroads, however, always have some of the compartment cars available in the Washington area in the event of a hurry call from the White House.

A sudden railroad trip is extremely rare. These trips usually are planned weeks ahead with operational plans worked out in advance and in pinpoint detail.

The Plane

The Sacred Cow came into being during Mr. Roosevelt's war years and was first used in his transatlantic trips to Big Three meetings. Because of Secret Service objections and his own aversion to flying, Mr. Roosevelt never used the plane in this country.

Mr. Truman, however, liked the idea of the *Cow* and began using it frequently. His first major swing through the country after becoming President was in the plane.

From the outside, the *Cow* looks like any other C-54 transport except for one exceptionally large window on the port side.

Inside, the plane looks like a futuristic airline advertisement.

The President's stateroom has a large sofa which is converted into a bed at night, two comfortable club chairs, a large mahogany table, a super-de-luxe radio, a connection on the plane's intercom system and a small but fully equipped bathroom.

The rest of the plane is devoted to double seats which look very much like Pullman equipment and can be converted into bunks at night.

Just aft of the "office" or operating bridge of the ship is an unusually complete galley with electric stove, refrigerator, food warmer, electric mixer, hot and cold water, toaster, food storage lockers and a place for storing ice cubes made by the refrigerator.

Actually, few people have seen the plane's most novel feature in operation. It is an electric elevator which folds up, when not in use, between the floor and outer skin of the plane. This was installed for the benefit of the crippled Mr. Roosevelt, but has been left in the ship. Mr. Truman's aged mother used the elevator in boarding the ship for a flight between Washington and Grandview, Missouri.

The Ships

Mr. Roosevelt and Mr. Truman seemed to share a preference for heavy cruisers on ocean voyages. Mr. Roosevelt used the U.S.S. *Augusta* on several occasions, notably the Atlantic Charter conference with Churchill. Mr. Truman used the same vessel for his trip to Germany where the Big Three met in 1945.

When Mr. Roosevelt made an extended cruise on a naval vessel, it required the installation of special elevators between at least two decks. This was to prevent his virtual imprisonment on one deck, and only part of one deck at that.

Mr. Truman, however, requires no special equipment

and thus causes less trouble to the Navy when he is aboard.

Mr. Roosevelt had as his yacht for cruising on the Potomac River and in Chesapeake Bay the old U.S.S. *Potomac*. In making the *Potomac* a more comfortable ship for the President, the Navy also made her top-heavy and Mr. Roosevelt ordered her condemned in 1944.

The Navy issued orders forbidding the *Potomac* to leave the Chesapeake and Mr. Roosevelt continued to use the antiquated yacht for overnight river cruises.

When Mr. Truman, coming from an inland state, entered office, few people expected him to take to the water in the manner he did. He used the *Potomac* as frequently or more so than his predecessor, and the Navy was pleased.

During the latter part of 1945, the Navy assigned a new yacht to the President—the U.S.S. *Williamsburg*. She began her career as the luxurious ocean-going pleasure craft of an eastern industrialist. Then came the war and the Navy made a convoy flagship out of her.

After the war, she was refitted and turned over to the President as his yacht.

The *Williamsburg*'s interior is a beautiful arrangement of pastels. The walls of each stateroom are tinted plyboard, equipped with built-in beds patterned after Statler Hotel equipment, and glass-enclosed showers.

On the dresser of each stateroom are two large gold flagons of shaving lotion and toilet water which on a windy day can be smelled from ship to shore.

The present White House staff has requested that the *Williamsburg* be referred to as a "service craft" rather than as a yacht. Technically, they are right because the

Navy has no yachts on its lists. But the *Williamsburg* was built as a yacht and a yacht she will remain in the newspapers.

Mr. Truman set an interesting pattern in his use of the yacht. Frequently on a Friday afternoon, he picks up bag and baggage and goes aboard at the navy yard in Washington with members of his immediate staff. They cruise on the Potomac until shortly after lunch Saturday when the ship returns to her berth at the navy yard.

The staff—most of it—departs, but the President remains aboard. The yacht stays at the navy yard dock all Saturday night and on Sunday morning the President's wife and daughter, Margaret, go aboard and the family cruises on the river during the day, returning to port at sundown.

This gives Mr. Truman relief from the telephone and visitors who "must" be seen—old friends who pop up at the front gate of the White House with little or no warning. It also gives him an opportunity to read his beloved Mark Twain undisturbed.

The President can go aboard the *Williamsburg*, get into an old sweater and loaf, wandering occasionally into the wardroom—which has a phony fireplace—to play his favorite tunes on a little spinet piano thoughtfully supplied by the Navy.

Few newspapermen ever travel aboard the *Williamsburg*. And the few that travel aboard the yacht do it infrequently.

On occasion, Mr. Truman sets up a week-end cruise for what he calls the "Hardrock Club." This is a small, tight organization of men who covered him during his 1944 Vice-Presidential campaign and his Big Three trip to Germany.

Each member—about seventeen in all, including the President's secretaries and aides—wears a small gold pickax in his lapel as a badge of membership.

The club got its name from an incident during the 1944 campaign when a timid member of the party declined to join up with Truman in a tour of a Montana copper mine, but sat dolefully outside the mine on a large rock. This grew into a running gag, which in turn grew into one of the most exclusive clubs in the world.

Some Washington newspapermen, when they heard about the Hardrock Club, formed an opposition outfit, loosely organized but with a honey of a name—"The Association of Men Who Are Not Close to Truman."

They claimed during the process of organization that their membership was wide open, but only five people were eligible.

(The "Hardrock Club" is mentioned in connection with the *Williamsburg* because it was aboard the yacht that the first formal meeting was held.)

A discussion of modern White House travel necessitates a comparison between Presidents Roosevelt and Truman.

Mr. Roosevelt delighted in a slow speed train. He knew the various roadbeds of the country better than some railroad men. And he knew that reducing the rate of speed meant an easier ride. He also wanted the opportunity to sit by the window of his private car and study the passing countryside.

He loved to astound his guests with amazingly detailed knowledge of the geography of the country through which he was passing.

He kept before him a small, neatly folded road map on which he followed the progress of the train.

Passing through some ordinary milk stop, the President would roar out to the person nearest him:

"This is the town where General Blank did so-and-so."

Or moving through a wooded part of the Northwest, he would boom:

"Look at those trees—need cutting, but the Park Service won't let anybody in there."

When we went from Washington to San Diego with Mr. Roosevelt in 1944, the trip took more than five days. The speed of the train rarely went above thirty-five miles an hour. This was so slow that the batteries on the sleeping cars would not recharge themselves sufficiently and the train had to stop every two nights to pump power into the batteries from the big Diesels in the radio car.

In fact, the trip—off-record at the time—was so slow and boring, that I rode through most of Oklahoma atop the engine cab, waving to astonished trackwalkers who never before saw a man riding on top of an engine.

But the President was happy. Nobody could reach him on the telephone. He followed his beloved hobby of geography. And he was able to bone up on the war situation before talking with Nimitz and MacArthur in Hawaii.

On a long railroad trip with Mr. Roosevelt there was a surprise at almost every meal. Often the train retained the same diner—usually from the Baltimore and Ohio Railroad—for the entire trip. Bigwigs in the states through which we passed showered down with local delicacies and since the President could not possibly eat all of them, many fine epicurean items found their way into the diner.

An unforgettable dinner was served to some of us in

Oregon in 1943 by Daniel W. Moorman, the B. & O. boss of Presidential trains.

After old-fashioneds made with thirty-five-year-old bourbon, there was a delicious fresh mushroom soup. Then followed a main course of Oregon fingerling trout, laid over broiled quail which rested on a bountiful layer of Smithfield ham. I forget the dessert. I think I went to sleep.

On the same trip, coming back through New Orleans, a gracious railroad executive put aboard the train a gallon of selected oysters for every person on the train. The B. & O. chef met the challenge, however, and served oysters in a dozen different styles during the following two days.

The leisure of Presidential travel—for the newspapermen—ended when trips changed from the secret, off-record variety to full-blown public travel.

When the President travels on the record, it means a grueling, around-the-clock routine for the reporters.

When Mr. Truman took Winston Churchill out to Fulton, Missouri, for a speech in the spring of 1946, I filed with Western Union more than 30,000 words between 2 P.M. when we left Washington and 2 A.M. the next morning.

When a President is moving through the nation by train, every stop is a new story, all this in addition to major speeches he makes at the more important stops. The big, set speeches are not too hard to handle because an advance text is furnished and the story written long before the actual performance.

Mr. Truman doesn't seem to get the same satisfaction from train travel that Mr. Roosevelt derived from rolling around the country in his private car.

Mr. Truman prefers speed. And when he gets where he's going, he likes to be surrounded by lots of people. If he is in a small town, he'll walk into the hotel lobby after dinner and shake hands with everybody in the room.

Mr. Truman has little or no taste for seclusion, but it is developing slowly. Mr. Roosevelt thrived on privacy and demanded it more the longer he was in the White House.

Mr. Roosevelt loved the out-of-doors. Mr. Truman can take it or leave it alone. He'd rather sit inside and talk with friends than hunt or fish.

On most train trips with Mr. Truman, the correspondents must stay in a state of perpetual alert because the President is relatively unpredictable. A few minutes after the train leaves Washington, he usually walks through each car, shouting greetings to everyone.

On one trip—to Fulton, Missouri—he went on up to the engine and drove it, donning gloves and cap to do the job in regulation style.

And the reporters never know when Mr. Truman is going to make an impromptu speech from the rear platform of his car.

The unscheduled platform appearances drive the reporters daffy, and make for many hours of nervous worry.

A traveling White House correspondent never knows when the President is going to say something newsworthy. Thus, at each stop, the reporters boil out of their cars and race for the rear end of the train. The President comes out on the platform of his car, waves and acknowledges the cheers of the station crowd.

And then he may speak. And the stop may last no more than three or four minutes. During that period, the newspapermen—the wire service reporters, at least—must record the President's words, dash back to their rooms, bat out a few paragraphs and hand them to a Western Union representative before the train pulls out.

The reporters have a traveling guardian angel in the person of Carroll S. Linkins, Washington press representative for Western Union. Linkins knows more about road requirements of the reporters than the reporters themselves. And he can find Morse wire in a tanktown where the town consists of nothing but a dilapidated railroad depot and a filling station.

The reporters have a major solace in Linkins. Once they hand their copy to him, they know it is as good as in their offices. "Link" alerts Western Union representatives all down the line ahead of the Presidential train, and if there is no stop, he puts the copy in a weighted canvas bag and hurls it at the stationmaster as the train speeds through the town.

Dewey E. Long and E. A. McMullin, the White House transportation officers, also are stars in their own right. They can recite page after page of intricate railroad and airline schedules by memory.

And when a Presidential train is being made up, it is the veteran Long who assigns space to the reporters. Long years of experience have taught him that Reporter Blank cannot stand the sight of Reporter Dash, and consequently he never puts them together in the same room.

Sharing a compartment or drawing room for two or three weeks with a man one detested would be a ghastly experience. It happened to one reporter I know. He hated his roommate who was extremely fastidious about his personal hygiene. So, the first reporter got even with him by not bathing or changing his clothes. The drawing room began to smell like a poorly ventilated gymnasium and finally the object of the campaign pleaded to be transferred to another room. He was.

On another Presidential trip there was a reporter named Bill who loved to spend his evenings in bourbon and multitudinous cigarettes. Because of a last-minute mix-up he was assigned to a room with a highly pious individual who neither smoked nor drank. What's more he started right off attempting to dissuade Bill from his dissolute habits.

Bill, however, was beyond redemption. Furthermore, he became increasingly incensed over the missionary efforts in his behalf. So, in a bourbon rage one night, when Bill realized that his companion had only one pair of shoes, he slipped into the compartment, purloined his roommate's only shoes and went to the end of the car.

He quietly opened the door and hurled the shoes from the speeding train out into the dark countryside of Massachusetts.

His roomie forgot most of his piety next morning and raised hell with the porter whom he accused of stealing his only shoes. And he had to cover the next two stops in bedroom slippers. Bill was happy for days.

The custom on the White House train of leaving one's shoes in the hall at night to be shined has led to a number of rather unpractical jokes. Just before the war, there was assigned to the train for one or two brief trips a highly objectionable character who attempted to entertain his colleagues with stories about his high and unmatched ability as a newspaperman.

After a session in the club car, the man retired early, leaving his shoes outside his room.

He arose early next morning, opened the compartment door and picked up his finely shined shoes. But when he slipped his feet into them, an expression of dull wonder spread over his face.

He walked around in the room for a few minutes, stamping his feet like a man trying on a new pair of shoes at a store. He shook his head and sat down. When he tried to take the shoes off, his feet came out trailing what looked like bubble gum.

During the night some fan of his had thoughtfully lined his shoes with LePage's Iron Glue.

Then there was the Jello.

The correspondents who made the frequent and boring trips to Hyde Park with Mr. Roosevelt organized the Hyde Park Protective Association, a device to while away boredom and, also, to needle unco-operative members of the party. For one dollar the association would leave you alone.

If you declined to pay, your next few days resembled Hell Week at a college fraternity house.

I remember one man who wouldn't pay. When he came back from dinner one night, he found in a basin of his hotel bathroom all his toilet articles—razor, brush, comb, toothbrush, etc. They were encased in a lovely strawberry gelatin, made double strength. The slippery mixture defied washing and the man promptly plunked his entire toilet kit in the wastebasket and stormed downstairs to the association headquarters. He paid his dollar, plus a dollar assessment—to cover the cost of the Jello.

All sorts of feuds and contests develop between the correspondents during lengthy road trips with the President, who rarely is aware of what is going on in the cars ahead of "the private."

One of the most memorable contests was waged between Fred Pasley of the New York *Daily News* and anybody who came within shouting distance.

On a quiet day in Poughkeepsie, New York, where the gang berthed when Mr. Roosevelt was in Hyde Park, Pasley went for a long walk and came back to the hotel with a live, red rooster.

The hotel clerk, just after a night when somebody put a dozen live frogs in the bed of another reporter, was a little testy and offered generously to escort Pasley to the street if the chicken was not abandoned immediately.

"You, sir," Pasley said in his best foghorn voice that filled the lobby, "are speaking of the rooster I love."

The party was leaving that night anyway so the room clerk's threats were meaningless.

Pasley took the rooster aboard the special with him at departure time and proceeded to the diner where he ordered two Martinis—one to be served in a saucer.

Somehow, Pasley got the rooster to drink the Martini and then the betting began. As the besotted thing—the chicken, not Pasley—flopped over on the table, Pasley called for odds on when his pet would have to relieve himself in the middle of the crisp, white tablecloth of the B. & O. diner.

The diner steward was apoplectic, not knowing from one moment to the next when Mrs. Roosevelt or someone of equal rank would walk through the car and witness the contest. Pasley eventually collected all the bets, then retired to his compartment, after renting the upper berth for the chicken.

Lest people get the idea that White House correspondents are a crowd of irresponsible pixies, it should be pointed out that these farcical affairs never happen on a hard-working trip. The men on most trips have time only for their typewriters.

Covering a Presidential election campaign trip, for instance, is about as hard work as there is in all journalism. It means writing around the clock. It is not unusual for reporters writing for both day and night circulations to go two or three weeks with only two or three hours of sleep a night.

And then when the pressure lifts, they sit around the club car and figure out how to hex some man who has not been picking up his share of bar checks.

CHAPTER FOUR

The Three Ghouls

THE dictionary defines a ghoul as "a demon who robs graves and feeds on corpses."

That, according to President Roosevelt, was the proper description for the role played during the war by two colleagues and me.

He used the term affectionately—sometimes. And then again, when he felt a trifle miffed about our presence, he added the label, "vultures."

"You wire service men," the President said to us one night early in the war, "are just sitting around like vultures waiting for something to happen to me. Isn't that right?"

We told him:

"Not exactly, sir. We're here *in case* something happens."

Thousands of miles were traveled. Mr. Roosevelt's "ghouls" were with him, just like the little boy's shadow. And it was on one of his "ghoul" trips that he died and we were there to report it, fulfilling plans that had been made and changed a hundred times.

Before there was any suggestion that Mr. Roosevelt was not in tiptop health, White House correspondents rehearsed in their minds, over and over again, what they would do when "it" happened.

"It" was death or serious injury, from natural causes, accident or assassination.

"It" has to be thought about by the men who cover a President because when bodily harm or pain come to a Chief Executive, it is the hottest news an American reporter can possibly handle.

"It" is one big reason correspondents clamor to accompany Mr. Truman on such inconsequential trips as to church in Washington, or to a boring banquet in the evening not three blocks away from the White House.

Suppose a drunk driver smashed into the President's car? Suppose a run-down jalopy careened into the side of his limousine? If White House reporters were not on the spot to inform the world immediately, they would be severely criticized by their editors. The public would be bitter because it did not know exactly what happened.

It is possible to go on supposing for pages. Heart attack? Food poisoning? An injurious fall?

All these things happen every hour to hundreds of Americans and there is no particular reason to believe that a President of the country is immune. And when "it" happens to him, the welfare of the nation is affected. The effect goes into every household, every family. And for that reason, the public has a right to know at all times what the President is doing and where he is.

During the war this public right was abrogated by military security; i.e., the fear that an enemy agent would assassinate Mr. Roosevelt.

The ghouls—the White House reporters for the United Press, Associated Press and International News Service— got their start early in the war. For some months after Pearl Harbor, Mr. Roosevelt would not permit a newspaperman aboard his train.

Even the President's trips to Hyde Park were put off-record and reporters told that they would incur high White House disfavor if they attempted to proceed to Hyde Park independently of the White House train.

The President issued orders for his staff to break up its headquarters in Poughkeepsie and move out to the bleak, drafty and rococo old Hyde Park mansion of the late Frederick Vanderbilt.

The government had taken over the Vanderbilt house as an historic show place. The first two ornately furnished floors were set aside for sightseers, and the President's staff was assigned to what had been the servants' quarters on the two upper floors.

The stall-like rooms were depressing and the sub-zero winds which swept down the Hudson Valley in the winter made the house a melancholy place. But the President was snug and happy in his own house two miles away. Why his staff had to stay secluded at the Vanderbilt place was a mystery, since each time the President arrived for a week end his procession of automobiles drove through the heart of downtown Poughkeepsie in full view of the public.

The President thought he was getting away with a lot more than he really was. Reporters assigned to the White House knew every time he left town, but, because of the voluntary censorship code, printed nothing.

The first publication to break the wartime secrecy was the college paper at Catholic University, the young editor of which saw the President driving with only a small escort to the railroad station at Silver Spring, Maryland. He printed a brief story about it, and a few days later received a visit from Secret Service agents whose very presence nearly frightened the young journalist out of his wits.

Then Leonard Lyons, the New York *Post* columnist who delighted in "exclusives," printed a Hyde Park trip that was known but not published by at least two hundred Washington correspondents who were well conversant with the censorship code.

This made the reporters increasingly restive and Steve Early was under constant fire about the situation. Steve, however, could not do much about it because the President liked the secrecy of security, and it also made things a lot easier for the Secret Service.

The three press associations, between them responsible for the news to every American newspaper and radio station, argued most incessantly for some form of coverage on all of Mr. Roosevelt's trips.

The *first* break in Mr. Roosevelt's determination to travel sans reporters became evident on September 16, 1942. Early asked for a secret conference with the wire service men that afternoon. Bill Theis of I.N.S., Doug Cornell of A.P. and I went into his office through separate entrances. Early locked the doors.

Then he told us the President would leave the next day for an extended tour of the war plants and military installations of the nation. The trip would be kept secret until October 1 when he returned to Washington. Only the three wire service men would be allowed to accompany the Chief Executive. No syndicate photographers, but navy cameramen.

Steve also issued us credentials as Secret Service agents —the engraved commission book with our pictures and the silver badge of authority.

He admonished us not to say a word to our offices beyond the fact that we would be gone for more than two weeks. He would not give us the itinerary, but told us only the first stop—the Chrysler tank plant at Detroit.

"And don't say anything more than you absolutely have to to your families," Steve said.

I went to my office and asked Lyle Wilson for eight hundred dollars.

"Going somewhere?" he said calmly.

"Yes, but don't ask me where because I don't know."

"Can't you give me an idea?"

"Well, for God's sake don't breathe this to anyone, but we'll be at the Chrysler tank plant in Detroit day after tomorrow. The President will be gone about two weeks, on a swing around the country, an inspection trip of war plants and army camps. But that is all Steve will tell us now."

I told Lyle the other skimpy details, and we got out a map.

"If the first stop is Detroit," the boy reasoned, "he'll probably go on out to Chicago, and then take the northern route to the west coast."

Between us, and just speculating, we figured in advance almost every stop the President would make, with the exception of one in southern California and one in Mississippi.

My wife, Eleanor, was puzzled, to put it mildly, when I went home that night and began packing heavy suits and light suits, sweaters and swimming trunks.

We reached the Chrysler plant shortly after noon on September 18. The workers gathered around the end of the President's private car at the plant entrance. They whooped and whistled when the President eased down the ramp to an automobile.

Mr. Roosevelt was openly pleased with their reaction of surprise, and commented about it all through the tour of the plant where he saw General Lee M-4 tanks under construction.

I walked through the plant just at the rear of the President's automobile, primarily to listen to what the workers said when they first saw him.

Most of them were surprised.

"By God if it ain't old Frank!" roared one smudge-faced boring mill operator.

The President laughed loudly and waved his hat at the man.

We reboarded the train after a brief visit at Chrysler and moved over to the sprawling Ford Motor Company bomber plant at Willow Run.

Henry Ford met the President and Mrs. Roosevelt at the train and piloted them, in an automobile, through the huge plant, which was not yet in anything like substantial production.

We returned to the train in the late afternoon and started to board the cars, thinking the President was about to do the same thing. But suddenly, his car started away from the train. We leaped back into our car and set out after him.

It turned out that Ford wanted to show him the Ford Engineers' School, and a small chapel for army men stationed at Willow Run.

This got us underway, and as the train pulled out of Detroit for Chicago, the three press association reporters, out of habit more than anything else, rushed to their typewriters and pounded out long stories about the start of the President's tour.

When I finished my piece, I confronted Cornell.

"Now that you've got it written, what are you going to do with it?" he jibed.

"I don't know, Doug. I feel a little silly. I guess I'll just stick it away in the bank."

Steve came around that night and gravely informed us that the next stop would be the Great Lakes Naval Training Station, outside Chicago. And he told us, too, that Mr. Roosevelt wanted to see every line we wrote before returning to Washington.

Great Lakes was miserable and raining. And we were glad to move on to Milwaukee, Wisconsin, for a tour of the Allis-Chalmers plant.

There we encountered our first "leak." Walter Geist, president of Allis-Chalmers, reported upon our arrival that the wire services had called him all the previous night, wanting to know what time Mr. Roosevelt's train would arrive.

Steve hit the ceiling. But he refused to believe that we had been responsible for the leak. His confidence in us was supported before we left Milwaukee. The Secret Service learned that the press associations in Milwaukee found out about the trip from railroad personnel.

With typical Roosevelt drama, he paid a midnight visit to an ordnance plant at New Brighton, Minnesota, then headed toward the northwest with the next scheduled stop at Athol, Idaho.

It was amazing to see a huge naval station high in the mountains of the Idaho Panhandle. The water of Lake Pend Oreille, on which Camp Farragut was located, was

2,200 feet deep just off the station, which gave comparatively large craft plenty of room in which to operate.

Life on the train began to get a little cramped. The porters burned incense in the Pullmans as the dirty laundry piled up. The Navy kept a meticulous log which was submitted to the President for his approval.

The log entry on the stop at Fort Lewis, Washington, where the President reviewed units of the Thirty-Third Division, made this report:

The units which did pass before the President are given below:
Time of
Passing
10:09   First Car
10:10   Band, with a good sized dog . . . at the leader's heels.

The President's schedule took him to the Puget Sound Navy Yard at Bremerton, Washington, where, although moving in secret, and our families not supposed to know where we were, he made a speech to more than five thousand shipworkers.

Leaning over the side of his open convertible and speaking into a hand microphone, Mr. Roosevelt blandly told the assembled workers:

"I can only say a word or two to you. The first is that I am not really here, because I am taking this trip under navy orders and that means that my cruise is not published in the papers, so just remember that for about ten days, you haven't seen me."

The President drove all through Seattle and waved gaily to cheering thousands—an entire city off the record.

But this was nothing to compare with what he did at

Portland, Oregon, when he visited one of the Kaiser ship-yards the following day.

After his daughter, Mrs. John Boettiger, had launched a ship—on the record and in full view of cameras—the President took over the meeting. There must have been twenty thousand people swarmed around a high ramp on which the President's open automobile was parked.

"You know," he said to the people over the loud-speaker system, "you know I am not supposed to be here today."

The crowd laughed and the President joined in the merriment. Damned if I saw anything to laugh about. Here was the President of the United States making an important public appearance in front of twenty thousand people, yet the newspapers and radio stations had to play like they knew nothing about it.

Although three reporters whose normal duty was to send news to thousands of outlets around the world were standing only a few feet from him, the President went on with his joke:

"You are the possessors of a secret which even the newspapers of the United States don't know," he told the shipworkers.

"I hope you will keep the secret because I am under military and naval orders, and like the ship that we have just seen go overboard, my motions and movements are supposed to be secret."

After several stops on the west coast, Mr. Roosevelt's secret circus reached Uvalde, Texas, on September 27, a quiet, hot Sunday morning. The President stopped there for his first word in more than two years with John Nance

Garner, who served as Vice President for the first eight years of the New Deal.

Garner was pretty bitter when he left Washington, having been discarded in favor of Henry Wallace. But there was nothing apparent that morning in Uvalde but friendship.

White-haired and then seventy-three years old, Garner drove from his ranch to the little, deserted railroad station in his rattletrap 1929 roadster. The train arrived ahead of him, but a few minutes later his little car pulled up in front of the Casey Jones Café just across from the depot.

Garner ducked beneath a sign proclaiming Uvalde to be THE HONEY CAPITAL OF THE WORLD and hotfooted it down the tracks to Mr. Roosevelt's private car.

There he swung up the steps, shouting as he saw the President, "Well, God bless you, sir. I'm glad to see you."

Mr. Roosevelt held Garner off at a distance to survey him from head to toe.

"Gosh, you look well."

They joshed each other about local affairs.

"How are things going around here?" the President asked.

Garner slapped his hat against his leg and roared, "They're one hundred per cent for you."

They exchanged a few jokes, and just before they parted, asked, like courteous country gentlemen, about each other's "missus."

As "Cactus Jack" walked back toward his car, he spotted Ross McIntire. He stopped to urge the President's doctor to "keep that man in good health and all the rest will take care of itself."

I have devoted so much space to Mr. Roosevelt's first war plant tour because it set the pattern for coverage of all his other wartime trips, continuing through to his death.

When we returned from that first trip, each reporter had about eighteen thousand words of copy to be filed. Most of it was sent back to the areas where the President had visited, and several general interest dispatches were distributed nationally.

The newspapers fell on Mr. Roosevelt's neck with strongly worded editorials of protest. All agreed that in the interest of security there should be no advance publicity about the President's movements. But they protested against keeping these movements secret for weeks.

With the exception of one other trip—to Mexico in the spring of 1943—the three wire service men covered the Presidential trips exclusively from 1942 until the President began his active campaign tours in the early fall of 1944. Most of these trips were to Hyde Park and never printed. We were along for "protection."

Between the first war plant tour and the Mexican trip, there were a number of arguments in the White House about uncovered travel. In response to one plea for coverage of a particular Hyde Park trip, the President, through Early, sent us this message:

"What do you want to do—watch me take a bath or go with me to the toilet?"

In 1942 we made only one trip to Hyde Park. The President permitted only the wire services to go along when he went home to vote in the Congressional elections.

During that trip he was on the record for about five minutes—the five minutes it took to carry him up the steps of the old town hall, vote and depart. Yet we were in Hyde Park for a week.

This was the first experience our offices had had with reporters in this country disappearing with the President for a week. Immediately after this trip, the President disappeared into another news blackout. He would be on the record in the White House for a few days each week, but the White House offered nothing in the way of an explanation when he was out of town.

The public in Washington gradually got wise. When there were no White House callers, it meant the President was out of town. Cab drivers could report the minute he left and returned.

Before the President left for the Casablanca conference in January, 1943, I went to Early.

"Steve," I said, "it is ridiculous that the President is going to a far-off part of the world completely uncovered by the American press."

He agreed, but said there was not a thing he could do; that the President and Churchill had promised each other there would be no reporters on the scene.

I reminded Steve that the British had made the same promise in August, 1941, but that Churchill still included two "literary gentlemen" in his Atlantic Charter conference party and they both had written finely detailed books about the meeting at sea.

Early, however, was helpless. Because the British had played a little loose with the rules, he was not going to do the same thing. And the President certainly had no intention of violating what was represented to us as an agreement with Churchill.

The President would not accept the "three ghouls" as

part of his permanent, wartime entourage until late 1943. He went to Teheran and Cairo without us, much to everybody's anguish because the British again made the Americans look like idiots.

The British were able to keep the public fairly well informed on the conference by quoting "world travelers" as they arrived in Portugal.

As the 1944 campaign came nearer, however, the President's attitude seemed to soften. We were on hand for the first Quebec conference between Mr. Roosevelt and Churchill, but so little actual news was available that many ordinarily accurate reporters were forced to "thumb sucking"—dreamily speculating and writing what they thought Mr. Roosevelt and Churchill were discussing.

The ghouls began to find themselves in the unchosen position of being arrayed against their colleagues who could not travel with the President. Naturally, the men who were left behind were ripe for rumors, and consequently heard about many things which never happened on Mr. Roosevelt's secret trips.

When the rumors were not verified in our copy after the trips were over, the question often arose around the Press Club bar; did the wire service accounts tell everything?

The off-record trips to Hyde Park were perfect rumor breeders, because we rarely were allowed to file anything, even after returning to Washington. Mr. Roosevelt did not want anyone outside his official family to know how much time he spent at his family home.

In early 1944, the President did not like the idea of the ghouls accompanying him to South Carolina where he sought to throw off a series of nagging winter colds and bronchial attacks. Steve, however, was well aware of the spreading rumors about the President's health and realized that our presence in South Carolina would be the best possible rumor insurance the President could have.

The wire service men went with the President to the Pacific in the late summer of 1944. "The Boss" was then again a candidate and he knew he had to have us along. But I don't think he liked it because he made us fly to Hawaii instead of accompanying him on the large, new cruiser *Baltimore*. His excuse was that there was no room for the three of us on the ship.

Maybe so, but I doubt it. I think there were several reasons why he made us fly out independently. His physical appearance was getting worse. He had a cold. He might not have wanted us to have him under steady, extremely close surveillance just ahead of a hard campaign. And his naval aide, Rear Admiral Wilson Brown, certainly did not want us along and told me as much.

A practicing ghoul, however, has a thick skin and always comes back for more.

All reporters were quite welcome aboard Mr. Roosevelt's train during the fourth term campaign. Virtually every restriction on reporting his movements was lifted for the campaign. But the minute he was elected, slam went the lid again, and again I was a ghoul, riding thousands of unreported miles on the Presidential train between Washington and Hyde Park and rarely writing a line because of the military security which disappeared so amazingly when there were voters to be wooed, but reappeared when the ceremony was over.

The President, by the time of his fourth election, was

just about resigned to the fact that like the poor, we would always be with him.

When we set out for Warm Springs with him after the election, he offered no protest to us, and told Early mildly that there would be no news while he was in Georgia. We went anyway and froze for a month in a ramshackle cottage which was ill-fitted for the unusual cold spell which gripped the South during most of our stay.

Despite the discomforts, however, the wire service men felt glad about one thing—they thought they had heard the last of the White House arguments over coverage of the President on the road. But then we heard about another Big Three meeting to be held in the Crimea.

When the Yalta trip came up in early 1945, we had started our campaign for coverage a month ahead of time. For a brief period, it seemed that Mr. Roosevelt might change his mind and take us along. But he claimed that Stalin and Churchill did not want us there.

We even had a session one afternoon shortly before he left with his daughter, Anna, and she was entirely sympathetic. She promised to try to convince her father that such a historic meeting warranted an independently reported record. But she struck out, just as Early had. And the President went away, leaving us on the beach.

Early went with him, however, and the three wire service men received orders to rush to Africa to join the party. We joined it, all right, but after the Yalta conference was over, and all we knew about it was what we read in British and French newspapers. But more about how I "covered" Yalta in a later chapter.

I could understand the President's position on the Yalta conference, but I could not understand why he was unable to change it by telling Churchill that the American people did not want to be scooped again by the British and the Russians.

We had been with the President in the Pacific the summer before. We had been in South Carolina with him before the fourth term campaign. We lived with him and were never more than a short distance away all during 1944, spending endless and newsless week ends at Hyde Park.

So, I thought he had more than ample precedent to say to the British and the Russians that we were attached to his official party and there was nothing to be done about it. But he wouldn't do it.

Our trip to Africa was highly educational, but largely a waste of time as far as real news was concerned.

We had a pleasant sea voyage home. Then after a brief stay in Washington, made another trip to Warm Springs. The President was very tired and was just going down to Georgia for a quiet rest. No news, he told us, not a single bit of news.

It was April, 1945.

CHAPTER FIVE

The Boss

A LARGE portion of modern history will be, and to a large extent has been, saturated with evaluations of Mr. Roosevelt.

When he was alive, several new biographies a year were about average. All the great biographers took a try at it.

If some superhuman copy editor could take all these biographies and cull from each its best portions, he'd have quite a book. For Roosevelt was too big a man to be put into one book by one author.

Since Mr. Roosevelt's death, a few of his close associates have begun to tell in print the story of "the Boss" as they saw him. Ed Starling of the Secret Service, Harry L. Hopkins, and Jonathan Daniels. And each with a different viewpoint, a different slant.

Men like Hopkins loved the President so much that they could hardly be relied upon to go into any detail on the weaknesses of their idol. And most of the authors who to date have tried to write about Roosevelt's bad side have been so politically biased that they failed to do the job objectively.

I would not be so brash as to attempt a well-rounded historical picture of Mr. Roosevelt. But I would like to show some of his many sides; to show what he was really like as a person.

Mr. Roosevelt was good and he knew it. He was superbly confident that he was the best political strategist known in American history. He knew for a fact that he could outguess and outmaneuver his opponents. And he did, time and again. He lost specific battles on occasion, but he won the wars.

Actually he was a fabulous monarch, a dramatic king. He could be and usually was socially democratic, but always with a regal air that never let you doubt that he was in full command of the situation.

Probably from childhood there was never a gathering that he did not dominate.

He would have been a wonderful actor. He probably would have been a Shakespearean star who wore fur-collared overcoats, carried a gold-headed cane and lorded it over the rest of the troupe.

It was this dramatic sense, plus bullheaded determination, that helped him overcome the incredible handicap of infantile paralysis. He was virtually a hopeless cripple, but the public at large did not realize it until his death.

Not in his entire time in the White House could he stand unsupported. Yet, few people outside of Washington realized this. He always had to rely on heavy steel leg braces, canes and, more often, the support of someone's arm.

His legs were literally lifeless. He walked on his braces and with support only by tremendous effort which often made perspiration pop from his forehead on a cold day.

But when appearing in public, he was the champion,

the colorful leader with his chin arched upward and his big hand in the air.

He knew he could thrill a crowded stadium by just this simple wave of a hand, or his brown felt hat. That was all it took to jerk a hundred thousand people to their feet in a screaming frenzy.

Between the President and sympathetic Secret Service agents, a general routine was worked out so that he was screened from public view while rising from his wheel chair to his braces.

Newspaper stories never made reference to the wheel chair until shortly before his death when the President, weary of the strain of the braces, began appearing at semiprivate dinners and similar affairs in his wheel chair.

Neither were photographs ever made of the President in his wheel chair unless it was precisely understood that only the upper part of his body would be shown.

This all added up to a friendly conspiracy which was based on basic principles of American sportsmanship— not taking advantage of a man's physical infirmities.

While Mr. Roosevelt was highly sensitive to publicity about his physical condition, he was completely at ease in small groups and among friends. His personality was such that a person seeing him for the first time paid little attention to the emaciated under part of his body.

He loved to associate with royalty. They were his kind of folks. He was fascinated by the regality of exchanging gifts with other heads of state when they met. No one but a complete monarch would have had the courage to give King Ibn Saud of Saudi Arabia a wheel chair.

Saud had given Mr. Roosevelt the Arabian works —gold daggers in diamond-encrusted scabbards, gold embroidered Arabian clothes, incredibly valuable perfumes. And Mr. Roosevelt without batting an eye rewarded Saud with a fourth term inaugural medal. The medal sold normally for two dollars, but Mr. Roosevelt had a special gold one struck for the king. And knowing the Saud's eyes were failing and his step faltering as a result of many desert war wounds, the President blithely bestowed upon him a snappy chromium and leather wheel chair—collapsible.

This amazing gift exchange took place aboard the cruiser *Quincy* when the President was en route home from the Yalta conference in early 1945.

In regal style, the President had dispatched the destroyer *Murphy* to Jidda to pick up Saud and his party and bring them back to Great Bitter Lake, in the Suez, where the *Quincy* was anchored.

Members of Saud's court tried to drive a large herd of sheep aboard the *Murphy,* but the harried skipper protested. They finally settled for eight sheep which were slaughtered one by one during the trip to provide food for the Arabians.

The Arabs also confounded the Navy by insisting that they sleep on deck. This was done by rigging desert tents between the gun turrets. The steel deck was covered with gorgeous oriental rugs.

Roosevelt later told us that when the *Murphy* hove to off the *Quincy,* "It was the damnedest sight I ever saw— she looked like a sailing bazaar."

And when Saud came aboard the *Quincy,* Mr. Roosevelt had to have his daughter, Anna Boettiger, smuggled ashore to Cairo during the conference. Arabs, it seems, don't think highly of having their womenfolk around for other men to gaze upon. And so, the President went Arabian for a day.

During the war, there was a succession of visiting dignitaries at the White House. Most of them were presidents of Latin American countries. Their visits became so frequent that between the President and the State Department protocol division, a set formula was worked out for their entertainment.

The visiting president arrived, say at four o'clock in the afternoon. He would be met by the Secretary of State at the railroad station or airport and escorted to the White House where the President waited for him in the windowless little diplomatic reception room in the basement or ground floor.

Soldiers, sailors mariners drawn up on the South Grounds would present formal military honors; and the visitor would then be escorted into the reception room where the President met him.

Mr. Roosevelt was at his best in affairs like this. Maybe he had never met the person before, or at the most once. He would roll his massive, leonine head and with a broad smile roar, "Well, well, well. My old friend—how are you?"

Mr. Roosevelt knew how to say "my old friend" in a dozen different languages.

He then would present the visiting fireman to the Cabinet and various other government officials rounded up for the occasion.

Once, while sitting in the President's private car in the course of a long trip, I asked him what on earth did he find to talk about to these people.

He laughed heartily.

"I have a system. After the visiting president has met the Cabinet, we go upstairs together and I give him a chance to go to his room and freshen up before dinner.

"Then before dinner, he and I meet for a drink. I give him two or three Martinis, made four parts gin to one part vermouth.

"Then we go into the state dinner and there are the usual toasts and starchy conversation.

"After dinner, he and I go to my study, and I have a Scotch nightcap for him. By this time, he is pretty sleepy. We talk until midnight or so and then part.

"Next morning, I arrange to see him in my study at about ten o'clock. After we have been talking for about five minutes, Pa Watson (Major General Edwin M. Watson, the President's military aide) sticks his head in the door and says my first engagement of the day already is running late.

"So, I say to my visitor, 'Oh, I'm awfully sorry. I had hoped to spend the morning talking with you, but they just won't let me alone.'"

And within an hour, the visitor was moved out of the White House and across Pennsylvania Avenue to Blair House. The President, however, followed no such schedule when Winston Churchill visited the White House. Mr. Roosevelt liked Churchill a great deal, disagreed with many of his ideas and suggestions, but nevertheless, found his presence stimulating, often to the point of fatigue.

"Winston," the President once said, "is not Mid-Victorian—he is completely Victorian."

Mr. Roosevelt never was a heavy drinker and had no inclination to match Churchill's nightly habits of doing business over a Scotch or brandy glass until two or three in the morning. The President would stick with Churchill until midnight or shortly after, then leave the Prime Minister with Hopkins whose ideas of late hours and several drinks perfectly matched those of Churchill.

Churchill, to a large extent, was cut out of the same cloth as Mr. Roosevelt. Churchill was a great, dramatic showman and actually a better speaker than Mr. Roosevelt. Churchill's speeches during the war contained much finer rhetoric than the Roosevelt speeches, but when it came to radio technique, Churchill could not come close.

To Mr. Roosevelt, the microphone was as much of a political instrument as a ward leader. He knew how to use radio with quality rarely approached by political contemporaries. His deep resonant voice was an organ upon which he played with the skill of a fine musician.

Another one of his great talents was his ability to put over sheer, unadulterated hokum.

This ability made it possible for him literally to charm people he detested.

"Bring in the old bore and let's get it over with," he would say to his secretary just before an appointment. The secretary would then usher in the person in question.

"Well, well," Mr. Roosevelt would boom, "how in the world are you, Bill? And why has it been so long since you came to see me?"

If the caller had some topic to discuss which the President wanted to avoid, the poor man probably never got a chance to open his mouth. Mr. Roosevelt would start in immediately on some utterly unrelated subject, and literally filibuster.

There once was a governor of Alabama, Chauncey

Sparks, who tried for an hour and a half to talk politics with the President while they were touring an army air base at Montgomery, Alabama. Mr. Roosevelt had advance knowledge of the governor's desires and for a particular reason, did not want to discuss the matter.

Every time Sparks started to open his mouth, Mr. Roosevelt would tell him about the great progress being made by the Marines at Parris Island, South Carolina, in rehabilitating mental patients. And then when F.D.R. exhausted that subject, he started in on Sparks about wild life and how he would, so much, like to have some quail sent to his train.

Sparks got the quail.

Another one they tell on Mr. Roosevelt around the White House goes like this:

A Supreme Court justice called on him one evening just before dinner. The President told the usher he wanted the justice out by seven o'clock.

About ten minutes to seven, the usher went into the President's study and gravely announced there were other people waiting to see the President.

But the justice didn't budge.

About seven, the usher came in and in a tone of great formality, announced that the justice's car was waiting.

But still the justice kept his seat and continued talking.

In another ten minutes, the usher reappeared.

"Mr. Justice, we just received a telephone call and it sounded like your house is on fire."

The justice leaped from his seat and sped out of the White House.

Mr. Roosevelt didn't ask whether there really had been such a telephone call. He knew.

His sense of humor was marvelous. Sometimes subtle, sometimes caustic and sometimes as obvious as a burlesque comedian's pratt fall.

He once received a letter from the Odd Fellows of Hyde Park, reminding him that on a future date he would have been a member of their lodge for twenty-five years. They suggested it might be nice to have a letter from him on that occasion.

He turned over their letter to a secretary. Across the top of the letter and written in his distinctively illegible hand were these instructions: "Write 'em just like they were Knights of Columbus."

Early in the war, and on a dull afternoon in the White House press room, the wire service men concocted a brief poem and showed it to Marvin McIntyre, the President's secretary. Our poem, decorated with crude pictures of a railroad engine, was entitled, "Ode to the Spring or Expense Account, Oh, How I Miss You."

The title reflected the fact that we had not been on the road in some time and the boys were getting anxious to see the countryside again—from a drawing room window.

We had heard that Mr. Roosevelt was thinking about a long trip—it turned out to be Mexico—with a stop at Warm Springs. So, we wrote as follows:

> As we wish for sectors vernal
> Warm (like hope) Springs eternal.
> There we'd bask in liquid pleasure
> While piling up a modest treasure.
> The problem's simple, answer same—
> Let's jump to Georgia once again.

McIntyre laughed and said, "Let me have that for the Boss."

McIntyre went into the President's office. It was late in the day and Mr. Roosevelt was finishing his mail with Grace Tully, his personal secretary.

He studied the poem for a moment. He chuckled and asked Grace for a scratch pad. Without saying anything more, he scribbled on the pad for a few minutes. He ripped off the sheet and handed it to McIntyre.

"Here, Mac," he said. "Give them this."

Mr. Roosevelt had filled the entire sheet. McIntyre called us into his office and handed the reply to me. It said:

Mar 1943

Your touching deep desire
Arouses in me fire
To send a hasty wire
To Warm Springs in the mire
To scrape the roads,
Break out the corn.
The gals is waiting
Sho's yo born.

TO THE 3 PRESS ASSOCIATIONS
ONLY
NONE OTHER NEED
APPLY.

He loved puckish practical jokes. His staff never knew when "the Boss" would be up to some intricate gag.

One afternoon, his staff was just finishing work when the President called for Dorothy Brady, assistant to Grace Tully.

"Dorothy, I think I'll go out for a little ride," he told her, "and I thought you might like a lift home."

Grace went with them and Dorothy's neighbors got

quite a thrill seeing the long, black Presidential limousine, accompanied by the Secret Service cars and motorcycle police, moving through the Arlington residential district.

Mr. Roosevelt's car pulled into the Brady driveway. Dorothy got out and thanked the President very much.

"Won't you come in for a cup of tea, Mr. President?" she asked politely.

And then Dorothy had a horrible thought. It was her husband's day off. And it was the maid's day off. And she had a vision of the living room littered with newspapers and magazines, and Maurice in a sweatshirt.

Mr. Roosevelt toyed with her for a moment. Yes, that might be a fine idea. Yes, indeed. A good cup of tea. But when he saw a look of poorly disguised apprehension spreading over Dorothy's face, he roared with laughter and said thanks just the same, but he had to be running along.

Nothing helps an accomplished raconteur like the supreme confidence that his audience is utterly enchanted. When Mr. Roosevelt told a story, there was not a doubt in his mind that every person listening to him was literally hanging on each syllable. He loved to tell parables. And after he told them a few times, he was dead certain that they were true.

During the early stages of the war when inflationary trends were first showing themselves in force, he told a press conference a story. He swore it was true.

It seems a garage mechanic friend of his "dropped in" for a chat. Now, how in the world a mechanic ever dropped in on Mr. Roosevelt was beyond explanation. He claimed a lot of friends in comparatively low stations of life. I regarded them as his imaginary playmates

because I doubted seriously one of them ever existed. He
told often of a Chinese laundryman he knew, a baseball
player, a small dirt farmer, a garage man.

This mechanic, he said, had come to him complaining
about the high price of strawberries in February. His
"missus," the mechanic was alleged to have told the
President, was having to pay a God-awful price for strawberries.

The President said he lectured his mechanic friend
sharply. Since when could mechanics afford strawberries
out of season? Why didn't they eat something else? Why
throw away their defense plant wages in such a foolish
fashion?

The President used this to prove that the price line
actually was being held, but that too many people were
spending their money on unnecessary luxuries.

About six months later, the inflation question came
up again in a press conference. Someone wanted to know
whether the President really thought the price line was
being held, and how much longer it would last.

The President declined to comment directly. He
thought for a moment and added that there were too
many people like a master mechanic he knew.

This man, he said, had dropped in "to chat" and complain about the high price of asparagus. His "missus," the
President said of the mechanic, was complaining bitterly
about having to pay such a dear price for asparagus.

And since when, the President said he told the mechanic, did he find it necessary to have asparagus, out of
season, on his menu? Why didn't they eat something
else? Why contribute to inflation by wasting their defense plant wages on unnecessary luxury items?

I could not resist it. I knew it was presumptuous and

bordered on the disrespectful, but I had to ask the question.

"Mr. President," I said, "is that the same mechanic who came in a few months back complaining about the price of strawberries?"

The press conference exploded into roars of laughter.

Mr. Roosevelt turned a little pink and shouted over the guffaws:

"My God, Merriman. It's true. It *is* true. It was the same man."

But he could hardly finish the sentence because he was laughing too hard, himself.

When he heard a story that was halfway good, but just missed being terrific, he would dress it up to suit himself.

One of his favorites used to be about the old lady in Hyde Park who was inclined to imbibe a little heavily of a tonic with a high alcoholic content. One night in a full blizzard, she wandered out to her privy.

Just as the old lady got settled, a gust of wind hit the privy and down it rolled the full length of a snowy hill with the old lady inside.

I mentioned this story to one of the President's oldest friends not long after he died and his reaction was this: "Not a word of real truth to the story. Probably the only basis for it was that the President heard of how the wind blew open the old lady's privy door one day while she was inside and caused her some embarrassment. He told the story a number of times and began to add details, and you heard one of the later versions."

And this friend said as an afterthought:

"Isn't it a shame he died. A few years more, and there's no telling how that story might have ended."

If ever a man loved his home town, it was the squire of Hyde Park. He reveled in the role of squire and made a habit of keeping abreast of every trivial development in the township.

As he said in announcing that he would accept the fourth term nomination:

"All that is within me cries out to go back to my home on the Hudson River, to avoid public responsibilities, and to avoid also the publicity which in our democracy follows every step of the nation's Chief Executive."

But his love of power and his sincere belief that he was the best equipped person to lead this nation to victory overpowered the yearnings of the country squire.

Despite the Presidency, Mr. Roosevelt in his latter years was in Hyde Park as often as many American business executives were in their own homes. When the war pulled the shade of secrecy over his travels, he began going to Hyde Park virtually every week end.

It was while sitting in Hyde Park many years before that Mr. Roosevelt, watching the heavy traffic on the Albany Post Road, conceived the idea of a chain of roadside restaurants, all served by a central kitchen.

He wanted the restaurants to specialize in cold meats, sandwiches, salads, beer and ale, all of which would be delivered by truck from the central kitchen to the branch units.

But he never got around to starting this business. That may have been due to the memory of his unsuccessful venture in the lobster business.

His *Who's Who* listings don't show it, but the President told me about it—how he was set to make a fortune in lobsters but the business died on the sword of ideas that were too progressive—and admittedly impractical.

And again, this story may be in the same category of the old woman who rolled down the hill, but it went like this:

He and an unnamed associate got the idea of speeding fresh seafood from New England to the Middle West by rapid express. This was a new thing at the time—in the early twenties—and the President reasoned that an icy, fresh lobster would bring a fancy price in St. Louis.

So the business was started and for about a year it prospered. The partner handled most of the details.

Then infantile paralysis struck the President and the lobster business had to be handled entirely by the partner.

After the President recovered sufficiently to inquire about the business—about a year had passed—the partner informed him sheepishly that their bankroll of $20,000 had disappeared.

It seemed that Mr. Roosevelt's associate had the bright idea of leasing an entire bay on the Maine coast and fencing it in with wire. Soon, the partner reasoned, lobsters, being unable to escape to sea, would fill the small body of water and could be caught much more inexpensively than through the customary methods.

But, as the President explained, the poor man did not realize that lobsters have to go to sea to spawn. So the entire venture was lost.

Mr. Roosevelt always took great delight in voting at Hyde Park's old, white frame town hall. He joked with the election clerks and made a great to-do over whether he was a tree farmer, a tree grower or a plain farmer. He never identified himself as President.

I saw him vote in Hyde Park several times, but remember as most typical the November, 1942, Congressional elections and the day he cast his ballot.

Secret Service men carried him up the creaking wooden steps of the hall and then he stood up on his braces. He walked in slowly and stopped at the table presided over by J. W. Finch, chairman of District Three election board.

With one eye on the newsreel microphones and another on the President, Finch asked solemnly: "Name, please?"

"Franklin D. Roosevelt."

"Occupation?"

"Farmer," Mr. Roosevelt replied. "I think that's what I said last time."

Mr. Roosevelt leaned over to sign the registration book and received an enrollment blank from Mrs. Douglas Crapser, a clerk and an old friend.

Walking at his slow, stiff-legged and laborious gait, he entered the booth.

"They might," said the famous village squire, "raise the height of these booths."

Mrs. Roosevelt was in England at the time and her absentee ballot was supposed to be on the way.

When he came out of the booth, the President asked Finch, "Did my missus' ballot get in from London in time?"

"It is not included in the absentee ballots on hand," Finch said primly.

Mr. Roosevelt shrugged his shoulders and started for the door.

Outside he chatted for a bit with Moses Smith, one of the tenant farmers who had ceremoniously informed the Secret Service just before the President arrived, "I have to report there are no strangers in the block."

The squire got in his automobile and started for his big, gray house overlooking the Hudson. He asked the Secret Service to drive by the Hyde Park grade school where he had heard the children wanted to say hello.

The kids came boiling out of the school as the President's car rolled to a stop in front of the building. The yelling seven- and eight-year-olds broke through state troopers and agents and swarmed the car.

The children, instead of being overawed, joked with the President, and he teased back.

I never saw him laugh heartier than when a fluffy little blonde in a stiffly starched apron climbed the running board and piped up:

"I hope you have a nice election."

This man laughing and joking with grammar school children was the same man who on occasion could be as tough as a bare-knuckled prize fighter, a ruthless, storming despot.

The same Mr. Roosevelt in the space of twenty minutes in a press conference, damned the critical "parasites" who were cluttering up Washington and denounced Drew Pearson, the columnist, as a chronic liar.

This was the man who turned on some of his political associates with no warning, calling on the voters and the Democrats in particular to drum them out of office, as well as out of the party.

Yet, he was the man who found it almost impossible to fire a friend, no matter how incompetent.

He was a complex man—inconsistently harsh and gentle, alternately hard and soft, a wealthy, landed conservative who practiced radicalism. And in every action, good, bad or indifferent, a polished, urbane gentleman.

CHAPTER SIX

The House with the Talking Fence

THE new Ambassador moving up the White House reception line toward the President fumbled nervously in his trouser pocket for a cigarette lighter. A sharp-eyed young man standing near by moved quickly and tapped the Ambassador on his pocket. He jerked out his hand without a word being said. The wife of a Senator saw the incident.

"Goodness, do they think we're criminals?" she said, eying the young men who were scattered through the crowd.

These young men were too busy to explain that the United States Secret Service, White House detail, has a policy of "no chances taken" and relatively unfamiliar people are not allowed to approach the President with hands in their pockets.

That was the reason why the young men looked not at the faces of the White House guests, but at their pockets, their evening bags, and the handkerchiefs which some of the ladies carried in their hands.

Keeping the President safe from harm is an industry in itself. The Chief Executive is about the best protected man in the world. The wartime guard around Mr. Roosevelt was as careful as that around Hitler.

The same protection, although a little more informal, was continued for President Truman. He had a hard time at first becoming accustomed to the ever-present young man with a gun bulging in a hip pocket.

His attitude toward Secret Service agents was like the little boy in Stevenson's child poem: "I have a little shadow that goes in and out with me, and what can be the use of him is more than I can see."

But in a few months, Mr. Truman got the idea and resigned himself to it. He composed his own epitaph to private life: "Every time I go anywhere it is like moving a circus."

The protection of the President begins at the front gate of the White House and the wrought-iron fence around the spacious grounds.

For a time during the war the fence could talk—and eloquently. The man who first thought of the talking fence is happily anonymous because it didn't work very well.

In the early, scary days of the war, a horde of bright young electrical experts were called into consultation on a super alarm system for the White House. Within a few days they began stringing taut wire and installing mysterious little black boxes along the iron fence that encloses the White House grounds.

The idea was this: the mysterious electrical gadgets, the wire and the little black boxes made the fence as sensitive as a radio microphone. If someone tried to climb over the fence, the police could hear it through the loudspeakers.

The vocal operation of the fence was discontinued within a few days, however, because the device was so sensitive that squirrels moving around the fence made noises on the alarm system that sounded like human beings.

Another tricky wartime alarm device was abandoned the very day it was completed. This was an electric eye gun-and-knife detector installed at the main entrance to the executive offices.

The thing cost thousands of dollars, but never was actually used because the police officer who opened the door for visiting dignitaries carried a gun. This set off the warning system each time he went to the door.

The detector also was abandoned for other practical reasons. Suppose the British Ambassador passed through the invisible rays of the machine and the dial in the little office a few feet away indicated that he was carrying a gun?

To stop and search him would have created an international incident.

While frayed ends of installation wire were still being swept out of the doorway, the Secret Service decided to rely on its time-tested system of watching pockets and suspicious packages. The protocol risks of the detector were too great.

At first glance, the extreme precautions taken by the Secret Service to safeguard the President seem overdone. But their point is that they are charged by law with responsibility for his safety. Therefore, they say there cannot be too much security.

There is an ever-present threat of assassination hanging over any President. The week rarely passes that a crank somewhere does not write a letter threatening to blow the President to kingdom come, usually because of some imagined injustice.

Each letter of this type is carefully investigated and traced. If the writer is a known nut and harmless, he or persons responsible for him are warned. Also, in a number of these cases the person who makes the threat is committed to a mental institution for observation, and sometimes, long term detention.

The Secret Service is no respecter of individuals when it comes to the President.

Even Cabinet members who visit the White House once or twice a week are checked from the front gate to the door, and from the receptionist's desk into the President's office. Every minute a visitor is in the White House the Secret Service knows exactly where he is and what he is doing.

Walking through the spacious White House lobby outside Mr. Truman's office, a first-time visitor probably does not notice the young men who survey him from the red leather chairs that line the room. These men look, at first glance, more like visiting college boys than the highly trained experts they are.

On the porch outside the President's office—in good weather and bad—there are other agents on duty. They are in the lobby of the White House proper, and at least one unobtrusively on duty in the second-floor residential quarters of the President's family.

Three shifts a day, around the clock, they watch for the man or woman who might want to harm the President or some member of his family.

There is, of course, no actual "frisking" of White House visitors. The Secret Service men can tell at a glance whether a person is carrying a concealed weapon. They look for suspicious bulges. And they look at all pockets impersonally, treat all visitors alike.

No one—even close personal friends such as Reconversion Director John W. Snyder or the President's military aide, Brigadier General Harry H. Vaughan—actually is as close to the President as the alert young men whose lives are literally dedicated to preserving the President's safety.

Every minute of the day and night, there are several of them within a few feet of the President, regardless of whether he is in his White House bedroom, aboard a battleship or meeting with Stalin and Attlee at Potsdam.

Congress handed the responsibility of protecting the President and members of his family to the Secret Service shortly after the assassination of President McKinley. The first White House detail of the Secret Service, a unit of the Treasury Department, went to work during the administration of Theodore Roosevelt.

Since then there has not been a successful attempt on the life of a President, and this is largely due to the policy of "no chances taken."

(The Secret Service does not count the attempted assassination of F.D.R. in Miami by Zangara as an attempt on the life of a president. He had not been sworn into office when Zangara shot at him, killing Mayor Edward Cermak of Chicago instead of Mr. Roosevelt.)

Literally every foot the President covers outside the White House is "cased" thoroughly in advance. For example, a picked, trained crew of Secret Service agents spent ten days in Chicago in advance of Mr. Truman's one-day visit there on Army Day in April, 1946. They examined every foot of the routes to be traveled by the President during the eight hours he was in the city.

They checked hotel employees, particularly cooks and waiters. They went into the life histories of the men who would drive automobiles in the Presidential entourage. And they furnished Chicago police with pictures of letter-writing cranks known to live in the area.

(Three arrests were made in Chicago that trip—two of them Secret Service suspects of long standing. Police and agents caught the threateners in crowds gathered near the President's train and in the lobby of his hotel.)

Parade routes in cities other than Washington are carefully blueprinted and diagramed in advance.

And strangers who will be close to him are checked and investigated one by one. That goes for members of church congregations as well as luncheon guests.

When the President goes out to dine, every servant working in the building where the meal will be served is checked and double-checked by the Secret Service long before the date of the dinner. Even entertainers are investigated in advance.

When anyone with a criminal record is turned up, the host or person in charge is told that the one in question must be removed from the scene or the President stays in the White House. To date the Secret Service has had no argument on this point.

At a Washington hotel where Mr. Roosevelt was to dine the agents found among the employees fifty aliens, some with criminal records plus one man wanted for murder in Texas. The very proper and dignified hotel management was mortified.

(No President—Mr. Roosevelt or Mr. Truman—has been in that hotel since then.)

During his latter years, Mr. Roosevelt had little time to accept outside invitations because of the heavy press of his war chores. He went to church a few times during the year, however, and regardless of how many times he had been in a particular church, the Secret Service made an inch-by-inch check of the building. The pastor was asked to furnish in advance a list of the congregation members who would attend the service.

On New Year's Day, 1942, when the President and Winston Churchill went to Christ Church at Alexandria, Virginia, to worship in the pew once occupied by George Washington, members of the congregation permitted to attend the service were not notified until a few hours before the two famous men walked into the little red brick building. The rector had prepared a list of the parishioners whom he wanted to attend, selected on the basis of their past church attendance.

The Secret Service made its customary check and found no suspicious characters. Advance word of the service was withheld, however, until shortly before dawn on New Year's morning.

Then a messenger from the church rode through the picturesque streets of old Alexandria, knocking on the doors of the selected parishioners.

Each sleepy church member was a little confused when the messenger handed over a card of admission to the church. The card made no mention of the President or Churchill, but the messenger warned, "You'll certainly regret it if you don't come this morning."

Most of them were in the pews at ten o'clock despite

the fact that the night before was New Year's Eve. And a clearly audible gasp of amazement filled the small Episcopalian church when Mr. Roosevelt, on the arm of his aide, and Churchill walked down the aisle.

Outside, around the church, for hours soldiers with rifles and machine guns had been stationed on the house-tops. Similarly armed patrols covered near-by alleys and all possible approaches, allowing no one to come near the place without credentials.

When Mr. Truman goes to church, now that the war is over and the danger of enemy agents is apparently dissipated, the operation is much simpler. The President dislikes any publicity in connection with his church-going. He doesn't want reporters or photographers along, so when they accompany him they remain fairly well in the background.

The men who guard the President are for the most part young and husky. Great care is taken when they are selected from the Secret Service field forces for the White House assignment. They must be levelheaded and virtually immune from overexcitement in time of crisis.

They are crack shots, as good with a Tommy gun as with the .38 caliber revolvers which they wear every moment they are on duty. They dislike automatics because of their tendency to jam, and the fact, too, that the slide on an automatic must be pulled back before it can be fired. That split second might mean life or death for the President.

They spend several hours a month on the target range. Every agent on the White House detail must be able to shoot with amazing accuracy with either hand, because he never can tell on which side of the President's car he may be riding when trouble develops.

Their pistol marksmanship is tested on one of the toughest target ranges in the country. The bull's-eye of their target is about half the size of the one ordinarily used on police and army ranges. And on repeated occasions, I have seen an agent casually outshoot a marine sharpshooter without half trying.

Secret Service men assigned to the White House must qualify with an unusually high marksmanship score every thirty days. They make sort of a game of their shooting ability and unmercifully kid a man who has a bad score on the range.

Each agent during the war was schooled to expertness anent poison gas. All of them are graduate first-aid experts and prominent psychiatrists lecture them periodically on how to spot and cope with twisted mentalities.

As to their own physical condition, most of them tend toward the athletic type. Many of them were college sports stars. They keep in shape by working out frequently at a gymnasium near the White House with their own trainer.

Their favorite sport for keeping in physical trim is handball—they say it is the best way in the world to keep down the waistline and develop long-lasting wind.

If an agent gets a bad cold, he is sent home to recover completely because if one man of this highly co-ordinated White House job were not fully able to carry out his assignment, the efficiency of the entire detail might be thrown out of gear in an emergency.

The long sessions of handball build up lung power for the most grueling part of the Secret Service assignment—trotting alongside the President's car when it is moving slowly through crowds, or along parade routes. They have to dogtrot for miles on occasion, keeping a sharp lookout for people who might dash out to the President's car or suspicious persons lurking in upper windows.

In 1943, when Mr. Roosevelt drove through Monterrey, Mexico, with President Avila Camacho, the procession moved through block after block of excited, cheering Mexicans at a rate of speed slightly under ten miles an hour. But the Secret Service agents assigned to the Presidential automobile had to run virtually every step of the way.

Their total dogtrot mileage under a hot Mexican April sun was over five miles a man. And while on the run they had to snatch screaming Indian children from beneath the wheels of the car, bat down strange bouquets which hurtled down from the tops of houses and keep unauthorized photographers at a distance.

The Secret Service is at its colorful best when escorting the President through large crowds. The agents can quickly tell the difference between a crank who might be dangerous and an overenthusiastic "jumper"—a person, usually a girl or woman, who, suddenly finding the President of the United States before her eyes, jumps up and down screaming wildly, "It's *him!* It's *him!*"

In most crowds the problem is not keeping away would-be assassins, but controlling exuberant spectators. During the 1944 campaign with Mr. Roosevelt, I saw an agent painfully injured when he risked his life to shove a shouting old man out of the path of a trailing police squad car. The agent bounced the man out of the way, and in so doing, slipped on a wet cobblestone street and slid into the high, stone curbing.

When the President is on the road, the Secret Service

puts a line of agents around his car, railroad or motor, whenever it stops. This "cordon caution" is not always visible, but it is always there.

Frequently people—usually in small towns—resent the hovering watch of the Secret Service over the President. They think it is a slur on their community.

During the war, there were occasional army and navy officers whose resentment of the Secret Service surrounding the President in a military installation was beyond disguise.

I recall an exchange which took place between an agent and an army officer when Mr. Roosevelt was touring army camps during the war.

The officer, aide to a general, was offended by the presence of the agents, civilians who seemed to have rather good control of the situation.

"Why," said the officer, "is it necessary to have so much protection for the President when he is on an army post? He's safer here than in the White House."

The agent smiled politely. A full division of infantrymen was drawn up for review before the President.

"Just look at all those men with guns," commented the agent to no one in particular.

The close Secret Service guard around the President when he was in an army camp or a naval station was no reflection on the armed services. The agents reasoned, however, that conceivably among the millions of men in service were a few soreheads who might blame the President for their being in service. And such soreheads had guns.

On the other hand, during Mr. Roosevelt's two major wartime tours of factories and army camps in the fall of 1942 and the spring of 1943, Secret Service precautions were implemented by thousands of soldiers guarding the route of his train. Every inch of track from Washington to California and back again was inspected and switches were locked to make sure there could be no collision or derailment. Upward of 150,000 soldiers were used on each of these trips.

And several soldiers were killed while guarding the President's train tracks. These were unfortunate boys who tried to get a little nap along the right of way before the Presidential train came by. Their choice of a resting place was tragic.

Occasionally during the two big wartime inspection trips an army officer took his Presidential guard duty as something of a God-given assignment and consequently went well beyond the scope of his orders.

One night in April, 1943, when the train stopped over on a Missouri siding for a few hours, members of the Presidential party who attempted to leave their cars for a breath of fresh air found bayonets rammed at them when they stepped from the train.

As I started out of my car a young corporal ran out of the dark and pushed his bayonet to within an inch or so of my belt line.

"Get back on the train, buddy," he said.

"What in hell goes on here?" I asked, climbing back up the steep stairs of the car.

"My orders are that no one gets off, no one gets on," he told me, keeping his rifle pointed at my middle. "And those orders stand until the colonel tells me different."

I didn't have to ask where the colonel was because I could see and hear a full-fledged argument going on back near the entrance to Mr. Roosevelt's private car. I went back through the train and found that the colonel and his earnest young troops would not allow the Secret Service to put out the usual line of agents around that car. Neither would they allow a frantic railroad flagman to set out his flares at the end of the train as required by safety regulations.

Frank R. Wilson, chief of the entire Secret Service organization, finally argued the colonel into seeing the error of his ways. The colonel grudgingly let the Secret Service men take up their posts around the car where the President was sleeping.

Later the colonel heard from the War Department that the object of such an assignment was to keep unauthorized persons from approaching the train. He probably would not have heard that much about the incident if he had not compounded his felony by boarding the train and refusing to pay for whisky which was served to him in the Pullman club car.

Things are rarely dull around the Secret Service, particularly when the President is outside the White House.

There was the case of the bomb in the ball park.

Mr. Roosevelt was going out to Washington's Griffith Stadium to watch the opening baseball game of the season. And the Secret Service sent out an advance detail to guard the particular area around the Chief Executive's box.

One agent was assigned to the part of the grandstand directly above the box where the President would sit. As he took up his post an hour or so before Mr. Roosevelt arrived, the agent noticed three obvious foreigners sitting at the rail, peering down into the Presidential box.

They talked excitedly in a foreign language, gesturing frequently to an ominous little brown box held by the man in the middle.

Unsnapping his pocket holster and ready for trouble, the agent walked over to the three men. He was confident a bomb plot was brewing. He moved in fast and before the three foreigners knew what was happening, he planted himself in front of the middle man and demanded the box.

The three men conferred in a babbling conversation, then surrendered the box. The agent cautiously lifted the lid and found six sandwiches, some deviled eggs and salt and pepper inside. The three men were attachés at the Spanish Embassy attending their first baseball game. They had their lunch with them.

The men of the Secret Service had to change their routine when Mr. Truman entered the White House. After twelve years, there was again a President who could walk.

Following a few occasions when the President ducked out of his office by a rear door to go to lunch in his White House dining room without notifying the agents on guard at the front of his office, an agent was stationed just outside Mr. Truman's "back" door.

The job now is more difficult than it was with Mr. Roosevelt because Mr. Truman is highly active, likes to be on the go a great deal of the time and moves fast when he is moving.

The current President has no personal bodyguard as Mr. Roosevelt had. The personal man was rather necessary to the late President because he always needed someone near by to help with his braces, assist him from one chair to another, and also, to help him to the bathroom when his valet was not at immediate hand.

Mr. Truman, however, needs no individual care except a helping hand when his curiosity gets the better of him and he climbs into railroad engines or scrambles up into the fire control tower of a fighting ship.

His first encounter with his "shadows" happened while he was still Vice President.

An agent, quietly assigned by the Secret Service, appeared at the Truman apartment every morning and accompanied him to his Senate office.

This went on for several weeks before the Vice President found out who was riding beside his driver in the front seat. He thought the agent was a friend of the chauffeur hitching a ride to town.

CHAPTER SEVEN

Pearly Gates

HOW would you like to live in a house where one minute a messenger from the Lord was at the front door, and the next minute a man with a gun who wanted to blow your head off?

That's the way things are at 1600 Pennsylvania Avenue most of the time and it takes alert White House police and Secret Service agents to see that these screwballs don't get by and raise pluperfect hell inside the White House.

One cold winter day up to the northwest gate came a man in a snappy double-breasted, wing lapel overcoat. He wanted to see the President and see him fast. He had a little proposition, said he out of the side of his mouth, to talk over with the big guy. Honestly, it really happened that way.

So, this man was sent into a little reception booth at the gate to talk with a Secret Service agent who immediately spotted a bulge under the man's left armpit which fairly shouted "shoulder holster."

"You better let me have that gun," the agent said.

The man chuckled, dipped inside his coat and handed over a Colt automatic .45.

"What's on your mind, buddy?" said the somewhat relieved agent.

"I want to see the President," was the reply, "and you think you're pretty smart, don't you? You think you've got all my guns?"

"Well, hand over what's left."

Then the man reached inside his coat and came up with a .38 revolver.

The agent's desk began to look like a pawnshop counter on Saturday night.

The man continued.

"You guys think you're so smart. You haven't found all my guns yet."

Before the astonished agent could say anything more, the man reached into each hip pocket and pulled out two more guns. And within a few minutes he was on his way to St. Elizabeth's Hospital for observation.

The White House police will never forget the day the white-winged Angel of the Lord came to call. He was a tall, lithe colored man who came skipping up to the front gate on tiptoe and flapping large and shimmery white wings.

Watching the strange figure glide through the summer heat to the White House entrance, one of the guards remarked to his buddy:

"This heat is getting me. I'd swear the guy comin' there was wearing wings."

He was. Not only king-size wings, but ankle-length flowing white robes and an ornate scroll tucked under one wing.

Stopping before the popeyed policeman, the "angel" proclaimed in Gabrielian tones, "I have a message from the Lord—a message of peace for the President."

Letting the angel cool his wings for a minute, the guards called for James Sloan, then the crank expert of

the Secret Service who was in the business of listening to
the impassioned pleas of unexpected White House callers from the days of Teddy Roosevelt until he died in
1945.

Sloan, from his experience, could see that the angel
was harmless, so he impressed on the deadly serious herald that the message from the Lord to the President would
be accepted with pleasure, but not by the Chief Executive in person. The angel walked away disconsolately, his
pretty white wings drooping in the hot sun that baked
Pennsylvania Avenue.

There's hardly a day that someone doesn't come to the
White House with a message of burning importance for
the President. Sometimes it is a Cabinet officer and he
gets in. But often it is a zealous inventor with a radio
death ray or a woman who thinks the O.P.A. is con-
trolled from Moscow. They don't get in.

The white-winged Angel of the Lord was a colorful
example of the thousands of people who believe the
world will stop unless they have a heart-to-heart chat with
the Number One man of the nation. They come to the
White House in person every day. They send gifts and
models of Goldbergish inventions. They write letters by
the thousand and when they have the money they telephone from all parts of the country.

Most of these people are profoundly sincere and a
great many of them would never be classed as zanies if
they stopped to realize that any President of the United
States is a tremendously busy man and can see only a
relatively few and important people each day.

The White House for years has maintained a kindly
attitude toward the "uninvited" except when they are

clearly dangerous or write threatening letters. Then the Secret Service moves in fast with action ranging from prosecution or commitment in a mental institution to stern warnings. Even the authors of threatening anonymous letters are usually tracked down in a surprisingly short time.

One afternoon during the war I received a long distance call in the White House press room from a small town in Canada. The strange voice, explaining that he had seen my by-line over White House news stories, wanted to let me in on something good.

"You can be of great help in ending the war within sixty days, Mr. Smith."

"How?" I asked.

"I have something here that, placed in the hands of the Allies, will crush Germany and Japan almost overnight. I want you to go to the President now—this afternoon—and tell him about it. Then the two of you get on a train tonight. You bring the President up here, but don't bring Harry Hopkins or General Marshall or any of those people. Just you and the President. And no Secret Service."

"Who are you and what is this thing that will end the war so rapidly?"

"Do you think," said the mysterious man in an "oh-you-poor-fool" tone of voice, "that I'd be so foolish as to tell you about it over the telephone? I'll tell one person —the President."

Then he gave a name and address, explaining that the name was fictitious, but the address was real.

"Why a real address but a phony name?"

"I am a writer, Mr. Smith," he said scornfully. "I use a *nom de plume*."

He hung up after warning me that if I failed my mission, the blame for years of bloody war would be on my head. I reported the call to the Secret Service right away. Within three hours officers of the Royal Canadian Mounted Police were talking to the man in his apartment.

His peace plan? No one could figure it out from the mass of scrawled manuscript that littered the man's lodgings.

Before Pearl Harbor most people with an "I-got-to-see-the-President" story could get inside the White House grounds and up to the entrance of the executive offices. Wartime restrictions, however, closed the grounds to the public and the folks with a burning story must tell it to the guards and the Secret Service men at the front gate.

Often it is difficult for the officers to draw the line between the dangerously unbalanced and the overzealous.

A hard-faced young man in denim trousers and a dirty woolen pullover swaggered up to the White House gates shortly after Pearl Harbor and demanded in a loud, angry voice to see the President.

"By God," he said, "I'm gonna see that guy and shake it out of him. I got money comin' to me and nobody's gonna do me out of it, not even the President."

At first the youth looked to the White House guards like a dangerous person. A Secret Service agent talked to him and after much patient effort, drew from the boy the story of his life in the merchant marine and how he had been torpedoed three times. In his last sinking the young man lost all of his papers and, so he said, had coming to him three months' pay which his company was withholding until they verified his employment record.

The agent had the youth wait in another room while he checked the story. Most of it turned out to be true; all of it, in fact, except the young seaman's idea that the company was deliberately trying to cheat him.

The seaman was sent to a merchant marine rest home near Washington. A week or so later he turned up again at the White House gates to tell his "friends" that everything was straightened out and he was anxious to go to sea again.

A little old lady lugging a shoe box and clutching a shawl around her neck showed up one night with the same old plea: "Must see the President."

She had come all the way from the Tennessee mountains by day coach to tell the President about the death of her fifth husband. She wanted Mr. Roosevelt to release her son from the Army "so he can help with the farm until I marry up again."

They told her at the gate that the President was mighty busy running the war and there was a special part of the War Department to handle cases like hers.

It was a different story on another night several years ago, New Year's Eve to be exact. This happened in the prewar days when entrances to the White House were not completely barred to outsiders as they are today.

The President and Mrs. Roosevelt were giving a small party for their younger sons and a few of their friends. Among the guests was Secretary of the Treasury Henry Morgenthau, Jr., who told the guards that he expected his son and daughter to arrive shortly.

A short time later a nice-looking young couple—they seemed to be about seventeen or eighteen years old—presented themselves at the White House door and announced they had come to see the President. Those in charge bowed them in, taking them for the Morgenthau children but not realizing that the boy and girl were complete strangers and storming the White House as part of a New Year's Eve dare.

The boy and girl scampered up the broad steps leading to the Roosevelts' personal living quarters where the small party was in progress. No one, even the President, paid much attention at first but it was only a few minutes before their secret was out, due to the arrival of the Morgenthau boy and girl.

The President did not think much of the prank and the kids were quickly hustled away by red-faced Secret Service men.

The White House was increasingly unhappy about the incident because the kids ran right to the local papers and boasted of their exploit which began when the girl dared her date to try to see the President.

The "uninvited" sometimes descend on the White House in mass formation. "Peace" pickets, for example, walked outside the Pennsylvania Avenue entrance for weeks before our entry into the war, carrying KEEP OUT OF WAR and THE YANKS ARE NOT COMING signs. After being called Communists, the pickets, as their critics were happy to point out, broke up their placards and moved away from the White House about the time the German attack on Russia was announced.

Various "Mothers" organizations were active in front of the executive mansion before Pearl Harbor, demanding frequent audience with the President and vowing that their boys should not be made to fight "for the British Empire."

The White House police suffered these people to picket as they liked, just so they kept moving.

Pickets came back to the White House right after VJ-Day, asking for the release of conscientious objectors.

The mail brings a daily avalanche of messages from folks all over the world. A surprising number of letters get to the Chief Executive, but of necessity most of them are handled by the staff or referred to the various government agencies.

Mr. Roosevelt often by a casual remark unwittingly caused the normally heavy mail to leap to mountainous proportions. He said in a press conference that he had a recipe for stretching coffee. Within a few days the White House mail room was knee deep in a flood of similar recipes, with a few coffeecakes and doughnuts thrown in for good measure.

Thoughtful ladies, mindful of Washington's foul weather, always shower a President, be he Republican or Democrat, with countless scarves and comforters. Frequently there are ornately stitched samplers in the mail proclaiming the President's good or bad points, depending on the political feelings of the seamstress.

Every year around January 30, Mr. Roosevelt's birthday, the mail room overflowed with extra special gifts aside from the thousands of dimes for the National Infantile Paralysis Fund. There always were a number of unusual portraits—pictures of the President done in bottle caps, canceled stamps, molded newsprint and bits of colored mirrors.

The White House, like a country newspaper, also gets its share of double-jointed potatoes, carrots grown in the shape of the Chief Executive's head and three-yolked eggs.

Each package is carefully inspected as it arrives on the theory that it is possible that sometimes the post office would fail to catch a cake which had been wired to explode.

Many of the Roosevelt gifts ended up at the President's museum in Hyde Park where the trophies range from a valuable tea set presented by the King of Norway to a donkey, symbol of the Democratic party, made of old 1940 Willkie buttons. There was a twenty-foot bull-whip from a rancher in Texas and a jeweled scimitar from the King of Arabia.

When a package looks the least bit questionable, before it is opened the bundle is put under a fluoroscope. If the fluoroscope shows anything suspicious, bomb disposal experts are put to work.

I was the source of extreme unhappiness to the White House mail room one afternoon. Several sacks of mail were delivered to the White House and when the mail room crew picked up one of the bags, it emitted a very mournful noise which sounded much like the love call of a lonesome cow. The men backed away from the mail sack in amazement and called for the experts.

They opened the bag gingerly and picked out the packages one by one. Finally they came to one that moaned every time it was moved. With steel tongs the package was lifted gently from the bag and address on it said: "Merriman Smith, Press Room, the White House." They shook it and turned it and the moaning continued.

Finally in desperation one of the bomb experts deftly slit open one end of the small package, and then a piece of the inner wrapping. There he saw a round red object with an open grillwork at one end. With his special iron tongs he eased the little red thing out of the paper and read with disgust, "Cow call—fool your friends."

When the thing was finally delivered to me, along with it was a profane message from the mail room to tell my wacky friends to confine their gags to my office or home, but not send them to the White House.

It didn't take Mr. Truman long to find out about White House mail.

On his first visit to Kansas City—his home stompin' grounds—after succeeding to the Presidency, the President one afternoon dropped in to see Eddie Jacobson, his old haberdashery partner. The President needed some new white shirts, size 15½, 33 sleeve. Eddie, much to his embarrassment, was out of that size as was most every men's clothing store during the latter stages of the war.

It made a nice little feature story and everybody printed it. And within a matter of hours, messengers began to arrive at the Muehlebach Hotel suite set aside for the President. Some brought six shirts. Some brought twelve. And inside of twenty-four hours, the President was receiving fancy numbers with red, white and blue monograms.

And while this was happening in Kansas City, the White House mail room back in Washington was getting groggy—shirts by the dozen in every mail. The President, since, won't admit to having received more than "a couple of hundred," but the fact is that he got nearer one thousand. Ask him about it and all he'll say is, "Well, I've sure got a closetful."

The President learned his lesson on the shirts. A few trips later, when he stopped by Eddie's to buy some socks, he whispered the size to Eddie and later refused to tell reporters what it was. But just to let the President know he can't get away with that sort of stuff—the size is 11 and go ahead, send him some socks.

(I wear 10½ and in a pinch could wear 11, and what he doesn't know won't hurt him. Maybe I might snag a pair or so.)

Any report on the many interesting people who "absolutely must" get in the White House should not overlook the classic case of Schwartz, the fire layer.

In the days of President Taft the White House was heated largely by fireplaces. It was the daily duty of a heavily bearded gentleman named Schwartz to lay the fires and have them ready for the touch of a match. Schwartz's job was understandably dirty. Instead of the white-coated costume worn by the other men servants in the mansion, he worked in a rather dirty pair of overalls and coat with grime to match. The bush black beard and the dingy costume gave Schwartz a sinister appearance.

When Mrs. Taft noticed Schwartz around the White House for the first time she was aghast. She stopped him in a hall, so the story goes, and exclaimed, "My good man, who are you and what do you do around here?"

"I'm Schwartz, ma'am," he said humbly. "I lay the fires."

Mrs. Taft said bluntly she couldn't have Schwartz around looking like that. She ordered him to put on a white coat like the rest of the help.

"And have that beard shaved off before you come in here again," she added.

Schwartz put aside his scuttle of coal and kindling and mournfully went to a barbershop down the street. When he returned his appearance was greatly changed by the oyster white of his freshly shaved jowls. The guards at the door looked at him with a glint of recognition, but refused to admit him.

A Secret Service man spotted Schwartz, however, and recognized him despite the prison pallor that underlies any beard of considerable vintage. The agent convoyed Schwartz inside where the President saw them.

"Who is that man?" Mr. Taft inquired of the agent. Told that "it" was Schwartz the fire layer, the President roared with laughter. When he saw a tear in Schwartz's eyes, he commiserated with him over the loss of the wonderful beard. "Go home," the President instructed, "and wait until the beard grows back. We'll keep your job for you, but we can't have you around looking like a ghost."

An hour or so later Schwartz was back at the White House, this time more mournful than ever. Without the beard, his wife had not recognized him and slammed the house door in his face.

An aide went back home with Schwartz and succeeded in convincing the missus that the white-jawed creature was really her husband, a victim of White House décor.

CHAPTER EIGHT

How the Fire Started

WHEN a house burns, the frequent case is that even the fire department has a hard time determining the cause of the blaze and how it started.

It is the same way with wars. The Congress for years will seek a clear cut account of how the last war actually began and why. And there will be almost as many reasons as there will be witnesses.

From the Washington end, I saw the last war start. I helped turn in the alarm.

On Saturday, November 30, 1941, there was the first clear indication so far as the public was concerned that actual conflict for this country was not far away.

For two weeks previous, the bulky, bearlike Japanese Ambassador, Admiral Kichisaburo Nomura, and his "peace" envoy-colleague sent from Tokyo on specific assignment, little Saburo Kurusu, talked at the State Department and at the White House, allegedly seeking a basis for easing the Japanese-American tension in the Pacific.

The talks produced nothing concrete except that the Japanese were fencing, shifting on their feet and demanding what they were certain the United States would not grant.

President Roosevelt had planned to go to Warm Springs, Georgia, his "other home" and site of the Infantile Paralysis Foundation, for a Thanksgiving holiday on November 20, the "New Deal" Thanksgiving. The Japanese situation caused him to move the trip back to the old-fashioned Thanksgiving a week later, and even then he found the Japanese situation too tense to leave even for a moment.

But the Chief Executive was weary and needed a rest, however brief. The disappointment of the polio patients at Warm Springs because of his absence weighed heavily on his mind, and he suddenly decided to make a quick trip to Warm Springs for a "third Thanksgiving" on November 30.

Those of us who made the trip were told confidentially we probably would remain in Warm Springs "four or five days," but on the way down, members of the official party said they expected the President to remain ten days at least, if the weather was good and the international situation did not take a turn for the worse.

The Presidential special reached the village of Newnan, Georgia, Saturday morning, November 30, after an overnight run from Washington. The weather was ideal and Mr. Roosevelt decided to ride the remaining forty miles of the trip to Warm Springs in an open car, waving frequently to farmers attracted to the highway by the far-carrying whine of the motorcycle escort.

Arriving at Warm Springs, the newspapermen split up into two cottages and provisioned them for at least a week. Everyone relaxed, had a few drinks and entered into the spirit of a much-needed holiday.

The President and the correspondents gathered in the

late afternoon at the cottage of Leighton McCarthy, then the Canadian Minister and a Warm Springs Foundation trustee, for a brief cocktail party before going to Georgia Hall and the traditional Thanksgiving dinner with the patients.

The President appeared gay and glad to be out of Washington when he arrived somewhat late at the Mc-Carthy party. Among the guests were some not in the official party and to whom the sight of the President was an awe-inspiring event. The President, when he was seated, looked around at some of the wide-eyed people and snorted, "Well, get me a drink—that's what I came for!"

This lusty, hail-fellow approach from the President broke what ice there was among the gape-jawed wall-flowers. The newspapermen took one quick drink and adjourned to their own cottage next door for dinner, spurning the heavy fixings of the Presidential dinner.

The President was scheduled to speak to the patients after the dinner and not too many of the newspapermen worried about catching his extemporaneous remarks because such addresses usually were very important to the patients but made little news in the outside world.

We elbowed our way into the packed dining hall just before Mr. Roosevelt spoke. The sight was half inspiring, half depressing. The patients, from little children to grownups, ate halfheartedly, fearing to take their eyes off their idol for a second lest he disappear as magically as he had appeared.

He rose to speak, the better the patients to see him. His speech began in customarily hackneyed channels: "Glad to be back . . . my other home . . . always inspired to be here." He interjected a few gentle wisecracks, but with an imperceptible change of direction, moved into a discussion of the war.

The newspapermen knew this sudden change in the tone of his remarks was intended for them rather than the polio patients; for the world rather than the roomful of cripples and invalids in their rolling beds and wheel chairs.

The President spoke of the oppressed people of Europe and how little they had to be thankful for. By next Thanksgiving, he said, we in America also may be "looking back on a peaceful past."

The newspapermen knew something ominous and world-shaking was about to be said. The Roosevelt build-up to a smashing remark was unmistakable.

The climax was slow and deceptive in its approach. Mr. Roosevelt suddenly veered to tell how he had spent part of the afternoon listening to the Army-Navy football broadcast. Where else in the world, he asked, could such a game be held except in the United States? Then the climax.

By next Thanksgiving, the President said, our boys in training at the naval and military academies "may actually be fighting in the defense of this country."

He stopped and as the echo of his voice fell before the thunderous applause, the newspapermen broke for the door, sidestepping around wheel chairs, skipping over crutches in a mad dash for the telegraph office.

I yelled to my wire operator as I hit the door of the telegraph office:

"Flash—Warm Springs, Georgia—Roosevelt says we may be fighting within a year."

Then I sat down with the fourteen other reporters and began to pound out a story. Sheet after sheet of copy, at least half consisting of background on the events that had happened in the previous two weeks, I poured into the wire, only to be heartsickened by a message from my bureau in Atlanta, where the story was being relayed to the nation, that I had started out too strong; that they were rewording my copy to tone it down.

I argued that this was the most definite thing said by Mr. Roosevelt in some time and amid the exchange of messages, a telephone call came to the telegraph office from the "Little White House" where the President lived while in Warm Springs.

Steve Early, the press secretary, had an announcement: The President, immediately after his speech, returned to the Little White House to find that Secretary of State Cordell Hull had been trying to reach him by telephone with an urgent message.

He talked to Hull at once about the grave Japanese situation. The result of this conference was that the President and his party probably would have to return to the capital at once. The definite decision would be made Sunday morning, then a few hours away.

This news touched off another flurry of writing; urgent bulletins were slammed down in front of the telegraph operators anew and away we rode on our typewriters again with more stories that forecast drastically serious developments.

We finally tied up the loose ends of our stories and went to our cottage, only to be roused from a few hours' sleep and told by the White House staff that the President had talked again with Hull early that morning. He decided to leave for Washington as soon as his train was ready.

We had time to write stories telling of the hasty return and to summarize the events of the night before. Then clothes were flung into bags, farewell drinks gulped with some of the old-time Foundation residents and we boarded our cars for the ride to Newnan where the train waited.

The return journey lacked the frivolity and high spirits of the trip down to Georgia. No one knew what was coming, but it was going to be bad. The Japanese Foreign Minister had made an insultingly militant speech the same night the President spoke in Warm Springs and this pointed to collapse of the peace talks in Washington.

At every stop on the fast trip to Washington, special White House telephone circuits were connected from the train to the capital and the President kept abreast of last-minute developments until he retired for the night.

The President sped from the railroad station to the White House next morning, Monday, December 2, and went into immediate conference with Hull. As we dumped our bags in the press room of the White House which we had left only two days before, we expected a diplomatic crisis to develop hurriedly, but no one dreamed that six days later we would be handling the news of Pearl Harbor.

I wasn't at Pearl Harbor on December 7, 1941, getting hit by Japanese bombs, but I must admit that I felt I was in a little hell of my own. Newspapermen for many days thought of that whirling Sunday and remarked gravely, "God, what a day!"

I was spending a leisurely Sunday at home and after

loafing all morning, decided to shave and look presentable for some relatives from the South whose arrival was expected momentarily. Whistling to the bathroom mirror, I thought back over the events of the previous week.

The hasty return from Warm Springs. The conferences with Kurusu and Nomura. A lot of conferences tied into the deepening crisis, but they didn't quite add up.

My wife, always a calm, levelheaded woman, knocked on the bathroom door about 2:25 P.M. and said rather puckishly:

"You know what the radio just said?"

"No, what?"

"It said the Japanese bombed Hawaii."

I nearly knocked her down coming out of the bathroom and grabbed the telephone. By an unusual quirk of the dial system the office was trying to get me at that very moment. I picked up the receiver to hear the Sunday night editor of the United Press in Washington bellowing:

"Japs just bombed Pearl Harbor. Get to the White House fastsyoucan."

Bang went his receiver and bang went mine. I pulled on a shirt, grabbed up a tie and coat and ran for my car. A few blocks from my house I spotted a motorcycle policeman and hailed him.

"Officer, the Japs have just attacked us in the Pacific and I've got to get to the White House right away. How about an escort?"

"Why, those little bastards," he replied, jamming down the starter lever on his motorbike. "What entrance do you want?"

"Just pull me in between the White House and the State Department."

We made the six-mile run from Arlington County to the White House in less than ten minutes, dodging through heavy Sunday afternoon traffic behind the cop and his howling motorcycle. I pulled into West Executive Avenue behind him, slammed the car into a parking space, yelled my thanks and ran into the White House.

Only a handful of men were in the press room. Steve Early had made the first announcement via telephone to the three press association offices, then started for the White House. The guard on the door told me that Early would have a press conference in a few minutes.

My breathing was about normal again when Steve held his first conference and gave us some details of the attack on Hawaii, including the first word of heavy casualties.

From then until about midnight there occurred the maddest scramble, the most rapid succession of world-shaking stories in the memory of the oldest old-timer in the newspaper business around Washington.

In a space of four hours I handled four flashes and eight bulletin stories. That means to a press association man that the heat was on about as hot as it ever will be. Men spend an entire lifetime in press association work without ever handling one flash story. I had four in four hours.

Much—too much—has been written in chronological accounts of that day at the White House. So I won't go into the hard details of when and what Mr. Roosevelt did. Newspapermen in harking back to that day think more of the other side of the picture.

For instance, no story at the White House ever brought

out the crowd of reporters that Pearl Harbor did. By five o'clock the afternoon of Pearl Harbor, there must have been one hundred reporters, radio men, newsreel and still photographers, assorted secretaries and Washington big shots trying to crowd into the press room where normally about a dozen men work.

The floor was soon carpeted with cigarette stubs. Radio newscasters coughed as they poured the story of the Japanese surprise into their microphones.

Men came rushing in from the professional football game, Sunday afternoon rides and the Press Club bar. New York papers flew in reinforcements for their Washington staffs and these men, entirely new to White House press room customs, tried repeatedly to grab private line telephones for their own use. Doug Cornell of the A.P., George Durno of the I.N.S. and I finally had to post big signs on our telephone booths, explaining carefully that these phones were for the exclusive use of the three press associations.

Every time anyone stepped out of Early's suite of offices it was the signal for a mad rush by the reporters. These men weren't rushing just to live up to the public's mistaken idea about journalistic behavior. They were rushing because extras were being printed all over the world. The world wanted the news of Pearl Harbor and new details when they were available. Fifteen seconds' margin might have made an earlier edition.

One girl started out of Steve Early's office in the direction of a women's toilet. But the hair-triggered crowd of newspapermen thought she had another anouncement and nearly ran her down. The girl retreated into Steve's office, blushing heavily.

The newsreels invaded Steve's office for one of the many press conferences of the afternoon and turned on a battery of floodlights. The sweat popped out on his red forehead and he squinted in the blinding light while announcing that the President had called in the Cabinet and a large group of Congressional leaders for conferences beginning at 8:30 P.M.

The camera crews swept their lights over the reporters who stood with bowed heads, scribbling nervously on wads of copy paper and the prim notebooks from the White House supply room.

When the conference broke up and the boys ran for their telephones, they encountered a banked battery of still photographers waiting for them in the main foyer of the executive offices.

The flash guns went off all at once. I was so blinded I couldn't read my notes for a few minutes and had to dictate to the office from memory.

The two and a half hours we spent standing on the north portico that night, watching high government officials come in, and waiting to interview them as they left, were impressive. Crowds gathered in Lafayette Park across Pennsylvania Avenue from the White House. The night was chilly and a cold damp wind swept in from the Potomac, but the shivering crowds remained.

They seemed to be waiting for someone to come out of the White House and tell them it was all a bad dream. Cars by the hundred drove by as slowly as traffic officers would permit, the occupants hanging from the windows just to stare at the graceful old white structure which all of them had seen many, many times before.

Many of the spectators, of course, were there to see

the celebrities come and go. It was throat-catching late that night to hear those cold people singing "God Bless America" and "My Country, 'Tis of Thee."

The words and music were faltering at first, but swelled up strong and I wondered at the time if Mr. Roosevelt and his Cabinet members could hear those unrehearsed songs coming spontaneously and from the hearts of the little people across his back lawn.

Standing and stamping in the cold, I realized late that night that I had not eaten since breakfast. That's what excitement will do for you.

Suddenly I wanted a drink and a sandwich badly and sent a Western Union messenger back into the press room to see what he could promote. Carroll Linkins, the Western Union press man, sent the skimpy remainder of a half pint of bourbon which I drank unashamedly in the shadow of the portico.

About eleven o'clock, fat, puffing Senator Barkley, the majority leader, stepped out into the cold long enough to announce that the President would go to Congress the following day to deliver a message to a joint session. Naturally he would ask for a declaration of war against Japan. He did and in that historic message he used words that will rank in history with some of the vigorous phrases of all times—"December 7, 1941—a day that will live long in infamy."

CHAPTER NINE

The White House at War

UP UNTIL Pearl Harbor, the White House was open and unafraid. Thousands of visitors streamed through the formal rooms every day. The only noticeable precaution was that the police asked the visitors to leave their cameras and packages in a checkroom.

The gates were wide open and no one had heard of a White House pass. Except for total strangers, reporters filing into the President's office for press conferences were not required to show any identification. The Secret Service and White House police relied entirely on their memory of faces.

There was no guardhouse or sentry box at any of the four gates leading into the White House grounds. Policemen were stationed at the gates, primarily to shepherd official traffic.

On Easter Monday, when Mrs. Roosevelt had her egg rolling on the beautiful, sloping South Grounds, as many as 50,000 people poured through the entrances. Mrs. Roosevelt had one rule—no adult admitted without a child. The result of this was a booming business for moppets who ushered in adults for fifty cents each, then went back through the gate for another one—until their faces became familiar to the police.

This peaceful, easygoing attitude around the White House changed abruptly. You could see the changes starting even as the people across Pennsylvania Avenue sang "God Bless America" on the night of the Pearl Harbor attack.

Reinforced details of police were rushed to each gate. The Secret Service threw together emergency plans in the event of an air attack.

Secretary of the Treasury Henry Morgenthau, Jr., called one of Washington's leading shade and drapery shops and demanded that his home be completely equipped with blackout curtains within twenty-four hours.

It was longer than that, however, before the White House got blackout curtains. A matter of a few days, at least. The President's residential quarters on the second floor of the house were the first to be curtained. Then the lower floors, and finally the offices.

Garden workers trundled into each office a large can of sand and a scoop with which to combat incendiaries. Gas masks were issued to the entire staff, from the President to the lowest file clerk. This was the only government agency so equipped in Washington, except for certain important units in the War and Navy departments.

The White House was sensitive about the gas masks and asked that nothing be printed about them. The President refused to try on his mask or test it. He felt he would look silly. That was the actor in him again.

Masks were issued to about ten reporters only after they were tested under tear gas on a hot afternoon when the gas turned each drop of perspiration on our bodies into a little rivulet of what felt like liquid fire.

Helmets—the World War I type—were issued to the police and other personnel whose presence in the grounds would be necessary during a raid.

Meantime, while the White House carpenters were tacking up long lengths of double-thickness black sateen at the windows, heavy steam shovels and bulldozers rumbled into the front grounds. Hordes of workmen filed in the front gates between ambassadors and Cabinet members. Lights were strung for night work and large board fences were erected to hide the work from public view.

But it took only a few days for us to see what was happening—the steam shovels were chewing a deep path toward the Treasury. Steve Early confirmed our suspicions—they were building a tunnel from the White House basement to the lower vaults of the Treasury. The President was to use the Treasury vaults as his air raid refuge until a White House shelter could be built.

The actual White House shelter formed the basement floor of the new east wing which was built during the early months of 1942 to house the offices of Admiral William D. Leahy, Harry Hopkins, the Secret Service and the White House police.

The walls of the shelter were nine feet thick and made of reinforced concrete. The ceiling was the same except for a protective thin sheet of steel to prevent chunks of mortar from tumbling down on the occupants in event of a near hit.

Special air-conditioning equipment with independent motors, power generators for short-wave radio, a small kitchen, two bathrooms, a first-aid room and double airtight steel doors were put into the shelter.

Unlike the luxurious shelters of other world leaders—

men who had good reason to use them—the White House shelter was Spartanly furnished. No couches, no beds, no decorations. Just a few plain chairs.

The lack of comfortable accommodations in the White House shelter was due to the military theory that if there was a raid on Washington, it would be a hit-and-run affair and that there was little possibility of sustained air attacks against the capital.

Mr. Roosevelt (and those responsible for his protection) began to worry about his personal safety. Hence the immediate censorship of news concerning his movements. There was some fear that the President's Hyde Park home would be bombed if the enemy knew of his presence there. Also, as a further safety measure, the Presidential route between Washington and Hyde Park was rearranged to avoid as many bridges as possible.

One night in the early stages of the war his train to Hyde Park was held up nearly two hours at a bridge. Shortly before his train had approached the bridge, an alert trackwalker spotted a jeweled cigarette case at the end of the bridge.

He made a quick report and it was transmitted to the Secret Service. They ordered the train stopped, fearful that a saboteur was working in the vicinity of the bridge which was far from near-by roads or farm homes.

The bridge was thoroughly inspected and the surrounding brush searched. Only when the Secret Service learned there had been a recent robbery in the neighborhood and the cigarette case was part of the loot was the train allowed to proceed.

The Hyde Park estate was turned into a land of electrical wizardry. An elaborate electric eye alarm system was installed, along with a complicated and geared-in system of floodlights which blazed on at the slightest suspicious sound.

Companies of specially trained—and investigated—military police were stationed both at the White House and at Hyde Park. They maintained encircling patrols twenty-four hours a day.

The public was prevented from approaching either house. In Washington, people were not allowed even to walk on the same side of Pennsylvania Avenue as the White House.

Huge steel cable barricades were installed at each entrance of the White House and mobile antitank units were added to the M.P. forces.

During this period the Secret Service ordered every member of the staff and each reporter and photographer allowed entrance to the White House photographed, fingerprinted and issued a pass. Without this pass, entrance was to be denied, regardless of how well the person seeking entrance was known to the guard on duty at the gate.

The process of accreditation took weeks. Applications were filed quickly for more than five hundred press and radio passes. My pass, issued on February 3, 1942, is Number 514. The passes—still in force and probably part of a permanent system now—carry the bearer's picture, his signature, right thumbprint and physical statistics for purposes of comparison should there be any attempt to change the picture and signature.

Admiral Leahy, brought out of retirement to be Mr. Roosevelt's chief of staff, was largely responsible for the establishment of "the map room" to help the President follow the war.

This room was in the basement of the White House and was one of the most forbidden secrets of the war. Steve Early became increasingly wroth each time reference to the room was made in public.

It was a nerve center where army and navy dispatches were co-ordinated so that the President could at all times have an up-to-the-minute picture of the war.

The map room also was a message center for the President. In it were elaborate and highly secret coding and decoding machines. Through this room passed the most secret dispatches of the war—messages from Churchill and Stalin; the President's answers.

Mr. Roosevelt usually paid two visits a day to the secret room where he saw latest fleet movements charted on huge wall diagrams. He also, like a factory executive spotting his salesmen on a map with red pins, could trace the movement of ground forces of this country and the Allies, and the enemy, too.

Like the White House pass, the map room probably will become a permanent part of the White House. At least it will remain there for a long time as the clearing house for confidential messages to and from the President. And, as during the war, it will continue to be staffed by the young army and navy men, most of them communications experts.

The map room is not stationary, but can be moved as it was to Yalta and Potsdam where the facilities operated with virtually the same equipment and speed as in the White House.

Mr. Roosevelt's feelings about his personal safety were

more than shared by Michael F. Reilly, wartime supervising agent of the White House Secret Service detail.

Mike was a superconscientious young Irishman who figured that with a war on and enemy agents about, no steps taken to protect the life of the President would be too many.

The danger of railroad travel to Hyde Park, plus Mr. Roosevelt's own desire for seclusion led to a search for a near-by hideaway. Mr. Roosevelt wanted it private and within two hours of Washington by automobile. Ross McIntire, the President's doctor, wanted altitude—a minimum of 2,000 feet, and coolness.

McIntire felt that the President needed altitude and a change in temperature to get relief from Washington's insufferable summer humidity which irritated the President's sinuses.

A circle was drawn around Washington and several places investigated, including some sites in Virginia. But the only place with all the qualities demanded by the President, Reilly and McIntire was seventy-five miles away at the Catoctin Recreational Area of the National Park Service.

This area is about three miles beyond the sleepy little Maryland mountain town of Thurmont. The specific site and its equipment were crude, but from the standpoint of seclusion and weather it was just what the doctors ordered.

The Catoctin area covers about eight million acres. During the early, unemployed thirties, the Civilian Conservation Corps and the Works Progress Administration developed a part of the area near Thurmont into three camps. Each camp consisted of a number of small, slab-oak cabins and a swimming pool. These facilities were rented to tourists and nature lovers for fifty cents a night a person.

With the start of the war, however, one camp was turned over to the Marine Corps as a rest station. Another camp was transformed from a peaceful rustic playground into a training site for the rough-and-tumble experts of the Office of Strategic Services, the "cloak-and-dagger" secret section of the Army.

The third camp became "Shangri-la," Mr. Roosevelt's favorite designation for anything secret.

After his first few trips to Shangri-la in the late summer of 1942, rumors began to spread around Washington. Some of the stories compared the place with Hitler's Berchtesgaden and every Washington barroom had its occasional story about the goings-on at Catoctin. These stories told of the incredible luxury and lavish living. And they were so much irresponsible blather.

The average tourist, aside from the hairy-chested individuals who like to soak up the great out-of-doors in moderate discomfort, would have complained about the accommodations.

The Big House—the President's own quarters—was made by moving three log cabins together. The result was a rather uninteresting cottage with a kitchen, butler's pantry, combination living room and dining room and four bedrooms. There are two baths—one for the President, one for the other three bedrooms.

The President's bathroom looks out on a beautiful valley—and what used to be Fala's dog pen. The room itself is small with a single bed, a green carpet, a dresser, a clothes locker and a chair. The furniture throughout the house all was discarded from the old Presidential yacht, the *Potomac,* or came out of the White House attic.

The bedroom furniture is flimsy and painted a low-luster white. The only touch of luxury to the President's room is a French-type telephone and a bedside box containing a row of four pushbuttons market SECRET SERVICE, VALET, SECRETARY and PANTRY.

A Washington newspaper wrote shortly after the end of wartime censorship that the President had an ultra-luxurious trout preserve right in front of his lodge. The story went on to tell how Mr. Roosevelt went boating on the pond, landing fat trout put there and kept hungry by the Interior Department.

Their correspondent must have been disappointed when he finally saw the pool. Actually, it is about fifteen feet square and was built to provide a reservoir of water in case of fire. The fish, about half of them goldfish and the rest bass and trout, were put in to make the place pretty. And if so much as a small dinghy were placed in the pool, most of the fish would be displaced into the gravel driveway.

Don't get the idea, however, that Shangri-la is a run-down tourist camp. It isn't. But it is not elaborate or luxurious. It is a fine place to sleep and play poker or swim, if you have the will power and strength to dip into a pool of 50-degree mountain spring water.

The only real touch of luxury at the Big House is the side porch overlooking a valley that leads down to Frederick, Maryland. The porch, aside from chairs and small tables, is equipped with a telescope on a tripod. The glass is very powerful but rather useless because of the perpetually poor visibility in the valley. And there are two adjustable fluorescent reading lamps.

A flagstone terrace off the porch has two tables with three wire and iron chairs at each one—the type of stuff usually found in ice cream parlors.

The rest of the Presidential camp consists of a guest cabin with twin beds, a coal stove and an explosive hot water heater over the bathtub.

There is a communications shack which contains a small switchboard with direct connections to the White House and short-wave radio facilities. Then there are accommodations for the help, including an office cottage for secretaries, a crude barracks for the Secret Service and a woodsy mess hall for the hired help.

It all adds up to something that looks like a medium quality boys' camp without horses or canoes.

At the end of one year in office, Mr. Truman had made only one brief visit to Shangri-la, although he planned to use it occasionally in the summers. Mrs. Truman visited it during October, 1945, but it was a rainy afternoon and a rainy October afternoon in the mountains is pretty dull business.

Winston Churchill visited Shangri-la on two occasions with Mr. Roosevelt, and the British Prime Minister was responsible for the first breach of censorship about the Presidential hideaway.

Churchill, so the story goes, could not resist making a trip into the village of Thurmont. Being a very inquisitive man, he wanted to see all of the town, including Thurmont's one social attraction, a beer parlor. Churchill went in for a cold one and allegedly gave the waitress some nickels to put in the juke organ.

The story got back to Washington society columnists who could not resist the temptation. They wrote the story, then pleaded ignorance about the supposed censorship.

Shangri-la was a source of consistent annoyance to the reporters who covered the White House every day. They knew all about it. They were thoroughly conversant with the censorship code which society page writers thought applied to everybody but them.

Igor Cassini, then a society gossiper for the Washington *Times Herald*, beat around the censorship code by breaking the first story on the planned establishment of a summer White House. But he picked the wrong site—an old estate in Virginia.

I showed Cassini's column to Steve Early the morning it was published, telling him, "This exclusive of Cassini's certainly makes us all look a little stupid since we've known about this project for weeks."

Steve got boiling mad, which was normal. On the hour, every hour Early erupted like an active young volcano. His low boiling point probably saved him from ulcers during the twelve years of his difficult job.

Early immediately called in the Secret Service, and a short time afterward an agent went to have a friendly little chat with Cassini.

But Cassini's sin was soon forgotten, thanks to Mrs. Roosevelt. Every reporter on the White House assignment was trying to co-operate with Steve and observe the censorship code which prevented any unauthorized publication of Presidential movement. And Mrs. Roosevelt helped them along by chatting gaily at one of her weekly conferences with newswomen about the summer White House "up the country."

We rushed in to Early again and told him what Mrs. Roosevelt had done. He just shrugged his shoulders. He was a sad-eyed picture of frustration. He knew he could not kill or withdraw Mrs. Roosevelt's statement.

And the Secret Service walked around the big White House lobby muttering. They were charged with the twenty-four-hour job of maintaining Presidential security. The President had said over and over again that he wanted no publicity about Shangri-la; that publicity would render the place useless from his standpoint.

But Mrs. Roosevelt was Mrs. Roosevelt.

She, however, was told about her loose talk within twenty-four hours. My best information was that it came in a nice, friendly note from Censorship Director Byron Price who later had several other occasions to wince at some of the contra-security items Mrs. Roosevelt unwittingly printed in her column.

Mrs. Roosevelt, in all her graciousness, apologized immediately to Early and the Secret Service, explaining that when the President told her about Shangri-la he had said nothing about the story being off the record.

(Imagine a situation in which the husband, chatting of an evening with his wife, has to say, "Oh, by the way, dear, what I just said is off the record.")

Columnists Pearson and Allen were the first to tell the public the story of the huge air-raid shelter being built under the White House. Here again was a case of reporters who abided by the rules being penalized for not breaking censorship. Neither Pearson nor Allen had been in the White House for weeks, maybe months. Yet every reporter on the assignment knew about the tunnel and the shelter and held back on publication at the request of censorship and the White House.

There were, however, two particularly well-kept secrets at the White House during the war. One was the first visit of Winston Churchill in December, 1941, and the 1942 visit of V. M. Molotov, the Soviet Foreign Commissar.

Knowledge that Churchill was en route to the White House was generally known among Washington reporters, but not a word was printed or broadcast until he arrived and Early made the official announcement.

The public was not aware of Molotov's visit until he had come and gone. He was back in Moscow before anything was published.

Molotov reached Washington on May 23, 1942, but most of the reporters, including this one, knew nothing about it.

I had lunch the following day with an old army friend who shocked me by saying, "I suppose you'll have quite a time with the Russian Foreign Minister."

"Oh sure," I replied uneasily. "Sure will."

"It certainly was funny," he continued, "the way Molotov arrived at Bolling Field yesterday afternoon—did you see it? Were you out there?"

"Nope, couldn't make it. Tied up at the White House."

"Well, his bomber—one of those big Russian babies—came in four hours ahead of schedule. There was only an army lieutenant to meet him when he stepped out of the plane. The Secretary of State finally got there, but not until old Molotov had cooled his heels for about thirty minutes."

As soon as I could wriggle away from the luncheon

table, I telephoned the office and the United Press put a watch on Blair House, across from the State Department, for signs of Molotov's coming and going.

That night at a cocktail party, I ran into Early and asked, "How's Molotov?"

He choked on his highball and wanted to know what the hell I was talking about.

After I convinced him it was no fishing expedition, Steve took me over to a quiet corner table. He told how Molotov, after meeting the President, had gone for a stroll before dinner. He walked around the lower White House grounds, peering out at the thousands of home-going government workers in the manner of a bear in the zoo playing to a Sunday audience.

Molotov did get away on one or two occasions while in Washington—once to buy peanuts from a vendor in the park across from the White House, and again, for an evening stroll through Washington's F Street shopping and theater district.

As the war continued, Mr. Roosevelt did virtually what he pleased, in public and in private, and in the secure knowledge it would not be on the radio or in the newspapers.

The week rarely passed that Early did not lecture us:

"Nothing must be printed or broadcast about the movements of the President without authority. Think of him as a battleship and report his movements just as carefully as you would the position of one of our battle-wagons at sea."

This was all very fine, but the President began to put on and take off security like winter underwear. When he wanted it, he ordered it. When he needed the publicity—

as in the 1944 election campaign—off came all the wraps.

Even before the 1944 campaign, the danger of air raids had virtually passed. And the Secret Service began to feel that as far as they were concerned, more publicity could be given in all safety to the President's whereabouts. But Mr. Roosevelt did not share their optimism.

He demanded secrecy for such minor things as a thirty-minute automobile ride in the Virginia or Maryland countryside. True the pressure of the Presidency is heavy and seclusion a welcome antidote, but Mr. Roosevelt made a fetish of his privacy during the war.

Now that the war is over, the White House is still at war. The blackout curtains and the sand bins have disappeared, but virtually wartime secrecy still covers many movements of President Truman.

Mr. Truman doesn't go in for secrecy for security purposes. He just likes to get up and go without too much fanfare. And there are people in his organization who are just learning the proper relationship between normal publicity and press coverage, and the Presidency.

For example, when Mr. Truman was making plans to attend the Army-Navy football game in Philadelphia during the fall of 1945, one of his top assistants expressed aghast amazement when he heard that the White House correspondents expected to cover the President's trip.

"What for?" he said. "They'll have sports writers there to cover the game. After all it's a football game, not a Presidential speech."

We attempted to explain to this important figure that the White House "regulars" had to accompany the President everywhere he went.

"The President," one correspondent pointed out to

the official, "will be sitting out in the open, in front of more than 100,000 people. Suppose somebody took a shot at him? What would the public know about it if the reporters assigned to the President weren't with him? After all, the President is a public figure. The public has an investment in him. And they have a right to know what's going on."

"A helluva lot of good it would do the President to have you reporters along if he were shot," replied the official. "I don't see where you would add to his protection."

I thought immediately of a time when about fifteen reporters accompanied Mr. Roosevelt to the theater. The Secret Service had remarkably good seats for us—in sort of a semicircle behind and to the side of the President's box.

We thanked the agent who supervised the theater visit for his fine treatment of us.

"Oh, think nothing of it, fellows," he said. "I'm pretty proud of this setup today. If you'll notice, it would be utterly impossible for anybody to shoot the President without hitting one or two of you guys first—and by that time we'd have him."

CHAPTER TEN

He's Dying

IN EARLY 1944 there were many people in and out of Washington who balefully forecast the death of President Roosevelt within a matter of months.

Their gospel largely was one of hope—and hatred. They were particularly active in the months immediately preceding the party conventions.

The gossips, however, overplayed their stories. They had Mr. Roosevelt dead before Election Day. They were wrong. But in the long run, they were right.

While the smart boys in 1944 insisted that Mr. Roosevelt was about to die, his doctors insisted he was all right.

Consequently, the rumors about his health were hard to accept. They were hard to accept because they were so easily disproved. Of course, the President had begun to look old and tired. Of course, his voice began to fail. But the rumor mongers threw us off track by telling so many lies.

For instance, when we returned from the Pacific with Mr. Roosevelt in 1944 just before the fourth term campaign got under formal way, we found our Washington offices stacked with messages telling of his having undergone surgery at Mayo Clinic in Rochester, Minnesota.

These people—men and women who talked behind

their hands—knew "for a matter of actual fact" that the President, en route from Seattle to Washington, stopped off at Rochester for surgical treatment of a cancerous rectum. They knew the time of day and the names of the nurses.

And they knew the reporters who were with the President—the three wire service men—were bribed liars.

Some day—with the aid of a rich fellowship—I would like to study political rumors, particularly the outlandish variety and discover the ingredient which makes them stand up after having been proved false.

The stories about Mr. Roosevelt being in Rochester were so much poppycock. I was with him. I knew at the time that it was utterly impossible for him to have stopped at Mayo Clinic. The train went nowhere near Rochester.

Yet, several relatively smart newspapermen in Washington told me immediately after the trip that I had been hoodwinked; that Mr. Roosevelt stopped in Rochester secretly.

Telling them that such a thing was impossible did no good. They wanted to believe he was dying.

And he was.

But they didn't know how right they were. They were wrong about Rochester, but right about his approaching death.

A key figure in Mr. Roosevelt's physical life was Ross McIntire. As the President's doctor, he had a hard time in 1944. He was torn between political considerations and his reputation as a physician. To his credit, McIntire never lied about Mr. Roosevelt's condition. He told the truth, but in language that could easily be misleading.

Just before the campaign began, McIntire gave what amounted to a "well as can be expected" diagnosis of the President's physical health. He said the President was in good shape for his age.

When I asked the doctor about the President's reported anal ailment, he said, "Merriman, if you have a rear end as good as his when you're as old as he is, you'll be mighty proud of it."

The first inkling I had that Mr. Roosevelt was slipping was in the spring of 1944. He found it necessary then to take the longest actual vacation he had had since becoming President.

He selected as his hideaway the 23,000-acre Hobcaw Barony, the plushy, Old South plantation of his friend and adviser, Bernard M. Baruch.

Hobcaw is one of twenty-seven similar plantations surrounding Georgetown, a South Carolina coastal village of about 5,000 population. Adjoining Hobcaw Barony is Bellefield, the plantation of Baruch's daughter, Belle. Together the two Baruch plantations form Waccamaw Neck which juts out into Winyah Bay, with some ocean frontage on the Bellefield side of the neck.

Mr. Roosevelt and the members of his immediate staff lived in Baruch's graceful old red brick Georgian home nestled in a clump of huge, aged and moss-hung live oaks. The President picked a ground floor bedroom on the northwest corner of the house which has nine bedrooms in all, in addition to a "gun room" which served as a study, a library, large living and dining rooms and individual baths for each bedroom.

Baruch bought Hobcaw Barony in 1905 and the original house burned in 1934. In rebuilding Baruch tried

to follow the pattern of his original home faithfully, even
to the graceful white columns on the porch facing the
bay and two narrow spits of land known as Rabbit and
Hare islands.

Of the 23,000 acres on Baruch's swamp and marsh-
pitted plantation, only one hundred were in cultivation.
This disturbed the President, but Hobcaw's primary
function was as a hunting preserve. In season, quail and
ducks were heavily plentiful around the abandoned rice
fields bordering the bay and the Waccamaw River.

Deer and wild boar are abundant on Baruch's plantation. A Secret Service agent killed one of the ferocious,
tusked boar with a Tommy gun a few nights after the
President arrived.

Baruch had approximately forty people—most of them
low country Gullah Negroes—working on his place.
They had their own clinic and a school presided over by
Josie Jackson, wife of a local mail carrier. There also was
a church on the plantation where African Baptist and
African Methodist services were conducted each Sunday.

Hobcaw Barony was one of ten original coastal baro-
nies totaling 119,000 acres and laid out in 1711.

Baruch does not live at Hobcaw the year around, but
comes down from Washington and New York periodically during the "season" which consists roughly of the
more unseasonable months in the East and the hunting
seasons in the South which had closed by the time Mr.
Roosevelt arrived.

Georgetown itself is a typical small, southern coastal
town. Everybody comes to town on Saturday night and
the nearest bar is in Charleston, some sixty miles away.
Reflecting the cosmopolitan atmosphere of the plantation

set, however, are the nine whisky stores for a population of 5,000.

Georgetown has two principal industries—fishing and a pine pulp paper plant which has given this community a solid industrial payroll every week for a decade. The businessmen of Georgetown belie the sleepy façade of the community and maintain a fast commercial pace.

The White House staff which increased the size of the town considerably was greeted enthusiastically and everybody from the storekeepers to the hotel bellhops had fun in playing the game of keeping the "big secret." Intent on displaying southern hospitality at its best, the people of the town staged fish fries and oyster roasts until the Presidential party started talking about taking out "first papers"; i.e., paying the poll tax and buying a house.

Only the three press association reporters "accompanied" the President. We were locked up as far as the public was concerned in the Prince George Hotel at Georgetown. We were about eight miles from the President and on hand just in case something world-shaking occurred or he decided to make his presence known.

It was Mr. Roosevelt's intense desire for seclusion that made the reporters wonder why. He did not take to fishing as he had a few years before and was content to catch catfish off a dock, when Roosevelt, the deep-sea angler, would have scorned such an humble pastime in his better physical days. He sunned behind a special glass windbreak on the bayside terrace of Baruch's handsome old colonial home.

I finally got the idea that after a winter of nagging colds and influenza, the President had decided to go off by himself and decide whether he could gather enough strength for a fourth term election campaign.

He looked ghastly and listless when we arrived, but perked up at the smell of the salt air blowing in from the marshes and Winyah Bay.

Mr. Roosevelt arrived in Georgetown on Easter, April 9, and next morning acted as though he meant to have a good time. A choppy wind kept him off the bay, so he fished with a hand line from the small pier jutting into the bay from Baruch's estate. The President had on a brown pullover sweater and a floppy white hat.

He fished from the pier again the next day, and went for a brief boat ride in the afternoon.

My notes for April 12 reported:

About every living soul in Georgetown and in the surrounding country knows "He" is here. They laugh at the so-called official secrecy. Ladies in the grocery stores say that not only the President, but Churchill and Stalin are out fishing.

The President's whaleboat moved out into North Inlet nearer the open sea today and big-time angler Roosevelt was mortified to pull in wicked-looking crabs on his line twice in the afternoon. Made the most of the plentiful crabs, however, and the party came back to Hobcaw with a bushel, but no fish.

With each day it became increasingly evident that Mr. Roosevelt was not his old self. The lights in his corner room blinked out not long after dinner most every night. He even scorned the movies which were shown in Baruch's stable, partly because of plentiful mosquitoes.

My notes for April 13 showed:

A cold snap that pulled the temperature down from the 70's to the 40's plus a sharp wind kept the boss ashore again. He tried bottom fishing with a hand line off the dock, and this time the man who prides himself on landing big, deep-water game fish, came up with a mess of eels.

As day went into day, we kept our distance from the President. The Secret Service impressed on us repeatedly to "stay out of the old man's way." He wanted seclusion and plenty of it.

When possible we followed his fishing excursions, but at a comfortable distance. Baruch invited us over to the plantation one afternoon—when the President was out —and later had his daughter prepare some written material about the estate for our stories to be filed when we returned to Washington.

But back to my notes:

April 21—There was joy in the stately halls of Hobcaw Barony tonight. Mr. Roosevelt caught his first fish. In the afternoon he drove over to George Vanderbilt's Arcadia plantation, seated himself by a specially stocked fresh-water pond and hauled in two bass. "My God," he said in awed amazement as he hauled in number one, "I've actually caught a fish."

April 22—The President's fishing stock continued to rise by leaps and bounds. He went deep-sea fishing today for the first time and the bag for his boat was 25 bluefish and 6 bonita. He had been trolling only a few minutes 15 miles offshore when he got his first strike—a five-pound blue. "That is more like it," he said. Spent nearly eight hours at sea. Heavily guarded. Blimps overhead.

April 23—The fishing tackle was put out for drying this Sunday and Mr. Roosevelt went for a long drive during the afternoon, along the ocean on Pauley's Island, past the beautiful Brook Green gardens to Myrtle Beach.

April 24—A ripping wind from the south that covered Winyah Bay with foamy rollers killed fishing plans and the President drove in the afternoon to Belle Isle gardens south of Georgetown for a leisurely inspection of the beautiful semitropical setting.

April 25—He remained indoors all day to greet Australian Prime Minister John Curtin and Costa Rican President-elect Teodoro Picado who flew down from Washington for lunch.

April 26—Rainy, stayed indoors.

April 27—Fishing from the dock in the afternoon at Bellefield. Caught a few whiskery catfish.

April 28—McIntire returned from Washington to tell the President of Secretary Knox's serious condition. Then the news of Knox's death and a brief press conference in the evening.

That actually was the first time during the trip we had seen the President to talk to, and he called for us about eight in the evening.

I had been in bed for several days with food poisoning, but the President mistook my pallor for a bad hangover and proceeded to rib me by describing in nauseating detail how Italian vermouth, a necessary ingredient for one of my favorite gin drinks, was made from vegetables which had rotted in Italian markets.

(He once nearly turned a group of White House correspondents into teetotalers by such tactics. They had taken on a heavy load of gin the night before and at a shipboard press conference in the Bay of Fundy the next day, he told them they probably had unknowingly gotten gin made from disintegrating fish heads salvaged from seafood wholesalers in the area.)

As we talked with the President about Knox, I wondered whether he had won his fight with himself.

He was fairly well tanned, but the color was muddy. You could see that he had been in the sun, but the results did not look particularly healthy.

The President, however, had lost his bronchial cough. He seemed in good spirits. In talking about the death of Knox, he was moderately serious. But he sounded more like a housewife who'd just lost a maid than a man who'd just lost a close assistant.

That may have been the Roosevelt breeding. I say that because I've been told that people of superior breeding never let their emotions come to the surface publicly.

The main reason we were called to Hobcaw that May night was to explain away the President's failure to attend the Knox funeral. The blame was finally placed on McIntire. He, the record said, wanted the President to remain in South Carolina lest his recovery from a bad, coughing winter be interrupted.

The President chatted gaily, once the business about Knox was out of the way. He talked about the Montgomery-Ward strike and his fishing luck. He asked about our hotel accommodations and we told him about having to pay $12.50 for a bottle of poor rye.

He roared in delight and called in his military aide, Major General Edwin M. (Pa) Watson, to hear the story. Pa in turn was instructed to pour some of Baruch's bourbon immediately lest the reporters feel poorly on their return to the "city."

We had a drink with Baruch on the way out of the house. He told us he wanted to give a party for us, a barbecue at his daughter's place.

Knowing that the President for some reason did not

want us around unless it was absolutely necessary, we thanked Baruch but explained that we felt we should stay out of the social picture as much as possible.

He scoffed at this and said he would cook up something more interesting than the hotel lobby for us in a few days.

I wrote a story that night, quoting McIntire as saying the President had thrown off the effects of his winter colds and that Mr. Roosevelt professed to be feeling fine. But for some reason—it certainly wasn't a conscious one—I hedged and wrote in documented and cautious phrases.

We returned to Washington on May 7—Saturday—and the President plunged immediately into the troublesome coal strike, scheduling a radio broadcast on the situation for Sunday night.

Largely to justify the expense of the trip, I wrote a long diary of the President's stay in Georgetown to accompany my main news story and it was printed on Saturday.

On the following Monday, Steve Early called me into his office and reported that the diary had incensed the President.

"He's convinced you bribed someone on his staff," Early told me. "Now, I know you didn't. But he says you have little, intimate details that are so accurate that they had to come from someone who lived with him at Hobcaw."

Steve was not on the trip, so he asked me, "Please, for your sake and mine, tell me where you got all this dope. He says he is going to put the F.B.I. on this thing and find out who was bribed."

I was flabbergasted.

"Steve," I said, "will you please explain to him first

that the United Press pays me to do the reporting and undoubtedly would fire me immediately if I had to resort to bribery on an assignment like this."

That morning I had received a letter from Baruch, complimenting and thanking me for the stories on Hobcaw which had appeared Saturday. And Baruch said he was sorry he had not been able to show us more hospitality and would we come back again.

I had the letter in my pocket.

"Show him this, Steve, and see if he still thinks bribery was necessary."

I ran out to my press room desk and got a copy of the blurb on Hobcaw which was prepared and delivered by Belle Baruch.

"Show him that, too."

"All this helps, but where did you find out—you don't have to tell me if you don't want to, but I think it would be best in the interest of future coverage—where did you find out about his fishing luck and the places he went?" he pleaded.

"Steve, this is foolish. His fishing guide dropped by the hotel virtually every night and volunteered to the whole lobby the details of the day. Also, Baruch invited quite a few people at one time or another to meet the President at Hobcaw and they always let us know about it."

Naturally, the F.B.I. investigation was dropped. But it started me wondering. Why was Mr. Roosevelt so suddenly touchy about publicity?

I wondered, too, why Ross McIntire was so cautious when he reported on the President's physical condition at the end of the trip.

"We have gained everything we hoped to gain in this four weeks' rest, and I am perfectly satisfied with his physical condition," McIntire said.

Meantime, I was being bombarded by rumors. The office had waiting for me two files of reports and tips from Rochester and Boston. The President had been "hospitalized" at both places while we were in the South.

After writing memos to deny both stories—which did not reach publication—I talked with Early again.

"Thank God," he said, "you guys were along on the trip. Although the Boss certainly did object to that diary, it was worth a million dollars to the Democratic party. It showed where he was every minute. It gave a perfect answer to the stories about his being in the hospital."

CHAPTER ELEVEN

The Fourth Term

MANY political experts to the contrary, Mr. Roosevelt did not want to run for a fourth term. Age was beginning to tell on him. He had lost much of his vitality. The specter of illness was increasingly visible.

But it was a thing he had to do. He was like a fire horse refusing to go to pasture. His love of political warfare, his vanity and his firm belief that the country needed him got the best of his judgment.

His attitude toward Governor Thomas E. Dewey, the 1944 Republican candidate, was one of unvarnished contempt. He shuddered at the thought of Dewey in the White House. But he knew, too, that if he did not run, the Democrats had little chance of winning against Dewey with any nominee they might select.

This was the situation on July 11 when he ordered the doors of his office locked and then read to more than two hundred sweating Washington correspondents the text of his letter to Democratic Chairman Robert E. Hannegan, agreeing to accept the nomination.

"You have written me," Mr. Roosevelt wrote Hannegan, "that . . . a majority of the delegates have been directed to vote for my renomination. . . ."

Reporters snickered. Who knew better than the President how the delegates were lined up?

Furthermore, the President said he would not run "in the usual partisan, political sense."

His dramatic voice boomed into the domelike ceiling of his office.

"But if the people command me to continue in this office and in this war, I have as little right to withdraw as the soldier has to leave his post in the line."

The President finished reading and grinned up at the reporters.

"Now," he said. "You've got your news—go on and get out!"

Shortly afterwards, we got the word to pack for a secret trip to the Pacific. Before leaving the country, the President would accept the nomination in a radio address on July 20, then sail quietly for Hawaii.

After a quiet five-day off-the-record train journey across the continent, we arrived at the marine base in San Diego at 2 A.M., July 19. I still don't understand the full reasons, but on this trip there was no press secretary. The President left Steve Early at home to keep an eye on the convention and other domestic developments. Steve's absence on the trip caused numerous difficulties.

It was difficult for the three wire service reporters and the one radio "pool" man—Carleton Smith of N.B.C.—to get information that would stick. There seemed to be a constantly broiling argument among the staff—Rear Admiral Wilson Brown, the naval aide; Major General Edwin M. Watson, the military aide, were the principal adversaries. Judge Samuel Rosenman and Grace Tully, the President's private secretary, were along, but they were in no position to cope with the Navy which was in control of the trip.

Brown one morning took apparent delight in trumpeting long and loud in the diner about the poor qualities of the press; why reporters should not be taken on trips of this kind. Brown was Mr. Navy of the old school and seemed to hate civilians with a passion.

Elmer Davis, then the director of O.W.I., was on the trip for the ride. He was headed for the far Pacific, and Roosevelt invited him to ride as far as Hawaii. Elmer, however, was unable to do very much about our particular problems.

As we reached San Diego, our big problem was the President's radio speech the following night. Brown told me that we would have to put a Washington dateline on the story and say nothing about the President's real whereabouts. I bucked at that; told him a Washington dateline would be an outright lie and that security or no security, the United Press could not go along with a project of such ridiculous proportions.

The President had been seen by thousands of people on the way to the west coast and I didn't get the point of the admiral's super secrecy.

About two hours before we were to be given copies of the speech on July 20, I went to Grace Tully and said,

"Grace, this situation is fouled up unbelievably and I have a hunch the Boss doesn't know about it. We can't put a Washington dateline on the acceptance speech. Everybody in Chicago (where the Democratic convention was being held) knows where the President is. What can we do about it?"

Grace said she did not want to project herself into the

affairs of the Navy, but with a twinkle in her eye, she suggested that I stick around the entrance of the President's car for a little bit.

I stood around talking with the Secret Service for awhile, then the heavy door to the President's car opened and Grace beckoned to me.

She told me to go on back to the President's bedroom.

I eased open the door of the tiny bedroom and found the President in bed. He looked very bad. He was breathing heavily and sniffling frequently. He was fighting a cold.

He turned and with a broad grin said, "Come on in, Merriman. What are they trying to do to you?"

"Mr. President," I said, "the Navy tells me that we must put a Washington dateline on your speech tonight. You know that would be outright dishonesty and we just can't do it."

The President chuckled.

"Oh damn, that's a lot of nonsense. I say in the first paragraph of my speech that I am speaking from a west coast naval base. Why not use that for a dateline?"

"That is fine, Mr. President. We'll use it."

"Now, what else is bothering you?"

"Well, sir, there's the question of what we do when we get to Hawaii."

The President explained that there was no room on the cruiser *Baltimore* for the four correspondents, but that he had ordered a plane made available for us at San Francisco and that we would beat him to Pearl Harbor by at least a day, and maybe more.

"When you get to Hawaii, you will be members of my party just as you are now. You will live and eat in the

same compound with me, and will go with me on all
my trips around Oahu. Now, Merriman, these are orders direct from me to you. Don't let anyone tell you
differently. We'll have a big press conference out there
at the end of the trip and you can release it when I get
back to the States."

Then the President cautioned me to say nothing to
anyone else about the plans for Hawaii.

"Don't tell anyone but your other reporters," he said.

I laughed, thinking of Brown, and General Watson,
who really suffered when he was left out of any secret.

The President and I chatted about the war and the
election and I learned that he had only one misgiving
about the campaign. He felt that his only danger lay in
the possibility of a light vote. He was already thinking
about ways to get the voters sufficiently angry and interested to assure their presence at the polls in November.

The first person I saw when I left the President's car
was Admiral Brown.

"Did you decide anything about locating the President?" Brown snapped at me.

"It was decided before I talked with him, Admiral," I
said. "He locates himself in his speech and we're going
to do the same thing in our stories."

Brown walked off muttering to himself.

Watson came up next and put his arm around my
shoulder.

"Smith, what went on in there—did you get everything settled?"

"I'm sorry, General, the President told me to talk to
no one, except the other reporters."

Watson swore at me and tramped off down the track

beside the President's special which was parked by marine freight sheds.

In Hawaii much was made of the fact that MacArthur was there to confer with the President. Admiral Nimitz was there, too, and the President saw much more of him than he did MacArthur. As a matter of fact, during the week Mr. Roosevelt was in Hawaii he actually conferred with MacArthur only once—from 10:15 to 12:45 o'clock on the morning of July 28. The President and MacArthur saw each other during the preceding two days at quasi-social affairs and during the course of inspection trips around the island. But there was only the one serious war conference involving the President and MacArthur.

There were many people in the States who thought the President's trip to Hawaii was primarily to emphasize his role as wartime Commander-in-Chief before undertaking an active political campaign. This definitely was one of the reasons for the trip, along with the desire to get a firsthand acquaintance with Pacific war problems.

After Hawaii, the President went to the Aleutians and we flew back to the west coast to wait for him at Seattle. On August 3 he lunched in the petty officers' mess on Adak and made a speech which did not come to light for more than a year afterward. In fact, I did not see the speech until long after Roosevelt's death and the end of the war.

Over a dish of boiled ham, stewed tomatoes and mashed potatoes in a steamy Quonset hut, the President, mindful of the hot weather back in Washington, got a laugh from the army men when he told them, "You don't realize the thousands upon thousands of people who would give anything in the world to swap places with you people."

Outside a frigid, wet wind beat against the turtle-back sides of the Quonset hut.

"Live and learn," the President said as a commentary on the way the Japanese surprised this country at Pearl Harbor and later by moving into the Aleutians.

"In the days to come," he said, "I won't trust the Japs around the corner. We have got to make it impossible for them to repeat this particular route of access to the United States. We are going to make it humanly possible to deny access to or aggressive attack by the Japanese of another generation against any part of the United States."

The President told the men of Adak that he couldn't be with them longer because he had to get back to the White House.

"By the time I get back home next week I will have been gone thirty days—my limit when Congress is left in Washington all alone," he said.

Roosevelt loved to make jokes like this and he meant this one sincerely. He honestly did not like the idea of leaving Congress alone in Washington for too long a time—particularly during an election year.

The President, sailing down the Inside Passage aboard the destroyer *Cummings*, arrived at the Bremerton, Washington, Navy Yard on the afternoon of August 12. The weather was overcast and misty. Thousands of navy yard workers waited a long time to hear the President speak from the forecastle deck of the destroyer.

It was a long, windy and poorly organized speech. It seemed at the time the President had committed a glaring political error in not having his speech assistants—Rosenman and Robert E. Sherwood—meet him off the Canadian coast to polish up the address.

But a few days afterward, it was apparent what Mr. Roosevelt did in the Bremerton speech. He made a travelogue address aimed at people who thought or knew little about Hawaii or the Aleutians. He was trying in homey terms to make them Pacific-conscious.

In the last half of the Pacific trip the President's party encountered spotty weather. I was talking with him in his private car two days after we left Seattle, bound for the East again, and he had his own explanation. He later became so attached to this explanation of the weather that he dictated it to a stenographer.

And here, as far as I know, for the first time published is Roosevelt's "Mary Had a Little Lamb—1944 Version" or "Admiral Brown Had a Low and Everywhere the Admiral Went the Low Was Sure to Go."

Shortly after leaving Honolulu, clear blue sky, calm sea, no wind, there appeared over the horizon a cloud as small as a man's hand. It saw us and approached slowly.

It turned out to be one of those rare animals known as a "low." The party was on deck and as soon as the "low" saw us it recognized Rear Admiral Wilson Brown, U.S.N., and headed straight for us.

We cannot shake it off.

It smiled all over, circled us several times and took a position just off the stern. It followed us all night and the next day and the next.

After three more days, we reached Adak, where it went ashore and played happily in the wake of Admiral Brown. With it came wind and rain and fog.

We all realized that it was a nice little cloud but to be accompanied everywhere by a "low" was getting to be monotonous. Its presence became so persistent that the tug boats were prevented by it from pulling us off the dock. In other words, it was an annoying "low." Our expert said it would pass us to the eastward and finally when it went off to gambol on the horizon for a few minutes, we got underway and had only been headed for Kodiak for an hour or two when the little "low" turned up again from nowhere and accompanied us.

All the way to Kodiak it hovered around us and while it was kind enough to run away while we caught a fish, there it was back again all the rest of the day and all the next day and accompanied us to Auke Bay.

By unanimous cursing, we persuaded it to go away while we caught some more fish and the sun actually came out. But having transferred to a destroyer, Admiral Brown seemed to be somewhat worried and sure enough his little "low" appeared again that evening. He was so glad to see it that it never left us. We think he fed it surreptitiously under the table.

It was with us all the way down the Inland Passage day after day and actually followed us into Puget Sound Navy Yard. We pleaded with the Admiral to say goodbye and leave it there. He said he would do his best and we think he did do his best, but to no avail.

In the late afternoon, we went to Seattle and boarded the train and to our horror the next morning after we woke up across the Cascade Mountains there was the little "low" following us. It kept on going all the way into Montana and the following day across Montana and into North Dakota.

What can we do about it?

The trouble is that it has lots of friends in the party. For instance, it has encouraged Admiral McIntire (the President's doctor) to use a new word with almost every sentence. If we cannot see the horizon we are told it is an "occluded front." It seems to me that is a very long word to apply to a little lamb or a little "low." Anna (his daughter) and the girls (two cousins, the Misses Laura Delano and Margaret

Suckley) had never seen an occlusion. They think it is just a nautical term for bad weather and we tell them it is just an old navy custom.

So here we are approaching the Twin Cities and we have got the bright idea that Admiral Brown should continue to feed his little "low" and bring it with us all the way to Washington. Washington needs a little "low" and so we must never forget that Wilson (Admiral Brown) had a little "low" and write a new children's book about it.

The official log of the trip bore this notation: "The consistently adverse weather that we encountered from the night of July 31st until August 16th was the subject of much conversation at mess by members of the President's party."

The Pacific trip was the first phase of the 1944 campaign. Mr. Roosevelt came back to Washington physically tired, but mentally refreshed. He faced a knotty problem in just how to campaign. Throughout the war, his public appearances were virtually discontinued. Security governed everything. And everything was secret. But the President realized that a candidate cannot run off the record.

He decided to make four major campaign appearances: New York, Philadelphia, Chicago and Boston.

He opened his campaign in Washington in late September with an address to the Teamsters Union. It was a banquet at the Statler Hotel. It was like any other Presidential banquet until the President started to speak.

He set out deliberately to pick a dock-walloping brawl with the Republicans, knowing that a political battle of such proportions would turn out a heavy vote. Also, he wanted to make Dewey lose his temper, knowing that an opponent moved by anger is more easily tripped than one who is campaigning coolly.

The President accused the Republicans of being liars, cheats and swindlers. And the teamsters went wild.

One excited teamster-Democrat behind me showed his approval of Roosevelt's nastily sharp lines by beating a silver bread tray with a soup ladle. The noise was terrific.

Two tables away from me, another loyal teamster applauded by smashing glasses with a wine bottle, taking a full swing for each of the President's punch lines and sending a shower of glass over the near-by tables.

The President reveled in the thunderous ovation, bread trays and all. And he was never in better form. His sarcasm reached an all-time Roosevelt high when in a mocking voice he protested the Republican attacks against "my little dog, Fala."

Shortly before he died, I asked the President if he had set out deliberately to get Dewey mad. He laughed, taunting me with a remark that he thought the results made the answer obvious. Dewey, it must be remembered, blasted back at him two nights after the teamsters speech in an address which the Democrats used during the rest of the campaign to accuse the Republican of twisting the truth. (Thus Dewey seemed to have taken the bait just as Mr. Roosevelt had hoped *and expected* he would.)

Next came the horrible New York City trip. The President was determined to show the people of New York that he was not a dying man as the campaign whisperers were picturing him. And in so proving, he nearly killed off his staff and the reporters with him.

It was a cold, rainy day in late October. And in this

murderous weather, the President toured the boroughs of New York for nearly five hours. He had a special heater under his legs in the rear seat of the car, a flannel under-suit, a fur robe around most of his body and his heavy navy cape. And he stopped once during the trip to go to the bathroom and change his upper garments which were soaked by water oozing down his neck.

I rode in an open Secret Service car just behind the President, sans heater, fur robe, flannel undersuit or a change of clothes. All I had was a raincoat and hat. Even with this protection I was drenched to the waist by the time the procession reached upper Broadway to begin the slow journey down to Times Square.

After speaking that night at the Waldorf, the President went to Hyde Park for a week end. He was loudly gleeful next morning when the doctor couldn't find a trace of a sniffle in him, but reported that several of the brawny Secret Service men had picked up bad colds.

Admiral Brown's "low" stayed with Mr. Roosevelt all during the campaign. Chicago was cold and nasty. Phila-delphia was a repeat on New York with daylong cold rain. And Boston was cold and damp.

The President wound up his campaign the Monday before the Tuesday Election Day by making his tradi-tional tour of the Hudson Valley. He drove from town to town with Secretary of the Treasury Morgenthau, say-ing a neighborly "how'do" and poking fun at the Repub-licans.

The temperature was barely above freezing on this last motor tour and again the President was prepared for bad weather. He wore a coat with a great fur collar and planted himself over the back-seat heater as he had done in other campaign appearances.

Morgenthau, for some unexplained reason, had on only a light topcoat and by the time the procession reached Newburgh, he was a cobalt blue. His teeth chattered constantly and his shivering was noticeable.

During a brief stop a Secret Service man ran back to the car I was in and barked, "Smitty, the Secretary is about to freeze to death and wants to know if you have a drink."

I explained that there was one in the car back of me, but it was a quart bottle and I couldn't imagine the Secretary taking a pull at the jug in front of several thousand people.

There was a hurried conference in the President's car and I heard the short-wave in our car start exploding with Secret Service orders. The advance car in front of the President was told to pick out a nice secluded hot dog stand where the party could get coffee and sandwiches.

Down the road about five miles from the Presidential party an old couple dozed before the fire in the front room of their little drive-in restaurant, dreaming of the days when gas rationing would end and they could make a living again.

Suddenly their front door banged open and in walked a crew of hard-faced young men who without much ado proceeded to look over the place, kitchen, refrigerator, back rooms and all.

The poor old woman nearly fainted when one of the young men said in a "now-I've-got-you-covered" tone of voice, "Will you please get some coffee and hot dogs ready? The President and about fifty people will be here in five minutes."

For months the old lady had had wieners frozen in the refrigerator and when we arrived they had just started to thaw. We smuggled the bottle of whisky up to the front car where Morgenthau poured himself a two-inch jolt into a cup of coffee. In a few minutes, due to the whisky and a lot of ungentle kidding by the President, there was some trace of restored circulation in the Secretary's face.

Election night was loud in Poughkeepsie and well ordered at Hyde Park. The White House staff and correspondents stayed at the Nelson House in Poughkeepsie until about 10 P.M., starting the usual all-election-night party. Steve Early was quite expansive about ordering drinks for the party and telling the waiters to charge them to the rooms of various reporters.

Early found out next morning, however, that with each round reporters had grabbed the checks and signed them with a flourish—"Stephen T. Early, Room 229."

I went out to the President's house in time to hear him talk to the Hyde Park villagers who whooped into his estate with red flares and the school band shortly before midnight. I was shocked when he came out on his porch. He looked older than I had ever seen him. Anna pulled his great cape around him and he wore a tweedy sort of broadbrimmed hat at a cockeyed angle.

The President's speech was irrelevant much of the time as he looked out at the crowd from the village. He talked about old times, pointed to a tree he used to climb and went from that right into a discussion of the Connecticut election, expressing a hope and belief that Clare Booth Luce had been defeated for Congress.

After the "speech" he went inside the house. The President rolled into his little dining room to continue his personal computation of returns, while in the other downstairs rooms, Mrs. Roosevelt swirled around among the guests, seeing that everybody had cider and doughnuts.

In the living room a collection of Mrs. Roosevelt's more colorful friends—arty old ladies in tweed, or evening gowns of two decades before—sat rather glumly around a radio listening to the returns put their neighbor back in the White House.

More than anything else at the moment, I wanted a drink to cure a fine state of exhaustion. But every time I asked any of the servants, all I got was another glass of the sweet cider.

Finally I gave up and went back to the Nelson House in Poughkeepsie to finish my story for the evening. The New York *News* had conceded for Dewey and the shouting was over.

When I finished filing, I wandered into the first room where I heard voices. It was a bunch of our people from Washington, sitting down over a bottle to second-guess the election. Strangely, it seemed then, they didn't appear to be much concerned about the various factors which brought Roosevelt another national victory. Instead they were arguing quietly the chances of his living out the fourth term. And those who believed he would were in a decided minority.

CHAPTER TWELVE

I Falter at Yalta

THE Mediterranean twinkled in the warm afternoon sun as we sat in the little sidewalk café of the Hotel Aletti. It was spring in Algiers. The sprawling Casbah actually looked clean—from a distance.

The man sitting across the small table from me sloshed his *vin rosé* reflectively in a small clay cup as he turned the pages of *Union Jack*, the British service paper.

"Well, well," he said, "look at this."

He handed me the paper, pointing to the lead article which told of the Big Three meeting at Yalta. The text of the Roosevelt-Stalin-Churchill communiqué was printed in full.

"Hmm," I said, "who paid for the last wine? Is it my turn?"

"It is your turn for the next two times."

"How come?"

"I paid for the shoeshines."

The waiter came to the table.

"Bring us two double bourbons, please."

The waiter smiled, murmured *"merci"* and returned in a few minutes with two more cups of the watery pink wine.

An Arab fell off a passing streetcar. He bounced like

a dried pea on linoleum, finally coming to a painful halt against the corner flower stand.

My table companion tired of watching Arabs fall off streetcars and resumed the conversation.

"You, sir," he said gravely, "are not you the great White House correspondent for the United Press?"

"Sh-h, that is top secret. Speak of me only as a scientist in search of a sure cure for Arabian cradle cap."

"Why is it, my good man, that you are not at Yalta with the President, reporting this tremendous news referred to here?"

He tapped the copy of *Union Jack*.

"Top secret," I insisted.

"Do you call sitting in an Algerian juke joint covering the President?"

I thought for a minute, groping for a good answer. Finally I had it.

"Call the waiter and ask him in your best French if the hour has arrived for the sale of *eau de vie de prunes*."

"*Garçon*," shouted my companion, using his entire French vocabulary at once.

"*Oui?*"

"Two more bourbons."

Evidently the hour for *eau de vie* had not arrived, because the waiter brought more *vin rosé*.

"And you, sir," I thundered at my companion who was then busy picking a tired fly out of his wine cup, "are not you the great White House correspondent for the Associated Press?"

"Top secret and confidential," answered Douglas B. Cornell.

"And why aren't you at Yalta?"

"Restricted."

Another Arab fell off another streetcar. This man did not roll very much. It turned out that he wanted to get off anyway. Since the streetcars in Algiers never stop except at the end of the line, the only way the Arabs can get off is to leap like flying bundles of dirty bed sheets and hope they land on their feet.

The Arab dusted the street manure from his robes, explored underneath his top sheet to see if his purse was still there and walked away.

"Where is Nixon?" Doug asked.

He referred to the third ghoul—Robert G. Nixon of I.N.S., a member of our pleasant little safari across the shifting sands of Africa.

"I think Bob is in his room practicing typing. It has been so long since we've handled a story he's afraid he'll lose his touch."

To understand our secret, strange life in Algiers, it is necessary to understand how it started.

We—the three White House reporters for the press associations—found out in December, 1944, that another Big Three meeting as in the wind. By early January we knew where it would be held. Censorship prevented publication of that fact.

The way I found out about Yalta started with a talkative member of our armed services who met another United Press man at a cocktail party in Washington. This was weeks before the trip started, but the officer advised the U.P. man to bet on a little Crimean town named Yalta as the site of the next Big Three conference. I had known previously that the meeting site was somewhere in the Black Sea area, so the Yalta tip fitted perfectly.

The press association men had been traveling everywhere with Mr. Roosevelt and naturally we raised the
question of Yalta with Steve Early. He said it looked
hopeless for us; that Mr. Roosevelt had agreed with Stalin
and Churchill to have no reporters of any nationality
present at the conference.

Steve said he would make the trip himself and send
whatever news he could back to Washington.

"Steve, in all due respects to you," we told him, "the
papers and the radio stations don't want the Big Three
covered by a spokesman for any government. They want
their own people there to call all the shots."

He agreed with this thesis, but said his hands were
tied. We talked it over then with the President and got
nowhere. His answer was always the same—he had committed himself and he could not, or would not change
the plan.

At 10:20 P.M. on the night of January 22, the President
went secretly to the basement of the Bureau of Engraving
and Printing in Washington to a special railroad siding
which he used during the war. He boarded his train
and started for Newport News, Virginia.

He could have gone in broad daylight and behind a
brass band as far as we were concerned because we knew
when he left, from where he would depart and where he
was going and who was with him. But censorship said no;
we couldn't print a line or even speculate.

Steve left Jonathan Daniels behind to serve as press
secretary at the White House.

The President and his party went aboard the cruiser
Quincy at Newport News next morning.

The official log of the President's journey pictured the scene at Newport News:

The railroad tracks within this pier are sunken to afford egress from the train at platform level, and it was not necessary to use the special elevator (on the President's private car) or a special ramp.

This, together with the darkness that prevailed at the time of our arrival, afforded complete secrecy to cover the President's movements.

Which may have been a comforting thought to the President, but which was untrue. Even the bus drivers in Washington knew he was gone and when he left.

The *Quincy* installed special ramps and elevators between the superstructure and main decks to give the crippled President some freedom of movement about the fore part of the vessel. Some people in the Washington press corps knew the name of the ship he was using, having heard several days before he left about the installation of elevators aboard the cruiser. The Navy didn't put elevators aboard ships for anyone but the President.

As the ship pulled out of Hampton Roads, the President and his party adjourned to the flag cabin to see a movie, "Our Hearts Were Young and Gay."

Back in the press room at the White House, our hearts were anything but gay. Maybe a little young, but not gay because a good story was slipping away from us and we knew that if past history repeated itself, someone on the other side of the world would break it, censorship or no censorship.

On the night of January 24, the President and his staff saw "Here Come the Waves," and the next night, "The Lady in the Window."

Harry L. Hopkins soon arrived in Paris and the news

shuttled right back to Washington. The leaks had started. And Daniels refused at the White House to confirm that there was a Harry Hopkins, much less the fact that he was in Paris—apparently in plain view—and on his way to join the President.

On January 26, the President saw "The Princess and the Pirate" which was not shown to American movie-goers for some months later. On the 27th he saw "Fighting Lady" with members of his mess. On the 28th and 29th, he saw "Laura" and "To Have and Have Not." He liked movies.

Daniels refused to admit anything. The story was coming in from a number of spots around the world by this time, mostly in the form of educated rumors and speculation. But Jonathan's hands were tied. There must have been a lot of chafed wrists before the trip was over. The President said his hands were tied. So did Early, and then Daniels.

No movies on the 30th. It was the President's birthday and his staff held a little party for him in the flag cabin. Back home, there were the usual birthday balls to raise funds for polio. But no explanation of where the honor guest was. Mrs. Roosevelt read a speech for him.

On January 31, the President and his mess saw "The Unknown Guest," and celebrated the entrance into the Mediterranean next night by seeing "Dragon Seed." Most people go to the movies once a week.

Mr. Roosevelt reached Malta February 2, feeling a little uneasy because of messages he had received from Churchill who complained about unhealthy living conditions in Yalta and the difficulty of reaching it. Hopkins, in London, sent Mr. Roosevelt this message:

"He (the Prime Minister) says that if we had spent ten

years on research we could not have found a worse place in the world than Yalta. He claims it is good for typhus and deadly lice which thrive in those parts."

Churchill sent other messages telling the President how the Germans had left the buildings at Yalta infested with lice.

While the Presidential party switched at Malta into planes for the rest of the trip to Russia, the gin rummy game at the White House continued, with occasional interruptions to read more stories from abroad hinting about the conference.

All I know about what went on at Yalta is what I read in *Union Jack*, but there were some facts *Union Jack* missed. For example, the President had Stalin and Churchill to dinner on February 5 at Livadia Palace. Mr. Roosevelt served vodka, five kinds of wine, fresh caviar, bread, butter, consommé, sturgeon with tomatoes, beef and macaroni, sweet cake, tea, coffee and fruit.

On February 6, the Big Three decided to announce what most of the world already knew; that the Big Three, their foreign ministers and chiefs of staff were conferring "in the Black Sea area."

Back in Washington we tried to print the fact that the meeting was Yalta. But no; security.

We tried every new possible argument with Daniels, but he seemed to be in a helpless spot. He had messaged our various pleas and arguments, our protests about being scooped by the foreign press; all this had been sent to Early at Yalta.

On the afternoon of February 9, Daniels called the three wire service men into his office. His hand trembled as he handed a message from Early to me. The Big Three conference was about to end and Early wanted us to start for Africa right away where we would await orders and join the party somewhere in the Mediterranean.

Everything was to be very hush-hush. We were to speak only when spoken to. We were to proceed first to Casablanca, and wait there for orders to go to Algiers. We were either to meet the President there, or be told where to go.

We had all sorts of secret papers issued to us that night; Secret Service commissions, special War Department passes, secret letters from Daniels explaining our mission and to be opened only in case of something about as drastic as death, and passports for Jerusalem with way stops in Africa and several other countries.

Somehow, the combined efforts of the White House, the Army and the State Department got us properly ticketed by next morning and we took off in the late afternoon in a big C-54 transport of the Army Air Transport Command.

We landed at Casablanca late the night of February 11. We didn't know it then, but at about the same time the same day, the Big Three meeting was in the process of final adjournment.

An ATC colonel met us at the side of the plane and whisked us into an automobile. The Army did not want French customs to examine our papers, so most of the confidential stuff was in sealed packets which we kept constantly in hand.

As we drove away from the airport, the colonel turned in the front seat and said, "Well, men, I guess you're here on THE mission."

"Don't you know why we're here?" we chorused in amazement.

"Ho, ho, ho," he chortled. "Everybody in Casablanca knows about the mission. You should have seen the stream of people coming through here on the way to the other end. A big party of navy people got in here tonight just ahead of you. They're on the way back."

"Back? Back to Washington?"

"Yes, back to Washington."

We finally argued ourselves into believing this did not necessarily mean that the conference was over. But the suspicion lingered on.

We were put up in fine style at the Anfa Hotel where the colonel had reserved a big suite for us. As we entered the lobby, a friendly major asked me, "How was everything at Yalta?"

"I haven't the faintest idea, Major."

"Oh, come now, everybody knows about it—ask any Arab in town."

"I just got here. Haven't had a chance to talk to the Arabs."

We looked at the suite and decided Yalta or no Yalta, this was not a bad place to lie low. Our plans called for us to remain in Casablanca about a week.

We spent the next day in luxurious leisure, riding around Casablanca, visiting the native shops and lounging in the beautiful bar at the Anfa. By this time, we had gotten over our Washington habit of speaking of Yalta in hushed tones. We spoke up aloud just like the army officers.

Our second night in Casablanca was just about to start when the colonel came to us with a worried look. He had just received orders from the Navy for us to proceed to Algiers without delay. This was in conflict with previous orders, but shucks, orders can change. We took this as good news. Maybe the President was rushing things for us to join him in time to handle the break on the Big Three communiqué.

We took off early next morning with instructions to report to the senior naval officer at Algiers.

When we landed there, we were met again by a nice army colonel. All smiles but no information. He didn't have the remotest idea what we were doing on his base, but heard we were coming in and had come out just to say welcome and see what we needed.

He obviously wasn't the man to talk to, so we asked about the senior naval officer. The colonel scratched his head and said he, the naval commander, was sick over at Oran, and he had not seen anything of his acting successor. He made a few telephone calls and shortly there arrived at the airfield a serious young naval lieutenant (j.g.).

He didn't know anything either, and hadn't heard anything, not even gossip. He recalled, after a bit, that his senior officer, a two-stripe lieutenant, had said something about billets for three civilians at the Aletti Hotel.

So, off to the Aletti we drove.

The young j.g. deposited us at the front desk and said the officer in command would get in touch with us immediately.

"Immediately" is a funny word in Algiers. The officer was having lunch with a French admiral. That was 1 P.M. At four, his office said he was still having lunch. At seven, his office said they hadn't heard from him since lunch.

We were getting a little worried, not knowing what change in plans had taken place and whether at that moment the *Quincy* might be steaming by the Algiers breakwater.

Sometime in the early evening, a bland young man appeared at my room and introduced himself. He was the senior naval officer at Algiers. I gathered my colleagues and we went into a huddle with him. All he knew was that he had been told by Admiral Hewitt in Naples that we would arrive and should be steered to accommodations. That was all he knew.

"Have you any idea why we're here?"

"Yes, I do, but since no one has said anything to me, I don't know anything official."

"Well, let us know if you pick up any dope."

"Sure thing, I'll keep in touch with you."

Which brings us back to the sidewalk café at the Aletti. Within a matter of days, we covered every inch of Algiers, and had started to work on the suburbs and outlying towns. We checked the lieutenant each morning, heard that he had heard nothing, then set out for the day, sometimes together, sometimes individually.

We found a fuel dump where we could get gas for such automobiles as we were able to obtain from day to day. All we had to do to get the tank filled was sign the name of the driver and the tag number.

February 16 was a pleasant sunny Friday. We were at our usual post at the sidewalk café in the midafternoon, sunning ourselves and thinking dreamily of the Press Club bar as we stared into the *vin rosé*.

"Look at that man coming up the walk," Cornell said. "Looks just like Judge Rosenman."

The thrilling sight of a face from home was too much. We jumped up and ran toward him.

The judge greeted us jovially.

"Why did you get here so soon?" he asked. "The admiral was sore as the devil—wanted to know who gave you orders to come up here right away?"

We explained that the orders we got allegedly came from the admiral.

But everybody was having fun and we forgot the tribulations when the judge said we were invited to the admiral's villa for dinner. The President would arrive on the 19th and we would have a ten-day voyage home, starting with a good news story right at Algiers. DeGaulle was to meet the President there for a conference.

We were quite interested in the invitation to the villa where Admiral Hewitt was staying. The villa was normally occupied by the naval officers stationed at Algiers and the lieutenant in charge told us bluntly that we could not have any meals there because they were rationed down to the last man. He also told us pretty pointedly that they had run out of liquor months before, so he was sorry he could not have us even for a cocktail.

When we walked in, the admiral greeted us at the door and steered us to a bountiful bar—bourbon, rye, Scotch —just about anything.

The admiral waved over toward the lieutenant and said to us, "Has he been taking good care of you—has he gotten everything you wanted?"

We smiled and said yes, sure, everything. The lieutenant left hurriedly, explaining that he had business in town.

I didn't blame the young officer, however. An admiral can dispense navy hospitality with nothing like the risk a junior officer might run.

Judge Rosenman had come from London where he had been on a special job for the President, to return to the States aboard the *Quincy* and work on a speech the President was to deliver immediately upon his return.

Steve Early welcomed us aboard the *Quincy* on Sunday and ushered us to his cabin.

No sooner was I inside the room than Steve handed me six bottles of Johnny Walker Black Label.

"Here," he said, shoving the bottles at me.

"Gosh, Steve, this is wonderful. You're really too kind."

"What the hell are you talking about, Smith? I want you to hold those for me while I tie them together. I'm taking them to Paris for Eisenhower."

Steve left the ship at Algiers to go to SHAEF and advise Eisenhower on public relations. Before he left, he briefed us on what had happened since the President left Yalta. In the first place, DeGaulle was not going to meet "the Boss." He had gotten sore because he was not asked to Yalta. Steve had a long memorandum which he showed us. It was packed with interesting things—the President's conferences after he left Yalta and a lot of brand new angles.

"That will make fine copy, Steve. Worth the trip."

Steve looked at us questioningly.

"I don't think you understand," he said. "This stuff was sent to the White House today and will be released there. You fellows won't be able to file anything until you return to Washington."

That night the movie was "Phantom Lady."

The next day after we passed through Gibraltar with all the guns manned ready for enemy submarines lurking in the area, the President received us in his cabin for a brief chat. The trip log called it a press conference. The President said he would discuss Yalta with us at greater length later in the trip.

That night, the movie was "Janie."

The next day, a bosun taught us to tie knots.

On February 20, Major General Watson died of a cerebral hemorrhage. A destroyer was detached from the task force to proceed one hundred miles south before sending the news back to Watson's widow.

The next two movies were "Frenchman's Creek" and "Mrs. Parkington." Cornell learned to toot a bosun's pipe.

The President spent a good part of each day basking in the sun on deck, playing solitaire in his cabin and reading mystery books. He devoted several hours daily to conferences with Rosenman and Admiral Leahy.

I learned to tie a double Carrick bend. The next two movies were "Enter Arsene Lupin" and "Going My Way" which Mr. Roosevelt had seen before.

We finally held a real press conference on February 23 when the President told us of his plans to go before Congress right away with a report on Yalta, that there had been no secret agreements reached at the meeting. The conference lasted an hour, but at least half of what he said was off the record and unpublishable.

The next two nights the President saw "Broadway Rhythm" and "The Pearl of Death." The movies seemed to be running low.

February 26 was a truly significant and important day. The President spurned the movie, "I'll Be Seeing You," and worked instead with Judge Rosenman on the speech.

The next day the President had the ghouls for lunch and we talked with him for more than two hours.

We left the ship shortly after lunch, boarded our train at Newport News for an overnight trip to Washington.

Now, if there is anything you want to know about the Yalta conference, try and find a back copy of *Union Jack*. I think I left mine on the table at the Aletti.

CHAPTER THIRTEEN

The Champ Goes Down

HISTORY says Franklin D. Roosevelt died on April 12, 1945, in the Little White House at Warm Springs, Georgia. Cause: a massive cerebral hemorrhage.

The story of his death, however, is a great deal more.

Stalin shuddered at the thought. Churchill wept. Political enemies said, "We knew it was coming." Political allies said, "What will happen to us now?"

The people seemed to agree generally that it was a national, and yes, an international catastrophe. They were frightened. The Great White Father was gone. What was going to happen to the war?

Over the nation a great, hurting sorrow spread. Bartenders stopped the juke organs, took off their aprons and went to Mass. Movies closed. People cried on their streetcars and busses. The stock market wavered. The Democratic party suffered collective chills and fever.

The Russian Ambassador wanted to send flowers. Mrs. Roosevelt said no flowers, please. Moscow angrily asked the Ambassador what was wrong. They had said send flowers and they wanted them sent. The poor Ambassador asked, and asked again. No flowers, he was told.

This led to rumor that Stalin demanded that his Ambassador be allowed to see the corpse so there could be no mistake about who died.

Mrs. Harry S. Truman cried and Mrs. Roosevelt tried to comfort her. The gray hair of the new President seemed grayer still as he peered through his thick glasses at the Supreme Court justice who swore him in.

The death of Franklin D. Roosevelt caused incredible complications. And yet it was so simple. He just leaned over in a chair and died. Party leaders could not do a damned thing about it. After twelve years, it just didn't seem possible. But it was.

The Boss was dead.

I saw him start to die. And I was there to report his death.

It was a beautiful April afternoon at Warm Springs and Bill Hassett and I were lazing away on the front porch of his cottage talking about hush puppies and Brunswick stew. Hassett was the secretary who made most of the trips with Mr. Roosevelt.

"I'll bet," Hassett said, "the President hasn't had any Brunswick stew in years. He'd enjoy some, too."

"Why don't we have one of the Meriwether County barbecue experts run up a pot of stew for the old man?" I asked.

The next thing: Hassett and I were talking over barbecue plans with Ruth Stevens, the manageress of the small Warm Springs Hotel who endeared herself to Roosevelt when she first met him by blurting, "Jesus sakes alike—it's the PRESIDENT!"

"We," said Ruthie, "will have us one damned good barbecue."

Ruth and the owner of the hotel, Frank Allcorn, worked like demons for several days lining up the chef, his assistants and some hillbilly musicians. Allcorn got two small hogs, a lamb and a side of beef. The Brunswick stew specialist was imported from near-by Newnan.

Finally, the magic day. Hassett came tearing down the side of Pine Mountain in his station wagon just before lunch. A smartly uniformed marine leaped from the car in front of the hotel. He carried a glistening bugle.

The marine took up his position inside the lobby while Hassett sent for me. He gave me my instructions. I was to announce him as he entered the lobby.

Bill signaled the marine who then proceeded to assail the eardrums of the lobby loafers with four blasts of "Attention." I strode in just as Ruth burst in from the kitchen.

"I bear a message for the Countess of Meriwether," I shouted with all courtly vigor.

Hassett handed a brown envelope to the marine who bore it across the lobby to Ruth. She turned a dull white.

Ruth's hands trembled as she opened the envelope.

"The President of the United States," she read, "accepts with pleasure your kind invitation to barbecue . . ."

"Jesus Christ," Ruth muttered, "I'll be a . . ."

(Ruth Stevens, it should be pointed out here and now, is one of the finest, most saintly women of our time. It just happens, however, that she cusses like a sailor, particularly when she is nervous. The good people of Warm Springs understand this and pay no attention.)

April 12, 1945, was the date of the barbecue, to be given at the Pine Mountain home of Allcorn, an Atlanta broker who bought the Warm Springs Hotel to satisfy his love of small-town life.

We decided to limit the party to the travel crew—the President's staff, the three wire service men and, of course,

Ruth and the mayor. This was to avoid social complications on Warm Springs Foundation where an invitation to eat with the President established a person's social position for years to come.

The party was supposed to start at four o'clock. The staff was to come thirty minutes ahead of the President to permit a few head-start drinks before the Boss arrived. He was scheduled to reach the mountain cottage at four-thirty.

I spent most of the morning of April 12 on the mountain, helping Ruth and Allcorn get organized. We tasted the barbecue—and the old-fashioneds—and by three in the afternoon we seemed to be squared away.

I had to go down the mountain to the Foundation for a few minutes and ran into Alice Winegar, Hassett's secretary. Alice looked a little strange as she darted across one of the Foundation's clay streets. I yelled at her.

"You folks better be getting ready," I told her. "Don't be a minute later than four o'clock."

Alice didn't say anything. She just looked terrified.

"What's the matter?" I asked her.

"Nothing, Smitty," she said. But I knew she was lying. I thought at the time something big must be brewing; that she was a little preoccupied, but it never occurred to me that anything truly earth-shaking was about to happen.

I went to the hotel, changed clothes and drove on to the Allcorn cottage.

At four o'clock the country fiddlers began to play. The first few guests were arriving. These included the Western Union people with us, Don Fisher of N.B.C. who had come in about an hour before to handle a Jefferson Day address for all networks, and Allcorn's family.

Four-ten came and Major Dewitt Greer, head of the White House Signal Corps unit, arrived. He made a quick check on the short-wave radio units which were placed in Allcorn's barn for the Secret Service.

Greer came over to me and said, "Where does a fellow get a drink?" I ushered him to the improvised bar and while he was having his first one, the two telephone company men who were part of the party arrived.

At four-twenty I became a little irritated because the secretarial staff had not arrived. I had visions of their cars clogging traffic for the President on the narrow one-way road leading up the mountain to Allcorn's house.

I excused myself from the party and walked back to the barn where Wayne Shell, a Signal Corps sergeant, was sitting by his short-wave portable, reading a Western magazine and waiting patiently for the end of his shift.

"Wayne," I asked, "how about letting me call the Little White House to see if the Boss is on his way?"

Waiting for the radio check, I looked out at the party. It was one of the happiest gatherings I'd ever seen. A warm spring sun bathed the valley below the small mountain and the air was an appetizing combination of odors —the crisp, crackling fat of the hogs, the warm pungency of the Brunswick stew and the added touch of civilization—the slightly barroom smell coming from a table laden with old-fashioneds.

The President, Hassett had said, will stay for about an hour, then he will have to go to a minstrel show being staged for him by the children of the Foundation. We had arranged a special chair from which Mr. Roosevelt could gaze down the beautiful valley, and still hear the country fiddlers. He was to be served no barbecue, but just a bowl of the stew and a drink or two.

The sergeant mumbled into his hand microphone.

"Indiana to Pine—Indiana to Pine—come in please."

"Pine to Indiana—Pine to Indiana—go ahead."

"Is there any sign of movement?"

"No—no sign of movement."

I leaned over to Shell.

"Let me have the mike a minute, please."

"Pine—who is this please?"

"This is Anderson. Who is this?"

"This is Smitty, Andy. What the hell is going on down there?"

"Smitty, I honestly don't know. No cars have arrived. There just isn't anything doing."

"The President is supposed to be here in a few minutes."

"Yeah, I know. But there's nothing moving as yet. Want me to give you a call?"

"No, Andy, I'll get on the phone and talk to Hackie."

Anderson was the Secret Service agent on duty at the front gate of the Little White House. Hackie was—and still is—Louise Hackmeister, the chief White House telephone operator.

I trotted to the door of Allcorn's cottage and asked his pretty daughter if they had a telephone. Yes, she said, on the wall in the next room.

It was a coffee-grinder type of set and it took several minutes to reach the Foundation switchboard.

"Ring the White House board," I asked.

A few seconds and Hackie's crisp "Yes, please" came in through the receiver.

"Hackie, this is Smitty. Why aren't you people on the way? What's holding things up?"

Hackie's voice sounded almost unreal. Usually, she was very levelheaded. But this time her voice was panicky. She was shouting.

"I don't know, Smitty," she said. "But Mr. Hassett wants to see you. Get the other two boys and go to his cottage as fast as you can."

"Hackie, for Christ's sakes, what's going on?"

"Smitty, I can't say any more. Just get down here as fast as you can."

I put down the phone and ran out into the driveway. I saw Bob Nixon of I.N.S. and Harry Oliver of A.P. standing together. I went over quietly and said, "Come with me."

We walked toward Greer's big fast Signal Corps Lincoln. He saw us and came running.

"What's up?"

"Can you take us down to Hassett's cottage right away? Something awful big is going on."

We saw Ed Clement, of the Southern Bell Telephone and Telegraph Company.

"Ed," I shouted, "get some circuits lined up to Washington, will you?"

(Ray Hoover of Western Union probably will never forgive me for not telling him at the same time, but I honestly didn't see Hoover and we were in much, too much of a hurry to stop and look for people.)

We started down the narrow, twisting mountain road, all speculating about what the big break would be. We agreed it was the capitulation of Germany.

Greer drove the car and when we hit the paved road leading to the Foundation, the speedometer needle was tickling ninety miles an hour.

In a cloud of dust, Greer pulled up in front of Hassett's cottage and we dashed inside.

I was the first one through the door. Hassett was standing near the fireplace of his living room, his face gray and mournful. I looked over to the couch and saw Grace Tully and her assistant, Dorothy Brady. Both of them were crying softly and literally wiping their eyes on each other's shoulder.

When I saw Grace Tully's tear-swollen eyes, I knew she was not crying about the end of the war. I remembered there were four telephones in Hassett's cottage. And one was only about two feet away from me—on the radiator of his living room.

I honestly had no exact idea of what was happening, but I knew it was big and tragic.

Hassett cleared his throat and fiddled with two or three small pieces of paper in his hands. He stepped away from the fireplace into the middle of the room, and I picked up the telephone.

"Gentlemen," he said, "it is my sad duty to inform you that the President . . ."

"Number please?" said the operator in my ear.

"Priority one—Washington—" I said softly.

Hassett continued.

"The President died at 3:35 this afternoon."

"Executive 3430," I finished to the operator. "My name is Smith."

I heard telephone switchboards yanked apart, and then —it seemed hours, but it was only a few seconds—I heard the most welcome voice I ever heard in my life—Romilda Flanagan, our operator in Washington.

"United Press," she chirped.

"Flash!" I roared into the telephone. I could also hear Oliver and Nixon screaming because I had grabbed the living room telephone. Hassett quickly steered them into rooms where there were other instruments.

Julius Frandsen, U.P.'s extremely quiet and calm news editor in Washington, answered with a soft "yes?"

"Roosevelt died at 3:35 Warm Springs this is Smith," I jabbered.

"Dictate," Frandsen said and hung up his phone.

I started dictating to the typewriter girls in Washington, and I didn't find out until sometime later that Steve Early, the President's press secretary who was in Washington beat me by a few minutes with the first news.

Steve had telephoned the wire service offices in Washington at about the same time we were getting the news from Hassett.

We dictated for a few minutes, then stopped to make notes, continuing this stop-and-go process for several hours. A tired young man in a sweaty khaki shirt and trousers helped us. He was Howard G. Bruenn, the navy doctor who was with Mr. Roosevelt when he died.

Bruenn mopped his face with a limp handkerchief and said with a hopeless shrug, "It was just like a bolt of lightning or getting hit by a train."

"One minute he was alive and laughing. The next minute—wham!"

"Howard," we asked, "did you see this thing coming?"

"This wasn't the sort of thing you could forecast. Doctors just can't say 'this man is going to have a cerebral.' It doesn't happen that way. He'd been feeling fine. He was awfully tired when we first came down here. You saw him the other day—wasn't he in fine spirits?"

Yes, the President was in fine spirits that day, but he looked unhealthy.

I had been horseback riding near the President's cottage most of the morning of April 5 when a marine courier found me on a back road and told me to proceed to the President's quarters immediately.

I didn't know what to do with the horse, so I tied him to a tree in the garden behind Bill Hassett's cottage—and found later that the horse hungrily did away with the owner's prized bed of pansies and lilies.

The three press association reporters were ushered into the small, comfortable living room of the Little White House at about two o'clock in the afternoon of April 5. The President had been in daylong conference with Sergio Osmena, then President of the Philippine Commonwealth.

Mr. Roosevelt was sitting in his favorite spot in the house—before the living room fireplace. The President was in a friendly and easy mood, but his hands seemed to tremble more than ever as he fitted a cigarette into his famous, scorched ivory holder.

If we had only known it was his last press conference, we would have better noted the smallest details.

Osmena was Mr. Roosevelt's guest only for the day. They had discussed distant plans for a day they hoped would not be too distant—the day of complete Philippine independence.

The President said that Japan, like Germany, would not be allowed to retain or build up any force capable of waging war. Japan, he said calmly but firmly, would be policed just like Germany.

He told of plans for ousting the Japanese forever from

their mandated islands and how these islands would be used as bases for the United Nations, primarily the United States, to keep the Pacific at peace.

Little Osmena, looking frail after a recent operation in Florida, nodded and smiled agreement as the President talked.

Mr. Roosevelt coughed lightly at frequent intervals, but he smoked chain fashion. It was a beautiful, tranquil afternoon and I could not understand why the President, the great lover of the outdoors, was not out with Osmena in the small convertible.

The warm Georgia sunshine streamed in through the windows at Mr. Roosevelt's back. Occasionally, he had to raise his voice to be heard over the measured snoring of a large Irish setter which slept blissfully at one end of the room. The setter belonged to Miss Laura Delano, the President's cousin who was with him.

Fala, the famous Scotty, waddled from person to person, sniffing trouser cuffs and trying to take some of the spotlight away from the snoring setter.

The interview was about over. Mr. Roosevelt began to fiddle with various papers on the card table beside him. And the reporters saw that one of the greatest news wells the world has ever known was about to go dry—for the moment at least.

"There are some other things," a reporter said, "such as what happened with the one vote versus three votes for Russia at San Francisco?"

"That," the President said with a roaring laugh, "is not even subtle."

Instead he kidded us about the bad golf that was being played on the Warm Springs course.

"Have a cig?" he said, shoving his pack of Camels across the card table toward me.

He used that expression often and it was so out of character. "Have a cig" seemed to belong more to the flappers and sheiks in John Held, Jr., cartoons than in the vocabulary of a Roosevelt.

His hands shook so badly he could hardly get the cigarette out of the package. I leaned over to light it for him, but he said no thanks, he had some kitchen matches of his own.

He seemed to gather all his strength and control into the lighting of the cigarette. It was an intense thing. I wanted not to watch.

I didn't see him again to talk with before he died. Two days before his death, however, the President was taking a quiet afternoon drive in his little open coupé and nearly ran me down. I was riding a very nasty horse which I had rented for the afternoon at the village drugstore. They had everything in that store.

As I reined in the horse to let the President and the accompanying Secret Service car pass, Mr. Roosevelt bowed majestically to me. The car was moving slowly and the President spoke. His voice was wonderful and resonant. It sounded like the Roosevelt of old. In tones that must have been audible a block away, Roosevelt hailed me with: "Heigh-O, Silver!"

As far as I was concerned, those were his last words.

Actually, however, he spoke his last words on April 12, just before 1:15 P.M. (Central War time).

It was before lunch and the President was killing two birds with one stone. He was at work on official papers which had arrived from Washington that morning, and posing at the same time for Elizabeth Shumatov, one of his favorite artists.

He had been in gay spirits. He was feeling so much better than he had in previous weeks that Bruenn that morning had telephoned an enthusiastic report on his condition to Admiral McIntire, who was in Washington.

Mr. Roosevelt sat where he could see the sun-bathed valley of dogwood trees west of his little cottage. He remarked what a fine day it would be at the barbecue. The war news was good that morning. The Washington dispatches looked fine. Let's see—there were two more bills Hassett had brought for his signature. The President leafed through the papers in front of him.

Suddenly, he clapped his hand to the back of his head like a man slapping a fly. His face wrinkled into a heavy frown.

The President said softly, "I have a terrific headache."

Then he collapsed. The massive, heavy upper part of his body rolled over against the side of the chair. The artist leaped to her feet. The President's cousin, Laura Delano, ran from the rear of the room.

"The President!" they called. "The President has fainted!"

Into the pleasant, sunny room dashed Arthur Prettyman, the President's valet. Miss Delano grabbed a telephone and called for Bruenn who was just leaving the swimming pool a mile or so away.

Prettyman ran into the kitchen and summoned a Filipino messboy. They lifted the President's sagging body from the chair and bore it into his small bedroom a few feet away.

Prettyman did what he could to see that his chief was

comfortable. He loosened Mr. Roosevelt's belt and his tie. The President looked very sick.

His tortured breathing could be heard throughout the cottage. His tremendous chest rose and fell as though a large pump were operating it. He was in his last fight.

Within a few minutes, Bruenn rushed into the cottage with George Fox, the navy pharmacist who gave the President nightly rubdowns and always traveled with him as a first-aid or emergency specialist.

They gently removed Mr. Roosevelt's blue suit and put pajamas on his limp body.

Bruenn immediately telephoned his chief in Washington. McIntire in turn telephoned Atlanta and asked Dr. James Paullin, famous southern internist who had consulted with McIntire before on Mr. Roosevelt's health, to hurry to Warm Springs.

While Paullin was en route, Bruenn did everything possible to keep the President alive. Fox tried gentle massage and moved the President's arms. Mr. Roosevelt's eyes were open, but they were unseeing eyes.

Fox called to the President, asking him to show some sign of recognition if he could hear his voice. But the eyes just stared straight ahead.

Paullin arrived after a wild automobile ride and his diagnosis agreed with Bruenn's—a massive cerebral hemorrhage. It was just a matter of time. And at 3:35, Warm Springs time, Mr. Roosevelt's tortured breathing stopped.

Bruenn, Fox and Paullin were the only ones in the room. The doctors bent over the bed. They looked at each other. The President was dead.

The news was given first to Mr. Roosevelt's two cousins, Laura Delano and Margaret Suckley, who were waiting in the living room outside the President's bedchamber. At the same time, Bruenn telephoned the sad news to McIntire in Washington. McIntire immediately told Steve Early who had the task of telling Mrs. Roosevelt.

The night of April 12 was truly a nightmare. It was a horrible, discordant symphony of people shouting for telephones, automobiles racing along dusty clay roads, the clatter of telegraph instruments and typewriters.

The three White House correspondents, having to carry almost the entire brunt of the coverage because the White House was loath to have the sorrowing Foundation overrun by strange reporters and photographers, wrote all night. I wrote until I thought another word could not come out of my typewriter. Then would come a message from Washington—"We now need a piece about . . . ." And the typewriter would go on.

Mrs. Roosevelt, McIntire and Early arrived around midnight. Steve gave us the funeral train plans as they developed. Shortly before dawn, the Southern Bell people informed me they had completed the installation of a special telephone for me at the little Warm Springs station where Mr. Roosevelt's body would be put aboard the train.

I still had to pack and check out of the hotel, so I signed off my wire to Washington and went into the village. Sorrowing, miserable people sat along the high curbstones, talking in low voices. Their faces were pictures of fear.

When I reached the hotel, the dawn was starting. It was a fiery red dawn signaling an unusually hot day for spring. The long funeral train was switched into position and the windows knocked out of the rear car to permit entrance of the casket which was brought down during the night from Atlanta.

The interior of the hotel was an unsightly mess. Ruth Stevens and Allcorn had graciously moved the barbecue into the hotel for the all-night workers and the lobby was littered with half-finished bowls of Brunswick stew and plates of barbecue scraps.

I went up to my room and started to get in bed, but I shook off the impulse, knowing that once I put my head down, nothing short of an explosion could awake me for ten or twelve hours.

Packing consisted of ramming clothes into bags wherever they would fit. I was momentarily overjoyed to find two bottles of bourbon in my gear and thought with amazement that during the entire night of grueling work by reporters, operators, linemen and others, I had seen only one pint. I cautiously tried a straight drink, but got only about half of it down.

As I trundled my gear down the stairs, Mrs. Stevens ran to help me.

"Come on in the kitchen, Smith," she said, "and let me give you some hot stew and a cup of coffee."

I gagged at the thought.

"Well, don't be a fool. You've got to eat sometime."

"Ruth, thanks a million, but I've got a hard day and night ahead of me and I'm so knotted up that food now would just make me sick."

When my bags were loaded aboard the train, I looked to my communications. The telephone was ready, so I put in a call to Washington and had a U.P. staff man, Fowler, from Atlanta stay on the call continuously until the train left. This was done to avoid wire jams that were certain to develop later in the day.

Shortly after nine o'clock, the Secret Service notified the three White House reporters to get in a car and go to the Little White House. We were to come back to the train in the funeral procession.

The cortege left the Little White House at nine-thirty. A hot southern sun bathed the green hills and valleys the President loved so well. The route was down a winding clay road to Georgia Hall, the central building of the Warm Springs Foundation, and thence about a mile to the little railroad station.

Troops from Fort Benning, most of them combat veterans, stood shoulder to shoulder at present arms along the way. An honor guard walked ahead of the hearse. In a limousine behind the President's body were Mrs. Roosevelt, the Misses Suckley and Delano and Grace Tully. The women were composed, but puffy eyes behind their black veils gave proof of their mourning through the night.

The square at Georgia Hall was thronged with hundreds of the President's close friends. They looked at the procession with tearful eyes, then bowed their heads in silence as the cortege passed.

First into the square was the United States Army band from Fort Benning. The roll of its muffled drums sounded dolefully through the soft, still country air. The white columns of Georgia Hall glistened in the brilliant southern sun.

One thousand infantrymen carrying carbines, then troops with rifles marched behind the band. The colors of each company carried black streamers to signify the mourning for their Commander-in-Chief. Then came the hearse. The President's body was in a copper-lined, flag-draped mahogany coffin.

The patients at Georgia Hall were drawn up in a large semicircle around the driveway. Some were on crutches. Others in wheel chairs. And others confined to their beds. There were no restrained emotions in this group. Their idol, their hope was dead. The world was at an end.

Mrs. Roosevelt had requested that the hearse stop momentarily at the entrance of Georgia Hall—just a brief stop, the kind the President had made every time he left Warm Springs in the past. The President always had waved and assured the patients of his return within a few months.

This morning, they knew too well he would not be back. Just as the hearse stopped, a Negro Coast Guards-man, Chief Petty Officer Graham Jackson, stepped from behind the columns. Jackson was one of the President's favorite musicians and he had his accordion with him.

Tears were streaming down Jackson's black cheeks as he lifted his accordion and began the soft strains of Dvo-řák's "Going Home." Kids buried their faces in their elbows and wept loudly. Case-hardened nurses and doc-tors sniffled and looked at the ground. Only the very young—those too young to know—seemed to be tearless.

There was old Tom Logan on the edge of the crowd. For fourteen years he had waited on the President at Warm Springs. As the white-haired Negro stared at the hearse bearing the body of his friend, his frail frame shook with sobs and he prayed, "Lawd Gawd, take care of him now."

As the procession started to move again, Jackson edged

closer to the slow-moving automobiles and began "Nearer, My God, to Thee," the most solemn song of the Protestant faith.

Many of the soldiers along the line of march cried softly as they stood at rigid attention. The tension and emotion of the moment was too much for one corporal who pitched over backwards into a drainage ditch.

At five minutes to ten, the hearse reached the train siding and eight enlisted men, picked as a guard of honor for the casket on the trip to Washington, loaded the casket into the rear car.

In the distance, a country church bell rang its sad farewell.

It was about fifteen minutes before the train left, so I dictated during that period to Washington. I was so choked with emotion, myself, that it was difficult to speak coherent sentences.

I saw the conductor wave his arm to the engineer, so I turned the telephone over to Fowler and sprinted for the train. It was beginning to move as I climbed aboard. I walked back to my drawing room and flopped in the seat.

The train passed a cotton field where Negro women were working on spring planting. I looked out and saw four of them kneeling near the edge of the field. Their hands were clasped together and raised in prayerful supplication.

I thought of the President's prayer on D-Day when he went to God in behalf of our troops pouring ashore in Normandy.

"Some will never return," he prayed. "Embrace these, Father, and receive them, Thy heroic servants, into Thy kingdom."

CHAPTER FOURTEEN

Post-Mortem

THE ride back to Washington was sad and slow.

At every stop, from Atlanta to Alexandria, people thronged the railroad stations large and small. Men stood with their arms around the shoulders of their wives and mothers. Men and women wept openly. Church choirs gathered at the trackside and sang "Rock of Ages" and "Abide with Me." Boy Scout troops and home guard units stood in salute behind lowered flags.

The train did not stop at most of the smaller towns. But Steve Early ordered the engineer to slow down for each village so the people could pay their last respects to the President.

At night the casket was easily visible to the crowds. It stood on a high catafalque in the lounge of the last car on the train. The only visible decoration was an American flag drawn neatly over the casket which rested on a pad of Marine Corps blankets. A soldier, a sailor, a marine and a Coast Guard seaman stood rigidly at each corner of the coffin.

The only undrawn shades on the entire train were those of the small lounge. Bright ceiling lights made the casket and the serious young men of the honor guard fully visible to people in the stations and along the right of way.

At first there were only a few flowers. But by dusk the forward end of the room was filled with large and ornate funeral wreaths, and with expensive sprays of beautiful southern spring blossoms.

At each stop, local officials and leaders of civic organizations brought their floral offerings to the side of the train. Early would allow a small delegation to go aboard to place the wreath personally at the head of the coffin.

The train in the early evening slowed for a small town in Carolina. The schedule did not call for a stop, so we rolled through at about ten miles an hour. I watched from an open door at the end of our car.

It was just after suppertime. The few street lights of the town blinked at the intersections. The streets were packed for two and three blocks away from the railroad. The people stood in the darkness, exchanging notes in hushed voices about the honor guard and the casket as it rolled into view.

As we passed through the small depot, a few Boy Scouts in front of the crowd began singing "Onward Christian Soldiers." A few grownups around them, probably their mothers and dads, joined in, rather hesitantly at first. But in a few seconds, the people for blocks around took up the song. They sang softly at the start, then their voices seemed to grow.

That was the most impressive moment of the trip, hearing that little town with many of its people blocks away from the track, singing Christianity's wonderful, brave marching song. It was heartening to hear the little town tell itself that everything would be all right.

Like every person on the train, I was exhausted; at the saturation point when it came to writing anything more about the grieving South. By the time we reached Virginia, I felt that all the emotion in me had been pounded out. It was then early morning, probably one or two o'clock.

As we approached a small Virginia train service point which was to be the last stop of the night, I pulled on a pair of dirty pajamas and crawled into the top bunk of the drawing room I shared with Harry Oliver of the A.P.

He was beating his typewriter industriously.

"Harry, for God's sake, let's get some sleep for the first time in forty-eight hours."

"Right now," he said. He handed his copy to a waiting Western Union representative, then locked the door.

"You know what?" Harry said as he pulled off his socks. "For the first time I realize that the old man is dead."

Wearily, he slipped into the lower berth and I cut off the lights. At that very moment the door buzzer rang. Harry fumbled his way to the door. The porter said a man wanted to talk with him. The train had stopped.

Harry walked to the end of the car in his pajamas where an A.P. man from Richmond waited for him.

"Where's the story?" the man asked. "They sent me here to handle it."

"What story. It is two o'clock in the morning. I've filed every detail up to now."

"Well, what about the story of the stop here?"

Harry came back to the room grumbling. I laughed.

"Thank God, the U.P. is leaving me alone. I must have filed a million words today."

Then the door buzzer went off again. This time it was my turn. There stood a United Press representative, waiting for my copy, too. He also had some messages for me that required answers. I finally talked the U.P. man into sending the story himself and promised to answer the messages up the line. It certainly was hard to give up the idea of sleep again. If that stop had been fifteen minutes later, no power on earth could have gotten me awake.

Once the work was out of the way again, I dressed and shaved. By the time I stuffed my Warm Springs accumulation of dirty clothes into bags, we were almost in Washington.

I rode in an open Secret Service car from the Union Station to the White House. The U.P. had a large detail of reporters on hand, so I did not have to worry too much at that point about detail. I just watched the crowd as we rolled by at a speed paced by the horse-drawn army caisson bearing the casket.

The Negroes who idolized Mr. Roosevelt were out in full force. Hundreds of them wept along the curbs as the caisson went down Constitution Avenue. Passing the Justice Department, an old Negro woman broke through the police lines and ran sobbing a few feet out in the street.

"Lord God, take care of us now," she moaned.

Policemen pulled her back behind the ropes.

A wizened Negro movie photographer ran alongside our car almost the entire distance from Union Station to the White House. Each time he raised his ancient camera for a shot of the cortege, a policeman seemed to get in his way. But he did not leave us and kept trotting along with the procession. I don't know why I noticed the Negroes more than the white people. I suppose it was that they seemed to be showing their emotion more openly.

A burning sun popped from behind clouds as we started into the final blocks. From 15th Street, down

Pennsylvania Avenue to the White House, the crowd seemed thickest. Somewhere a band played a dirge and from our slow-moving automobile we could hear the crying, we could see the women dabbing at their eyes and trying to comfort their children. I felt weepy too.

The caisson moved into the White House grounds. I stood for a few minutes to watch the casket unloaded and borne into the house. Admiral Leahy and Mrs. Roosevelt, her sons and their wives in the severe black of mourning, walked up the steps slowly and followed the casket inside. I walked on over to the press room.

"Well, we're back," I told the office. "The casket has just been carried into the house through the North Portico and into the East Room."

Julius Frandsen, presiding over the U.P. news desk, cut in on my telephone conversation.

"Look, Smith, we've got everything covered. You go on home and get some sleep. I want you to get all the rest you can before you leave on the funeral train for Hyde Park tonight."

I went home in a cab and my wife took one look at me and insisted that I skip the trip to Hyde Park.

"I'm sorry, but I just came home for a nap," I told Eleanor. "Wake me at six o'clock."

That was a foolish hope, however. I hadn't been in bed more than ten minutes when the telephone rang. I could hear Eleanor arguing that I shouldn't be disturbed. I finally went to the telephone. It was Frandsen.

"I'm awfully sorry and I won't bother you again if I can possibly help it," he said, "but do you know if . . ."

I answered his question and tried the nap again. The night desk wanted to know something else. Finally, after

a series of calls not only from the U.P. but from other
reporters, too, I gave up and tried to soak away some of
the fatigue in the bathtub.

When I boarded the funeral train that night, the porter
told me that most of our party was in the diner. I went
in and sat down with William C. Murphy, Jr., then covering the White House for the Philadelphia *Inquirer* and
now the publicity director for the Republican National
Committee.

The train was so long and heavy that the crew found
it difficult to get it started. A coupling broke three times.
The third time, Murphy remarked laconically, "The
Republicans have always known that it would be difficult
to get Roosevelt out of Washington."

A lot of judgment was passed that night on the way to
Hyde Park.

One school of thought said the public had been misled
by not having a true and full report on Mr. Roosevelt's
health long before his death, particularly during the
fourth term campaign. Another group took the other side,
arguing that the public had been given the whole story;
that the President's death was as unexpected to his doctors
as it was to the public at large.

If Dr. McIntire was at fault for not telling the nation
more about the President's health, the fault was not his
alone. Due largely to the frequent prevalence of untrue
rumors about Mr. Roosevelt's health, members of his
staff and his close friends bent over backwards to deny any
suggestion of poor health.

To the best of my knowledge, Steve Early was completely honest in what he said about Mr. Roosevelt's condition. But Steve didn't say much about it, unless the

President had a cold or some other minor ailment which was sufficient to keep him away from the office. When this was the case, Steve always supplied bulletins, sometimes several daily, giving temperature readings and other details.

It seemed to me, however, and in retrospect, that the older Mr. Roosevelt got, the less his staff tried to say about his health.

The last public report on his health came from the President himself. On March 1, 1945, he reported to Congress on the Yalta conference. For the first time before such a large public audience, the President sat in his wheel chair and did not stand for his speech.

"I hope you will pardon me," he told a joint session of the House and Senate, "for the unusual posture of sitting down during the presentation of what I wish to say, but I know you will realize that it makes it a lot easier for me not having to carry ten pounds of steel around the bottom of my legs, and also, because of the fact that I have just completed a 14,000-mile trip.

". . . I am returning from this trip that took me so far, refreshed and inspired. I was well the entire time. I was not ill for a second until I arrived back in Washington and here I heard all the rumors which had occurred in my absence. Yes, I returned from the trip refreshed and inspired. The Roosevelts are not, as you may suspect, averse to travel. We seem to thrive on it."

The President might have been more convincing if he had looked better. His voice that day in the crowded House chamber was thin. He sounded poor on the radio. His delivery was listless and spotty. He misread sentences. His head sagged as he read from his big, black notebook.

He may have returned "fresh and inspired" but it didn't look that way to some of us who came back with him. The ten days at Yalta probably were the most difficult days of his Presidential career. On the trip home, he seemed to have aged ten years. Although he sat for hours in the sun, he appeared to tan very little. He had lost weight in Russia, but did not take it too seriously since he expected to make it up at Warm Springs.

As we passed second and third judgment in the diner of the funeral train that night on the way to Hyde Park, one reporter made the point that it was a mistake not to have performed an autopsy on the President's body and with a full, public disclosure of the results.

That would have been a sure antidote for the rumors that swept the country in the days following his death. There are today, for example, people who believe Mr. Roosevelt was murdered. Some swear that he committed suicide. One magazine actually printed an article alleging that the cerebral hemorrhage which killed him was the third he had suffered.

Then there were reports that he died of cancer, of tuberculosis and/or poisoning. There was a rumor current in Harlem for a time that he had not died at all, but had gone raving mad. This rumor obviously fed on the fact that his body did not lie in state or in public view before the funeral.

Plainly these rumors are untrue. The world had the word of three distinguished medical men—McIntire, Bruenn and Paullin—for the cause of the President's death. Their reputations and their established integrity, plus the lack of any established facts to the contrary, make it necessary to accept their stated cause of death.

But the record does not seem as unquestionable on reports of his health in advance of the President's death.

McIntire reported at the end of the Yalta trip that Mr. Roosevelt was in "tiptop" condition. Yet, it was during that same period that Secret Service agents were assigned to protect Vice President Truman.

Mr. Truman did not ask for the agents. McIntire did not request or recommend them. So, what was the answer? The higher-ups of the United States Secret Service obviously were worried about the President's health. To be on the safe side, they assigned a detail of agents to guard the Vice President.

If the people close to the President did not believe he was in failing health, I think they were kidding themselves. As a layman I saw many indications, not of approaching death, but of sagging vitality. I realized, too, that we could not expect the Administration to be so politically inexpedient as to announce, for example, that "President Roosevelt is now a tired and worn out old man, and is having trouble regaining his strength and energy." But that seemed to me about the size of it.

I knew a man who was one of Mr. Roosevelt's closest friends and associates. Up until the time "the Boss" actually died, this man consistently pooh-poohed stories about the President's worsening health. But a few days after the President died, he admitted quite candidly that he could see the Chief Executive "slipping" for the previous eighteen months.

This was an example of hindsight, of course, but it was typical. Many members of the Roosevelt administration felt the same way generally. Until the President died, they could see the pressure of his job slowly sapping his strength, but they refused to let themselves think about the possibility of his death in office.

With no job or political future at stake, I believed during that period that he would live out his fourth term. I thought he would become increasingly weary of the White House. I thought the Presidency would take a mounting physical toll. But I didn't think he would die. I anticipated spending more and more time in Warm Springs and Hyde Park and had so planned.

In various memoranda, I tried to keep my office up to date on various indications of poor health. I reported months before he died that his hearing seemed to be failing rapidly because of sinus trouble. In his last six months, probably the most obvious deterioration was in his voice. It was very noticeable in press conferences and in his speeches. In talking with reporters, his voice a few years before was powerful enough to shake the windows. But shortly before the end, he was often inaudible to persons a few feet from his desk.

Everybody on the funeral train from Washington to Hyde Park, at least in the press cars, had his own theory. The talk in the diner and the club car continued until late in the evening.

It was one of those conversations where everyone is absorbed with his own thoughts—not really listening to what other people are saying. But one remark I was to remember long after.

"What about this Truman? He's certainly in a tough spot."

CHAPTER FIFTEEN

Early to Rise

I SAW Senator Harry S. Truman, Democrat, Missouri, several times at the White House during the war. He made routine visits to President Roosevelt every now and then to report on the progress of his war investigating committee.

The visit that seemed to stick in my mind was not long after the Democratic convention in 1944 when Mr. Truman was nominated to be Vice President.

He had lunch out on the South Portico with the President, and Mrs. Roosevelt sat with them part of the time. When the Vice-Presidential nominee left the White House, he carried two roses in his hand.

To be frank about it, he did not look much like a big political figure as he stood in the White House lobby chatting in his mild manner with the reporters. He explained almost shyly that one rose was from Mrs. Roosevelt to Mrs. Truman, and the other from Anna Roosevelt Boettiger to Margaret Truman.

That wasn't very world-shaking news, so the correspondents pressed a little harder with their questions. It was the first time the President and his running mate had met since the convention. The campaign was on. It seemed they must have had something more important to discuss than roses.

It was a nice lunch, Mr. Truman said. Then he proceeded to describe every item on the menu. But as to what he and the President had discussed, Mr. Truman didn't say very much. When we heard later that Mrs. Roosevelt had been present much of the time, we could understand that the luncheon was on the level of a pleasant little visit, rather than a big-time political conference.

Then, on the April afternoon when they lowered Mr. Roosevelt's body into the simple grave at Hyde Park, I looked over the bank of funeral flowers and saw the new President.

I tried to wipe out of my mind the picture of him standing in the White House lobby with the two wilting roses in his hand. I knew it was an unfair picture.

Standing by the grave, the President seemed tired and a little uneasy. He stared down at the lowering casket through his heavy glasses. A bright spring sun made his hair seem whiter than it actually was, and his wife and daughter by him looked uncomfortable and sad.

A Secret Service man, one I'd never seen before, tapped him on the elbow and the party started for the train.

When I got aboard and settled down in the drawing room in which I had traveled so many thousands of miles with Mr. Roosevelt, I didn't feel at all like I was covering a new President. There just didn't seem to be any President at the moment.

Most of the people on the train were members of the Roosevelt staff. Before the train was out of sight of the crepe-hung Hyde Park depot, they started what turned out to be a post-funeral wake.

Liquor flowed in every compartment and drawing room. The shades were drawn throughout the train and from the outside, it looked like any train bearing mourners home. But behind those curtains, the Roosevelt staff had what they thought was a good time.

Their Boss would have approved. They were tired and exhaustingly sad. They had mourned with all their hearts and might for three days and nights and the tension had to give somewhere. Instead of crying—a few of them did —most of them got a little plastered.

I saw one of the top New Dealers hurl a tray of empty glasses into a toilet and shout in mock bravado, "Down the hatch, we won't need you any more."

Porters and club car stewards bustled up and down the corridors with gurgling, sloshing trays. If you hadn't known the people in the drawing rooms, you would have thought they were on their way home from a football game.

Some of the people were using whisky as an antidote for worry over their jobs. Many of the people on that train knew it was just a matter of days, weeks or months before their White House service would be over.

Back in a private car, however, there was a different scene. The new President and his staff gathered in the lounge and talked in low voices about the awesome tasks ahead.

When the train stopped in the railroad yards outside New York City to change engines, I walked back to the private car. Out on the observation platform were new men, most of them strangers to me. There was a chunky army colonel named Harry Vaughan. I had trouble spelling his name when someone told me. He would be the new military aide.

There was a good-looking young chap named Matt

Connelly. Someone said, "He'll be one of Truman's secretaries." And there was George Allen, whom we'd all
known before. Usually gay and laughing, George was
quiet and serious on this day.

I was introduced to Vaughan and we chatted on the
end of the car for a few minutes. I looked in through the
window at the lounge. I didn't see a single highball glass.
Just men with their heads together talking seriously.

Vaughan told us what little he could about the President's plans. Each time he said "President" he said it
carefully. The word was very new. The truth of the
matter was that there were very few plans to tell. The
President would return to his Connecticut Avenue apartment that night, but probably not move into the White
House for some time.

He told how Mr. Truman wanted the Roosevelt family
to have all the time they needed and wanted before
moving out of the White House.

The train started to move and I ran to my car. As I
swung up the steps, I could hear an alcoholic chorus of
"Auld Lang Syne."

A government official brushed by me in the corridor
and stopped to shake hands.

"Smitty, old boy," he said, "I guess this is the last time
this gang will ever travel together."

Most of the reporters were busy on pieces for the morning papers, forecasting government changes and the
people Mr. Truman would retain; writing personality
pieces to tell the country about Mr. Truman's background.

Many feared a bad effect on the war effort. There was a
running argument about whether the new President

would be conservative or follow the Roosevelt course to the left.

Nobody referred to Mr. Truman as "the Boss" or "the old man."

The train reached Washington in the early evening. It seemed strange to see new faces riding in the President's automobile. As I recall, no reporters made a point of trailing the Truman car to the President's home. We had men stationed at the apartment but no reporters went with him.

As I crawled off the train with my bag and typewriter, I realized how tired I was. It was Sunday night. Since the previous Wednesday night I had slept a total of four hours. Everybody who had been in Warm Springs felt the same way. They were red-eyed and their shoulders drooped.

I got in a cab and went home after someone from the U.P. told me we had a man waiting at the Truman apartment.

When I threw my bags into our living room and flopped in a chair, my wife remarked about how dragged-through-the-keyhole I looked. She brought me a drink. I stared at it for a few minutes, then suddenly broke into uncontrollable tears. I tried to stop, but I couldn't. I walked all over the house cursing myself for being such a ninny; I told myself it was just nervous exhaustion; that, hell, I was tough. I argued with myself that the country would survive, that no man was indispensable; that it was so much idle talk that Roosevelt's death was equal to our losing ten divisions.

But I couldn't sell myself and locked myself in my den away from the family. I finally passed out from sheer fatigue. When I got up Monday morning, I felt a little lost and aimless.

On my way to the White House, I stopped at the office to talk with Lyle Wilson. I had asked him several times during the war to assign me as a combat correspondent, but he had declined on grounds that the White House was an important war front in itself and there I would remain.

When I repeated this request, Lyle rejected it. I told him that this would be an ideal time to change men at the White House; that the A.P. was doing it and sending in a man who was a personal friend of the new President.

Lyle heard me patiently, then said, "Get on over to the White House and start learning to know the new boss."

(It is interesting to me that I now know Mr. Truman far better than I ever knew the late President. He's a much easier man to know.)

When I got to the White House, I met my new competition, Ernest B. (Tony) Vaccaro of the Associated Press. The I.N.S., like the U.P., retained their White House man, Bob Nixon.

Tony, who had known Mr. Truman as a Senator, had caused quite a splash on Mr. Truman's first day as President by riding from the Truman apartment to the White House with the new Chief Executive.

I had visions of being scooped and beat for several weeks by Tony because of this personal advantage. But he realized shrewdly that his advantage would be temporary because there were other reporters who knew Mr. Truman, too. And that the President knew better than to hurt himself right at the start by playing favorites.

"You guys," Tony said in the press room that morning,

"have been around here too long for me to try any fast ones on you. Please forget this business about my being close to the President. Every one of you will be, too, before long."

The President scheduled no callers that day, but there was an endless procession of strangers through the lobby. Some went right on into the President's office. Others sat in the lobby and looked important.

New stenographers were in evidence. They were the President's staff from Capitol Hill. When they passed some of the late President's staff in the lobby or in the office corridors, they didn't speak. They didn't know each other and seemed to make little effort toward acquaintance.

During the day we were told that the President and his family would move immediately to Blair House, the government guest house just across Pennsylvania Avenue from the White House and the State Department. They would live there until the Roosevelts moved out with their accumulation of twelve years' trophies and personal belongings. Then the President wanted the house redecorated.

The President also scheduled a press conference for the following day.

Having heard about Mr. Truman's early rising habits, I got up two hours earlier than I usually did next morning and went to Blair House. Standing around the front gate were several sleepy photographers and Vaccaro. It was 7:45 A.M.

Smiling and wearing a trimly tailored topcoat, the President came down the steps about 8:15. A few people gathered on the streetcar loading platform in front of the house cheered him. A passing cab driver yelled, "Give 'em hell, Harry."

The President chuckled and waved. He walked at a rapid clip across Pennsylvania and into the White House grounds.

After the President went into his office, the reporters and photographers walked into the press room.

"Wonder how long this crazy business will keep up?" said a cameraman, rubbing his hand over his unshaven chin.

"I covered his Vice-Presidential campaign," Vaccaro said reassuringly, "and he must have overslept this morning. When he was in the Senate, lots of mornings he had walked two miles, had breakfast, read the newspapers and his mail by the time he got up this morning."

Mr. Truman's first press conference followed shortly, attracting the largest crowd ever to attend such a conference in any administration.

Steve Early and Jonathan Daniels had explained the procedures to the President, but their explanations must not have been too comforting. The President was as nervous as a Derby favorite at the barrier. He started three times before the reporters were all in the room.

The wire service men went in first. Behind them pushed more than three hundred other reporters. The crowd was so big that it spilled over onto the porch outside the President's office.

When we walked up to his desk, he jumped up from his chair. It was Mr. Roosevelt's old desk, but cleared of all the gadgets the late "Boss" loved to collect. The desk was as clear as the flight deck of an aircraft carrier about to receive planes, with the exception of one neat pile of letters and a little clock and fountain pen set. When Mr. Roosevelt was alive, the desk was so littered with gimcracks that there was not room for a hairpin.

Good morning, good morning, the President said as I reached his desk.

(Since Mr. Truman is still in office, I cannot quote his press conference remarks directly, in accordance with a long-established White House rule. Hence the third person or unquoted first person.)

Knowing his habit of speaking rapidly, I asked, "Will you take it sort of slow for us today?"

The President said he would; glad to do anything he could to accommodate the reporters.

Jonathan Daniels leaned over his shoulder to re-emphasize the necessity for speaking slowly. The President agreed. He sat down. Then he got up and asked if everybody was present.

"No sir," shouted a dozen reporters.

"They'll let you know, sir," I told him.

He sat back down, but was on his feet in another few seconds when someone observed that a full quorum had turned out for his debut. The President started to speak. I leaned over and explained that when it was time to start the conference, Bill Donaldson, superintendent of the House press gallery, would shout "all in" from the rear of the room.

The President sat down again. People were pushing us hard from behind. A girl reporter planted her notebook on my shoulder.

"Have you had any official complaints from the boys yet about the early hours you keep?" a reporter asked him.

Another reporter spoke up.

"Probably do some of us good to get up early—it will get us to bed earlier at night."

You just wait, the President said, adding that he had not started yet; that the hours would be even earlier once he got down to real work.

The President seemed to be a little self-conscious about the mob of people standing around his desk staring at him, and comparing notes about his suit and his tie.

He explained to one reporter who had known him in the Senate that he was waiting for the starter's gun. He said he wished he had a high chair so he could see the back of the room.

Finally Donaldson boomed out from the back of the room, "All in."

The President jumped up again and read a little memorandum prepared for him by Daniels and Early, explaining the press conference rules under which he would operate. The rules were exactly the same as those used in the Roosevelt conferences: no direct quotes, "background" material was for use but not for attribution, and "off the record" meant just that, an explanation or fact which was given for guidance and could not be printed or broadcast in any manner.

Then he shuffled the papers he held and read from another memorandum; that he had asked Early, Daniels, Hassett and Rosenman to stay on. He then announced that Leonard Reinsch would help with his press and radio affairs. Reinsch was a new one. Nobody knew him.

Then, speaking so rapidly that it was almost impossible to make notes either in long or shorthand, the President read a letter from Mrs. Roosevelt, endorsed the

Bretton Woods international monetary program, supported the reciprocal trade agreements program, endorsed the Missouri Valley Authority, reviewed his record on anti-discrimination and discussed the pending first conference of the United Nations at San Francisco.

A reporter broke in to ask whether the President, before the San Francisco conference, would see V. M. Molotov, the Soviet Foreign Minister.

The President said bluntly that Molotov would stop by and pay his respects to the President of the United States. And as he should, the President added.

The press conference erupted in a blast of applause at this remark, which still has me puzzled. I suppose the men who started the applause liked the idea of the President acting tough about Russia.

"Have you any plans for Mr. Byrnes to take any public office?"

For the President, this was a tricky one. It had been widely circulated that he would make Byrnes Secretary of State in the near future. The U.N. conference was just about to open and the Secretary of State, E. R. Stettinius, Jr., needed all the support he could muster because he was the top American delegate.

The President said flatly that he had no such plans; that when he wanted Byrnes's advice he would ask for it. Byrnes had been in Washington talking with the new President, and had returned to his home in South Carolina. Thus, the President's remarks sounded like a rebuke and were so reported in some papers.

But this was snap judgment and fast answers. Reporters were getting answers when a few months before they had gotten nothing from Mr. Roosevelt but evasion or negative information.

(In most of the stories about Mr. Truman's first news conference, the President received a laudatory press. He was praised lavishly for his directness and his hard-hitting manner.)

The conference settled down to rapid-fire questioning and rapid-fire answers.

A man in the back of the crowd wanted to know whether the President would lift the government ban on horse racing. Almost at the same second a reporter in another part of the room wanted to know whether the Cabinet would remain the same.

The President interrupted the questioning to say that a fellow in the back of the room had been trying to say something and deserved a chance because the men in the front row were asking most of the questions.

When these questions were answered, I yelled "Thank you, Mr. President." And the wire services started their drive through the thick crowd. As we moved out of the room, I heard the President laughing. I found out later he was amused by the way the wire service men bumped into their colleagues to clear a path to the door.

At first I thought there might be something of a farm-boy pose in Mr. Truman's early rising. That was before I got up every morning at six o'clock for the next three weeks in order to record his two-minute walk across Pennsylvania Avenue. Slowly and sleepily I began to realize this man was in earnest. He *liked* to get up early. He wasn't doing it for the publicity or the pictures.

When he saw us standing in front of Blair House each morning, he stopped and warned us, "Stick with me—I haven't started to get up early yet." And when somebody groaned, the President laughed and took out for the White House at a pace normally reserved for track stars.

By the time we made our first trip with him, I had changed my entire way of life. Midnight once had been a moderate bedtime and I didn't go to work until ten or ten-thirty in the morning. But things were different under the Truman administration. If I stayed up after nine-thirty, I was a yawning wreck. And by ten-thirty in the morning, I was ready for lunch.

While my life was changing, so was the White House staff. Daniels left, and so did Steve Early who became vice president of Pullman Company, Inc. Most of the women secretaries disappeared into other government jobs. Charlie Ross left the St. Louis *Post-Dispatch* to become press secretary.

As one White House stenographer said when she left her job, "My God, you'd think a Republican administration had taken over, the way they cleaned out this place."

The Roosevelts moved out behind truckloads of packing cases. And the Trumans moved in.

The task of literally rebuilding an administration took most of the President's time until June, 1945, when he decided to go to San Francisco for the conclusion of the U.N. conference. Before going to San Francisco, however, he planned a short vacation at Olympia, Washington, with his old Senate friend, Governor Mon C. Wallgren of Washington.

It was our first experience in Presidential air travel. The White House restricted coverage to the three ghouls, two other newspaper representatives, a radio man and a still and movie photographic pool.

We flew out to the coast nonstop in our own C-54. The President traveled aboard *The Sacred Cow*. We arrived late in the day. Next morning the reporters headed for the governor's mansion at six-thirty, thinking that would be in ample time to watch the start of the President's day.

But when we reached Wallgren's handsome home overlooking Puget Sound, we found the President strolling in the rose garden. He had been up for more than a half hour.

The day was active, including two side trips of about fifty miles each, and the reporting of several war developments which were put up to the President for his reaction. I finally eased into bed after eleven that night, having been assured by Ross and the President, himself, that nothing else would happen before daylight.

I realized at eleven-twenty, however, that to take such advice seriously was foolish. My telephone rang at that moment and a voice informed me that the President had just gone to the State Capitol Building, and was there playing the organ.

Is it hard to get to know Mr. Truman? That, my friends, depends entirely on your physique and endurance.

CHAPTER SIXTEEN

The Incurable Missourian

HARRY S. TRUMAN is a typical American.

That may be a statement barren of color and drama, but that is just the way Mr. Truman is. And he's proud of it.

There was nothing typical about Mr. Roosevelt. For twelve years, he fed the American people a straight diet of color and drama, of precedent and the unexpected.

When Mr. Truman entered the White House, people clamored: "Compare the two men for us—what is their big difference?"

One of the best answers was: "Franklin D. Roosevelt was for the people. Harry S. Truman is of the people."

One of Washington's veteran correspondents, assigned by his newspaper to write a color story about the new President, said, "This man's color lies in his utter lack of color. He's Mr. Average. You see him on your bus or streetcar. He sits next to you at the drugstore soda fountain. There must be millions like him."

In his quiet easygoing way, Mr. Truman is an awfully nice person. Smiling most of the time, he is very gregarious and likes to make and keep friends. He is shy around women, but loves nothing better than an evening with the boys, playing the piano, having a few drinks and playing cards.

Mr. Truman often says he did not want to be President. He means it. This fact can well prove to be a handicap in a future political campaign. But handicap or no handicap, the President does not like the imprisonment of the White House. He is irritated by being unable to go and come as he pleases.

Mr. Roosevelt in contrast *wanted* to be President. He loved the pomp and circumstance. But Mr. Truman is a man who is a bit shy about whether to salute, stand still or shake hands when a band plays "Hail to the Chief." I've seen him do all three.

(Usually, everyone present, including the President, stands at rigid attention while "Hail to the Chief" is played.)

Some of the great minds of daily and periodical journalism have devoted thousands of words to telling about Mr. Truman's weaknesses and his faults. As in the case of Mr. Roosevelt, this will be confined to what sort of human being Mr. Truman is, leaving the political factors to the commentators and columnists.

For example, many of Mr. Truman's early biographers went into great detail about his dislike for formality. To the extent of starchy, uninteresting ceremony, that is true. But no President before Mr. Truman has enjoyed so much dressing up in dinner clothes.

He is an impressive figure at evening in either dinner jacket or tails. He is meticulous about his clothes. The four sharp points of his breast pocket handkerchiefs in his business suits attest this.

He is proud of his trim physique and his physical hardiness. He has the rugged constitution of a man many years his junior. Before becoming President, he kept in physical trim by long walks. Now his walking is limited largely by the iron fence surrounding the White House grounds. Thus, most of his exercise is in the White House swimming pool, or pulling wall weights installed for him by the side of the pool.

About his only physical weakness is in his eyes. His eyesight has been poor almost from birth and he has had to wear glasses since grammar school. His eyes are examined by top specialists at fixed intervals, and thus far, the vast amount of reading required of a President has not hurt Mr. Truman.

Some writers have blown up to inane and inaccurate proportions Mr. Truman's alleged love for bourbon whisky. As a matter of fact, he prefers Scotch. He once favored bourbon, but someone gave him a case of Scotch several years back and he learned to like it.

Actually, most stories dealing with Mr. Truman's drinking habits are overdrawn. They tend to show him as a man who "likes" his whisky. For that matter, Mr. Roosevelt "liked" his whisky, too, and not much was ever made of it. Most people who know the two men closely would guess that Mr. Truman drinks no more than Mr. Roosevelt did.

Mr. Roosevelt was not, and certainly Mr. Truman is not, what the country generally regards as "the drinking type" or "heavy drinker."

Mr. Truman likes a highball or two before dinner. If he does not have them, it does not matter much. The only time he really wants a drink is when he is very tired. If he is with friends during a social evening, he may take one or two after dinner. But not on a nightly basis.

Men in the position of the President of the United States simply cannot let themselves use any stimulant to an excess. They have to keep their minds ready for highly important action on a split second's notice.

There are some segments of the public that look with horror upon Mr. Truman's poker playing. Nuts.

Mr. Roosevelt played poker, but I don't recall any church group ever adopting formal resolutions against it.

Poker is a relaxing hobby with Mr. Truman. He has another hobby, too—reading history. But because reading history is a rather colorless pastime, the public usually skips over this fact and reads with interest how the President dealt a few the other night with some of his friends.

Mr. Roosevelt had his stamp collection and his ship models. He also had his large collection of cheap detective mysteries. Mr. Truman has his bicycle deck. He also has his large collection of history books, dealing with past wars of the world, a particularly good collection on the Civil War and histories of the men who preceded him in the White House.

One reason Mr. Truman receives more public criticism than Mr. Roosevelt for doing exactly the same things is that the current President is more open about his social activities. Also, Mr. Roosevelt was a far more imposing, fearful figure than Mr. Truman, and consequently it took more courage to bait him than it does to throw brickbats at the man from Missouri.

The stakes seem to matter little when the President plays poker. He'd as soon play for nickels as for dollars.

He's a smart player, largely through his ability to size up his opponents in a hurry. When he's playing with old friends, he inclines toward recklessness and wild games, many of them known by their particular names only in Missouri.

After he wins a big pot, he usually feels a little sheepish and acts as though he is duty bound to give the losers a better than even chance to get it back. He will remain in succeeding pots far beyond what the mathematical odds would dictate just to put the nickels back in the game.

Mr. Roosevelt was not an excellent poker player. He loved to bluff, preferring to "steal" pots rather than win them. This was the strategist in him, the magnificent manipulator.

Mr. Truman's card-playing style reveals his manner of making quick decisions and sticking with them. But, actually he is not a gambler.

When Mr. Truman can get away from White House routine, he's as happy as a seventh grader let out for the summer holidays.

He finds living behind wired fences, police and Secret Service agents an unnatural existence. Most Presidents felt the same way, but sooner or later, gave in to the system. Mr. Truman has trouble accepting his role.

For one thing, he likes long walks before breakfast. The forty-odd acres of the White House grounds inhibit him, so for a brief time the President, accompanied by two Secret Service men, walked along the streets near the White House.

He took these walks early in the morning—starting out at seven o'clock or earlier. But he was soon discovered and there were stories in every newspaper of the nation.

The President was disappointed. He thought that the next time he went for a walk near the White House, he would be followed by photographers, reporters and assorted spectators.

Stubbornly refusing to walk under such circumstances,

the President figured out a new system. He got in his long, black limousine in the morning, and drove to the outskirts of Washington where he got out and did his walking in rural seclusion.

Because the President used different locations it became virtually impossible for the reporters and photographers to outguess or anticipate him. And the President felt good again.

He's the kind of man who liked to spend off hours in Missouri lodge meetings, or chewing the fat with political cronies in the Kansas City barbershop of Frank Spina.

Now, the lodge members have to come see Mr. Truman. They have to be checked in and out by the Secret Service. And when the President is in Kansas City, Spina comes to him.

When Mr. Roosevelt died, Mr. Truman thought as an average American would: When you move into a house that has been occupied by other people, the place could stand a coat of paint and general freshening.

While this was being done, the President and his family moved out of their $100-a-month apartment and into Blair House.

In the first few months Mr. Truman was quite naïve about the Presidency. This was first visibly demonstrated about a month after he took office.

He had business to do with his banker. So, with little warning to anyone, he called for his automobile and set out for the Hamilton National Bank at Fourteenth and G streets in Washington. He decided to do this at the lunch hour.

The Secret Service had hurriedly ordered escort cars and notified the District of Columbia police. When the entourage stopped in front of the bank, traffic was tied up during the busy lunch hour for blocks in four directions.

When the President came out of the bank and found a cheering crowd waiting for him, he was highly embarrassed. He waved his western-style hat at the people in sort of an apologetic way, and then literally leaped into the car.

A few days later, he wanted to go back to the Senate and have lunch with his old friend, Leslie L. Biffle, secretary of the Senate. Although he had been in the White House but a short time, Mr. Truman was a little homesick for his old home grounds.

But the President, remembering the trip to the bank, asked that there be as little fanfare as possible. When he got to the Capitol, however, Mr. Truman saw he was being accompanied by two carloads of Secret Service agents, a District motorcycle escort and two limousines (rented) of White House reporters.

The President said later to Biffle, "When I go anywhere there are *more* people who have to go with me!"

Mr. Truman discovered rapidly, too, that being President is a twenty-four-hour job. He learned that only on rare evenings can a President have a cold snack out of the icebox and slop around the house in his slippers.

Not long after Mr. Truman assumed office, Washington newspapermen planned a cocktail party and buffet supper for Steve Early who was preparing to leave the White House for his job with Pullman, Inc.

Mr. Truman was told about the party. He said he would like to come and join in paying tribute to Steve.

The President came early and strolled around the big

Presidential Room of the Statler Hotel, greeting friends and in general, having a fine time.

Graham Jackson, the Negro musician from Georgia, was there, playing alternately at the piano, and then at an electric organ. Graham wanted to play something special for the President and Mr. Truman sent word he'd like to hear the Chopin *Polonaise*.

Graham, whose greatest talent is boogie-woogie, but who prides himself on knowing from memory about every musical composition ever written, started in. He gave Chopin some new, hot touches and Mr. Truman smiled broadly throughout the number.

He applauded Graham enthusiastically when the music was done, remarking to a reporter standing by him, "Well, that might not be Chopin, but it was plenty loud."

A waiter brought the President a bountiful plate from the buffet and Mr. Truman sat at a table with Steve and some friends. Everybody was hungry and started eating immediately. Mr. Truman toyed with his food. He looked at his watch several times.

I saw him not eating and wondered why. I walked over to the table.

"Mr. President, can we get you something else?"

"No, Smitty," he said a little sadly. "I'll eat a little here and then I've got to go back to the White House and eat some more. We've got company for dinner and I just have to go back."

The President thought a moment and ate a shrimp.

"It seems," he said more to himself than to his companions, "that there's somebody for supper every night."

Mr. Truman's sense of humor borders on horseplay. Nothing cruel or sarcastic, but obvious.

There are some State Department protocol officers who still cringe a little when they think of the fun Mr. Truman had at a diplomatic reception in San Francisco.

The occasion was the conclusion of the first United Nations conference in June, 1945. Mr. Truman spent a five-day holiday at Olympia, Washington, with Governor Wallgren and flew down to San Francisco to end the conference with a speech.

The first night he arrived, the top item on his schedule was a reception for the heads of all the missions represented at the conference. Secretary of State Stettinius presided at the reception, introducing each delegate and not once missing a name.

A protocol officer greeted the delegates first, and then passed them on to Stettinius who in turn presented them to Mr. Truman.

Vaccaro of the A.P. and I stood just behind the President and Stettinius to hear what conversation, if any, took place. It was just a case of "How do you do' and "Glad to see you" until the protocol man said to Stettinius, "The British Ambassador, the Earl of Halifax.'

"Here's an old friend," Stettinius said as he presented the tall, lanky Ambassador to Mr. Truman who had known Halifax for years.

Then Stettinius turned on the protocol man and with subdued anger told him in certain terms not to make him look stupid by formally presenting people Stettinius knew and worked with almost every day.

The reception line was nearly over with few guests remaining but the large American delegation and staff to shake hands with the President.

Stettinius looked over his shoulder and saw me.

"How about a cigarette?" he asked.

As I handed the pack to him, the President turned around and laughed.

"Well, well, look who's here. How'm I doing, boys?"

We agreed that the President was getting along famously.

"Come on up here and get in the reception line with us," the President said to Vaccaro and me.

We offered faint, startled objections, but the President would have none of them. He grabbed me by one arm and Tony by the other and pulled us into line with Stettinius.

The protocol man coughed nervously and adjusted his tie. Stettinius roared with laughter, and as the last American staff members passed by the President, Stettinius wheeled out of line and passed by us.

In mock solemnity, the Secretary of State bowed and shook hands with each of us, including the President.

Then the President called his military aide, Brigadier General Vaughan who was standing a few feet away. He had Vaughan take his place in the line while the President followed Stettinius, shaking hands in fine diplomatic gravity with me, then the general and Vaccaro.

That ended the reception on a rather uproarious note. The diplomats, standing around sipping champagne punch and staring at us, seemed a little stunned and disbelieving. None of them had the slightest idea who Tony and I were, so the point of the joke was over, or under, as the case may be, their heads.

There was another reception the following day for the civic leaders of San Francisco who did so much to make the conference a success. About four hundred people came to meet the President, and again Stettinius made the presentations.

Stettinius had a new protocol man for the civic reception and he was introducing San Franciscans to the President as though he had known them all his life. The reception was about half over when the protocol man suggested that the President might be fatigued and the reception line could be ended.

This, he explained to Stettinius and Mr. Truman, was quite customary at White House receptions. The President *never* waited to shake hands with the entire line.

Mr. Truman's face clouded momentarily.

"Now wait a minute," he said. "Those people came here to meet me, to shake hands with me, didn't they?"

"Yes, Mr. President," the protocol man said a little nervously, as he sensed something wrong about his recommendation.

"Well, then," the President said, "bring them on. That's what I'm here for—to meet them."

One of Mr. Truman's first big problems was the Berlin meeting of the Big Three in the late summer of 1945.

Mr. Truman did not want to go to Berlin. He felt that with the war over in Europe, and apparently driving toward a successful conclusion in the Pacific, his place was at home.

What he wanted to do was tell Stalin and Churchill that if they wanted to see him, they knew how to get to Washington and he'd be glad to put them up at the White House.

But for many international reasons (most of them Stalin), that could not be done. He decided to go to Berlin only if he could leave there with the assured knowledge that Russia would enter the war against Japan. And before he made final plans for the trip, he had virtual assurance that Russia would agree.

Meantime, the State Department arranged for the President to visit Oslo, Copenhagen and London on his way home from Germany. Mr. Truman agreed reluctantly and we were told to take tails, as well as dinner jackets, for the court appearances.

Accompanying the President on the cruiser *Augusta* were the three wire service men—Bob Nixon of I.N.S., Vaccaro and me—and Morgan Beatty of N.B.C., representing the combined networks. There was also a photographic crew, Hugo Johnson and Al O'Eth of Paramount representing the newsreels, and Tommy Thompson of I.N.P., representing the still picture syndicates.

The ship was barely beyond the Virginia Capes when the President began to argue with himself about the ceremonious side trips to the three European capitals. He did not like the idea.

"I don't know what the American people would think of me," he told us a day out of Newport News, "if I were to go traipsing around Europe at parties with royalty when I should be home at work."

But the next day his mind was made up. He said the first thing he would do upon completion of the Big Three meeting would be to hurry back to Washington and report as soon as possible to Congress.

Mr. Truman has a number of moods, but his rarest one is anger. He almost never gets openly out of sorts or angry unless someone says something unkind or even the slightest bit uncomplimentary about his women folks —his mother, his wife and his daughter.

When a Washington columnist printed that Mr. Truman sent Margaret to their home in Independence, Missouri, for the summer to get her away from Washington parties, Mr. Truman was furious. The connotation was that Margaret had turned into quite a party-goer. The President regarded the column as an unwarranted lie.

This same columnist saw the President some months later and Mr. Truman's staff, knowing his elephantine memory, remained at very close hand. When they saw the President's jaw set and his face flush, they were literally afraid Mr. Truman might throw a punch at the man.

Mr. Truman did not mention the particular offending article to its author, but he gave him a good dressing down on another count.

The President's love for his mother is inspiring. He goes to her little, cream-colored frame cottage at Grandview, Missouri, not far from Independence, at every opportunity. He also talks with her on the telephone frequently.

And when he is with her, the relationship is entirely mother and son. Mrs. Martha Truman is not awed in the slightest by her son's high place in life.

She accepts him as President, but as her son first. Mrs. Truman still talks to him as though he were starting a new semester in high school.

And it's the same kind of motherly advice that women have been giving their sons for years—highly general advice and admonitions to "do what is right" and "take care of yourself." And the President loves it as he sits by her on the sofa of the little house in Grandview.

One time—and I hope it's one of the very few times—I incurred Mr. Truman's unmistaken wrath. And unfortunately, his mother was involved.

She was ninety-three years old in November, 1945, and we asked if Mr. Truman would fly out to see her. Inquiries of Press Secretary Ross brought no answer, however. The White House insisted Mr. Truman had no such plans.

On the morning of her birthday, however, the President got up early and took a look at the weather. It was just after dawn on Sunday and the weather was excellent. So, the President ordered his plane. And with no public announcement, he flew to Grandview.

Many newspapers, and particularly Washington newspapermen, first heard about the flight from radio broadcasts. While Mr. Truman was at his mother's home, he telephoned Roy Roberts, editor of the Kansas City *Star*, and announced his presence. Roy in turn, notified other news offices.

I shared the view of a number of reporters that the President, being the head of the country, is pretty much public property and should not make long plane flights without public knowledge.

The flight to Grandview and back to Washington is about eighteen hundred miles and a lot of things can happen to an airplane in eighteen hundred miles. The least we felt the White House should have done was to have notified the Washington offices of the press associations and networks of the President's trip when he took off.

Mr. Truman began his return flight in midafternoon, landing in Washington shortly after eight o'clock. I was at the airport to meet him, along with other reporters and photographers. When he stepped from the plane, we began questioning him.

With an uncanny ability of mine to speak up at the wrong time, I said to the President during the course of the questioning:

"Mr. President, some of our customers (papers and radio stations) were a little worried about your making a long plane flight without any advance knowledge. Is there any explanation?"

Mr. Truman's almost ever-present smile disappeared. I could see the sharp expression on his face in the light of flaring flashbulbs on the news cameras.

"No, there isn't any explanation. And I don't intend to make any. I don't have to."

Another reporter tried to put a question, but the President continued to talk.

"I just wanted to go out and see my mother without any fuss and fanfare. I just took a notion to go see her and I did."

I made the added mistake of continuing the conversation instead of backing away gracefully.

"But, Mr. President," I asked, "have we in any way ever caused any fuss or fanfare, or caused any interference with a visit to your mother? We were concerned only with the plane flight."

The President said no, that we had not caused any fuss.

"Well, what does this add up to?" said someone who was safely in the background.

"I just took a notion to go see my mother and I did," the President said firmly.

I saw that our point was poorly taken and started to walk away.

The President walked over behind me and tapped me on the shoulder.

"Never mind, Smitty," he said. His voice had changed to a much softer tone. "We'll make a good trip one of these days soon."

I wanted to turn around and tell him that I didn't care if I ever made another trip with a President, but that as long as I was assigned to report his activities for the United Press, I had to do it the best way I could, and as closely as possible.

But I just said, "Good night, Mr. President," and walked away.

Mr. Truman then spoke of "a good trip" to Vaccaro who was itching to say some of the things I wanted to say. And with that he drove away.

I thought we were doing our newspaper and radio clients a service in trying to keep close tabs on the President, and letting him know why we wanted to maintain close coverage. But most of the newspaper editorials I saw sided with him and stoutly defended his right to visit his mother whenever he felt good and ready.

I knew these editorials were being shown to him, so the next time I had a chance to chat with him informally, I confessed that I must have been wrong. And I stressed that I was not trying to pry into his relations with his mother, but only posing the question of whether he should make secret plane trips.

He chuckled and told me to forget it.

"Shucks, I wasn't mad," he said. "I knew you were just doing your job."

There isn't an ounce of pretense in Mr. Truman. He abhors sham.

This was demonstrated on the European trip aboard the *Augusta*. The first afternoon at sea the President wanted a breath of air, so he told his staff and some of the *Augusta*'s officers that he wanted to go out on "the front porch for a while."

The regular navy officers arched their eyebrows at the completely unnautical term "front porch." But his own naval aide smiled knowingly and escorted the President to the forecastle deck.

We later kidded the President about the term, and for saying upstairs and downstairs instead of above and below.

He had a very logical explanation.

"The only time I was at sea before was going to France and back in the last war. Now, wouldn't it be silly for me to try to ape the language of men whose business is ships?"

CHAPTER SEVENTEEN

Debut in the Big Time

THE music was "Japanese Sandman" and the band
had trouble with it.

A few feet away, a Russian captain was having trouble
with a German girl. His medals were carefully encased in
cellophane. He wanted to leave. She didn't. He slapped
her on the side of her head, and she decided he was right
after all. They left.

Then the little band tried "Chattanooga Choo-choo,"
but they played it in march time. The lights were low and
the place smelled like a well-patronized gymnasium.

A *fräulein* in a shedding white fur coat walked up to
me at the bar and asked for a cigarette. I told her to
scram. She yelled, so the interpreter told me, that she was
not German but Egyptian. It was like that all over
Berlin. No Nazis and few Germans. But a lot of Arabs,
Egyptians and Swiss.

It was just like Algiers for a moment when the bartender murmured, *"Bitte?"*

"Two double bourbons," I said.

"Danke," he said with a smile and glided over to the
end of the bar.

A rather potted American army officer overheard me
and staggered up belligerently.

"Did I hear you order bourbon, buddy?"

"That's right, buddy."

"These damned krauts got bourbon?"

"Sure. Just doesn't look like bourbon."

"Who the hell you tryin' to kid?"

"Myself, old man. Pay no attention."

In a few minutes the bartender served up two small glasses of a pink fluid, a watery and unsatisfactory version of cherry pop.

This was Berlin, July, 1945.

The spot: a bombed-out jive joint called *Femina*— the German equivalent of Roseland Ballroom. The girls at the *Femina* danced for fun and offered the hospitality of their unattractive bedrooms in return for a chocolate bar or a few sticks of chewing gum, and in the case of a beautiful favorite, maybe a pack of Camels.

In this joint the word *Schokolade* was our equivalent of "Come up and see my etchings."

My interpreter was an army captain from Chicago— Allen Hackner, who had been a civil engineer before the war. Hackner had a rather direct mind that at times was a little shaking.

Sniffing the cherry pop and promptly ignoring it, Hackner spoke (Algerian papers please copy):

"So you're the White House correspondent for the United Press?"

"Want to make something of it?"

"No, I just wondered."

"Wondered what?"

"Why you aren't out at Potsdam with the President."

It was all Stalin's fault.

I've got to hand it to that man. When he says he wants

no reporters on the premises, there are no reporters on the premises. He couldn't do much about our accompanying President Truman into the German capital, but he said no when it came to passing the barricade at Potsdam where the Big Three meeting was held in 1945.

The President went to the Big Three meeting against his wishes. For one thing, he believed that personal contacts between chiefs of state immediately after a war do not necessarily make for a smoother approach to peace. He thought the series of high-level conferences following the First World War hurt rather than helped the cause of peace.

He went to Berlin, however, convinced that his participation in the meeting would help shorten the war in the Pacific. He had asked Stalin and Churchill to come to Washington. Stalin had to decline, explaining to Mr. Truman that his doctor did not think he was in the proper physical health for a long trip.

It will be a long time again before Mr. Truman and Stalin meet. Possibly never again. Mr. Truman is determined, and has expressed himself on this subject repeatedly, that when and if the Big Three meet again, it will be in the White House. Since the Potsdam meeting, Stalin has turned down another request by Mr. Truman to visit Washington, and again for the same reason—poor health.

But this is no way to tell the story of what happened at Berlin. The best beginning from my point of view is found in the navy log of the President's trip to Germany. At the outset, the log says:

A striking innovation in the membership of the Presidential Party was the inclusion of newspaper men. With the end of the war in Europe, there was no longer so great a need for security as there had been during earlier conferences. The President had no reluctance in telling reporters in June that he expected to go abroad the following month and the news of the conference site was released in London at the end of June.

The President decided to take several reporters with him so that his journey could be fully reported to the American people, and although the President slipped out of Washington without any announcement on the evening of 6 July, there was no doubt in the public mind about his destination. . . .

The log officer's stuff about "a striking innovation" in having reporters along was amazingly naïve. The young man evidently didn't know about some of Mr. Roosevelt's wartime trips.

The phrase "so that his journey could be fully reported to the American people" is another dilly. If Drew Pearson had not cut a corner on censorship the night after Mr. Truman sailed, the entire voyage across the Atlantic would have been kept secret. Pearson, censorship or no censorship, broadcast the fact that the President was on the high seas bound for Antwerp.

Two days later Ross and the President decided that further efforts to keep secrecy were futile, so we were allowed to start filing stories from the cruiser *Augusta* on which we traveled. The reason I feel so strongly in this matter is that it cost me a fine vacation. Instead of riding across the Atlantic in high secrecy and without any work to do, I found myself suddenly projected into the same old White House routine—up at daylight and moving at a dogtrot all day long behind the President.

Before we left the wire service men, the pool photographers and the pool broadcasters were told to take long underwear, in addition to the dinner jackets and tails mentioned previously.

The long underwear was to guard against the severe cold in Berlin. It was July. I took this rather seriously, however, and took in addition to the underwear, a heavy fur-lined jacket borrowed from the skipper of the *Augusta*.

Before going further: future travelers to Berlin in July, heed my warning, hear my sad tale. There is about as much need for long underwear in Berlin in July as there is for a cork helmet in Minnesota in January.

Having spent an ample amount of United Press money on the two suits of evening clothes, I felt rather foolish when we were informed of the President's decision to forego his tour of the British, Norwegian and Danish capitals.

After filing the story of the President's change of plans, I spent a sad evening looking at my pretty tail coat. I was sitting on my bunk idly popping the opera hat that went with the outfit when a marine came in the room to deliver a message. His eyes popped at the sight of a high silk hat aboard a fighting ship.

"Jesus—I mean sir, you're wanted in the President's cabin."

With that, he stalked out, shaking his head. The stewards in the wardroom mess later passed the word that we had a magician aboard.

The trip actually began on July 6 when we left Washington by train and rode overnight to Newport News. We sailed early in the morning. The next day the President explained to the members of his small flag cabin mess that the breakfast hour would be 0700 every morning, but that the late sleepers did not have to abide by his rules.

There went our late sleeping because the reporters had to be on hand when the President was on the move about the ship. We were filing copy around the clock. It was worth at least a paragraph every time he ducked into the boiler room or the sick bay to say hello to the sailors.

At night the *Augusta* turned into a floating movie palace. Movies were shown in the cabin of Secretary of State Byrnes for the President's party, but Mr. Truman rarely attended. Movies also were shown nightly in the wardroom for the officers, and in the well deck for the crew.

Filing copy from the *Augusta* was quite a chore. The copy first had to be submitted to Ross who initialed the pages. Then it was submitted to Commodore James K. Vardaman, the naval aide, who added his endorsement. Finally the copy had to be presented to Captain H. Foskett, skipper of the ship. Foskett actually exercised no censorship, but he was a bear for nautical detail. When he got through with a page of copy it had the salty tang of a page from Jane's *Fighting Ships* or Lovett's *Naval Traditions and Customs.*

The log for July 11 showed:

2000: Motion pictures were shown in the Secretary's cabin. The President witnessed the newsreel and the Navy short subject, "The Fleet That Came to Stay," but did not remain for the feature picture, "Eadie Was A Lady."

All I can say about Mr. Truman's taste in movies is that Secretary Byrnes must be a glutton for punishment.

Byrnes sat through this one. In fact, I don't think he missed a night.

The movie the next night was "To Have and Have Not." The producer of this movie must have been waging a White House campaign because it also was shown to Mr. Roosevelt on the *Quincy* on January 29. Mr. Truman, however, wouldn't look.

Friday, July 13, was a momentous day. The President, Byrnes and Admiral Leahy spent most of the day in conference, preparing for the Big Three. But that night, according to the log:

> There was no movie show this evening. Instead, the President and the members of his mess engaged in a card party held in the President's cabin.

Hollywood seemed to be losing out.

Crossing the Atlantic, we were able to get an interesting insight into Mr. Truman's approach to his first big conference with other heads of state.

The wire service men stood with him one afternoon, watching a shuffleboard game on the forward deck of the cruiser. The brisk wind ripping over the bow fluttered his tweed cap.

The President said quite seriously that he would rather have done anything else in the world at that time than leave the country. The only reason he consented to make the trip, he said, was to shorten the war.

Germany had collapsed, and Japan was growing weaker. The President hammered repeatedly at the same theme—he was on his way to Europe for one primary reason—to save American lives. He wanted to avoid an invasion of the Japanese home islands if possible. The atomic bomb had yet to be tested, so the shortest route to a quick victory over Japan seemed to be Russian participation in the Pacific war.

The President said he was determined that Russia's entrance in the Pacific war would have to be guaranteed at the start of the Potsdam conference. He reasoned that American aid was indispensable to the rebuilding of Europe, but that not one American dime would go into that project until we were assured of more help in defeating the Japanese.

Mr. Truman had reason—he never did tell us what it was—to believe that Russia was ready and willing to enter the Japanese war. But he was taking no chances and planned to ask for it at the start of his meeting with Churchill and Stalin.

Mr. Truman did not like the idea of secret meetings with the British Prime Minister and the Russian Marshal. He thought the time had come for increasingly open discussions. But his conferees did not share his views. And reluctantly he accepted their viewpoint purely because he thought he had an opportunity to shorten the war.

For the first time, I really appreciated Mr. Truman's sincerity. We went to Potsdam understanding what it was all about. This was a far cry from the manner in which Mr. Roosevelt conducted himself in connection with the other wartime meetings of the Big Three. The President gave us no pin-point details of the Potsdam agenda, but he was willing and frank in his discussions of the broader problems.

He was rather serious about his meeting with Stalin and Churchill. I think he realized better than anyone his lack of experience in big time international discussions.

But he did not appear awed in the slightest. He relied heavily on the advice of Leahy and Byrnes and spent hours with them in studying the problems which awaited him in the old castle at Potsdam where he would meet his British and Russian colleagues.

Once we landed at Antwerp, July 15, we didn't see the President again to talk with him at any length until July 26 at Weinheim, Germany, just outside Frankfurt.

The President's party separated at the Brussels-Evere airport. Byrnes and his State Department advisers took off in one plane for Berlin. The President and his staff went in *The Sacred Cow*. And the reporters were assigned to another plane.

The President landed at Gatow airfield, near Potsdam, but our plane went into Templehof airdrome in Berlin.

General Vaughan had messaged ahead, asking that quarters, transportation and communication facilities be provided for us in Berlin. We were agreeably surprised a few hours later when Lieutenant Colonel John R. Redding, commanding the Berlin press camp, escorted us into a beautiful old home. It was in the suburbs of Berlin on the fringe of the press camp at Zehlendorf West. I had a large bedroom to myself. The house was finely furnished.

And on a table in one of the three parlors or living rooms on the main floor was the most important piece of equipment in the house—a telephone connecting us directly with the switchboard serving the White House party at Potsdam.

The house belonged to the head of a large German pharmaceutical firm and had been requisitioned by the Army. Redding informed us our meals would be served at a small restaurant down the street.

The President and his staff established a "Little White House" in Babelsberg, a suburb between Berlin and Potsdam. The house once belonged to a German movie executive who at that time was with a labor battalion in Russia. The entire Babelsberg-Potsdam zone was under Russian control, except for the small American "island" on which the President lived.

Censorship prevented our reporting the first night that Stalin had not arrived, so we marked time until the next morning. Instead of using the house telephone, I walked down the street to Redding's quarters and telephoned Ross. Stalin still had not arrived, so I sent a story saying that the Big Three meeting had been delayed for twenty-four hours. Almost at the same moment, the Berlin man for Reuter's, the British news service, sent a flash announcing the opening of the conference. He later had to kill his story.

Since Stalin had not arrived, the President took advantage of free time on July 16 and went for a brief tour of central Berlin. I got a chance to talk with him a few minutes underneath Hitler's famous balcony of the then-shattered Chancellery. Mr. Truman was moved by the utter destruction of downtown Berlin. Gazing up at the balcony from which Hitler set the world afire, the President waved toward the ruins.

"It just shows," he said, "what can happen when a man overreaches himself."

He looked around at the other buildings, once proud citadels of Nazism and now only burned out shells.

"I never saw such destruction," he told Byrnes who was sitting beside him in an open car. "I don't know whether they learned anything from it or not."

As the President drove back to Babelsberg over the *autobahn*, his car passed long and weary processions of old men, women and children laboring under heavy bundles of their few remaining belongings. These were people in constant search for food and shelter, and seldom did they seem to find anything.

There was an awful stench that covered Berlin shortly after VE-Day. It was the smell of death, rotting bodies and the charred remains of buildings. A rubble dust hung in the air most of the day. The people were dirty. Few smiled. Almost every block had its queue of silent, forlorn people waiting to buy a few slices of bread.

Stalin showed up on July 17, and the meetings got under way. It was evident the first day, however, that there would be little news. Redding and a British colleague held briefings twice a day, but usually the most they could report was that the Big Three and the Foreign Ministers met, or that they dined together and what they had to eat.

We had been told aboard the *Augusta* that the President would shortly send for Vice Admiral Emory S. Land, the American merchant marine boss during the war. After about three days of reporting timetable facts, we got together and decided to use the Land story. This was without any call to Ross at Babelsberg or word to anyone but the reporters who had accompanied the President.

The result was that next morning other correspondents stationed in Berlin received messages from their offices, asking why they had not handled the Land story. They formed a delegation and marched in hurt anger to Redding.

They accused us of having private pipelines into the

President's house. They said we were being shown undue favoritism in our quarters. They complained particularly about our having an electric refrigerator in our house.

We heard about the protests. But we wondered why. The special telephone to Babelsberg had yet to be used. Not one call was ever placed over that telephone. And the refrigerator? Well, it hadn't worked in over a year when we moved into the house. Some of the family men in our party got to tinkering with it, and as family men will do, got it to running.

Justice in this case meant little. Redding, after talking with Ross, regretfully sent over some Signal Corps men to cut the wires on our telephone. Since Redding had six bottles of champagne in our revitalized refrigerator, however, he took a more lenient attitude on that point and allowed the refrigerator to continue in operation.

The telephone was taken out with high ceremony. As soon as the Signal Corps men left the house, I jumped into a jeep and went downtown to what once was Hermann Goering's Air Ministry. I found a very handsome telephone, decorated with mother-of-pearl, and jerked it from its connections. The telephone was hauled immediately to our house and reinstalled. It wouldn't work, but the sign beneath it had the desired needle effect on some of our Berlin colleagues. The sign said: FOR THE USE OF WHITE HOUSE CORRESPONDENTS ONLY.

A few nights later, Ross slipped in from Babelsberg to see us. He was sorry about the protests and advocated patience on our part. From his viewpoint, he was right. He could not put himself in the position of favoring one group of American reporters against another.

"We were all set," one of our crowd told Charlie, "to give the world a fairly honest count on what was going on in Potsdam. Why should the protests of some prima donnas stop that?"

Charlie agreed to the theory, but not to the practical fact. He had to live every day with the Russian and British information men for Stalin and Churchill. The only hope he could offer was that on the way home we would get a full and accurate account of what had happened in Potsdam.

The only news of any appreciable detail came from the Americans. The British supplied even less. And the Russians gave absolutely nothing. The Russians also wanted their colleagues to keep quiet, but the Americans refused to remain bottled up completely.

The President did not like this situation, but there was nothing he could do about it without seriously offending Stalin.

Several interim communiqués could have been issued easily and without jeopardizing the necessary secrecy of the military discussions. But the Russians were adamant. As far as they were concerned, there would be one official announcement—the text of the communiqué at the close of the meeting and after Stalin was well on his way back to Moscow.

Thus the men who were assigned to the President were restricted, as far as the Lig Three meeting was concerned, to reporting the daily briefings which were sadly lacking in facts so important then to the world situation.

Every afternoon some of us, particularly Vaccaro and me, dropped in at Redding's quarters. There was always a drink on the dining room table and around this little table with its dirty cloth we bemoaned our current fate.

The first night our people had some drinks with Redding, he tried to give a presentable party. He was restricted, however, to some purloined French gin and a few drinks of low-proof Scotch. We realized the generosity of his gesture because any alcoholic drink in Berlin at that time was worth better than one hundred dollars a fifth.

The next morning, we canvassed our supply and tried to reciprocate. We gave Redding and his officers two bottles of bourbon brought from the States. He was visibly moved by the offering. It was the first bourbon he had seen, outside of the mess of a high-ranking general, since early in the war.

He graciously opened a bottle and the Washington crowd moved in. Jack Redding is a good friend of mine now, but I don't think he felt too kindly that night when he counted his blessings and found that the persons who had given him the bourbon had consumed same and gone home to bed.

The lack of hard news from Potsdam gave us a good bit of free time. I tried each afternoon to go into Berlin with Hackner who could speak Russian and German. I learned a lot about the war and the German people through this young Chicagoan.

We had a little game we called "Find the Nazi." We tried and tried, but couldn't find one. Every German we talked to either cursed Hitler or in a shoulder-shrugging manner, disclaimed any allegiance or responsibility for the Nazis.

Our search for our first Nazi ended right in our own house. It was the maid Gertrude. Until a few months before the Russians swept through Berlin, Gertrude had been a secretary and interpreter for I. G. Farbenindustrie in Frankfurt.

The surge of the Allied armies finally forced her into Berlin. Highly educated, she had to take domestic work in order to draw daily rations.

Gertrude was serving coffee one night when Hackner asked her how she felt about the Allied victory.

"It was a shame," Gertrude said in her guttural English. "Der Fuehrer made one mistake. He tried to take too much territory in too short a time."

Hackner gasped. Here was an unvarnished, unspoiled Nazi.

"Who started the war, Gertrude?" someone asked.

"That is foolishness," she spat. "The United States declared war on Germany."

"But you were at war before that."

"Not with the United States. What business did your country have in our affairs? Did Germany ever tell the United States how to live?"

A photographer who had been shot at by the Germans from Oran to Ardennes couldn't stand it.

"You God-damned bitch," he shouted. "You know you're lying."

Gertrude looked almost majestic for a moment. She stood at the head of the table, quietly passing coffee cups to us. She ignored the photographer for a few seconds, then set her tray on the table. She straightened up and looked at him.

"Mein Herr," she said deliberately, "you can put steel around my hands, chains on my legs, you can throw me in prison, but you cannot do anything about my mind.

What I believe in, you can do nothing about. I feel this in my heart."

A corporal who was living in the house with us jumped to his feet.

"Throw the bitch out," he roared. "Kick her out in the damned street. And I'll go down in the basement and run out all the other God-damned krauts."

(The doctor-owner of the house, his family and the servants lived in the basement of the house while we were in residence. They were not allowed above the first floor.)

"Wait a minute," Hackner advised as moderator. "Don't be angry with this girl. Look at her as a prime example of just how effective propaganda can be. She really believes what she says. She's been taught from childhood. Look on her as an interesting example, a clinical specimen of the poison Goebbels was able to generate."

Gertrude went ahead quietly serving coffee.

"Look, Gertrude," Hackner said to her softly. "We won't hurt you. We just want to talk. Now tell us how the war started, tell us about Poland."

Her eyes narrowed. She pushed back a falling lock of greasy black hair.

"We were," she said in her painful, slow English, "trying to get room for our people to live. England, Belgium and France were trying to strangle us. Der Fuehrer saw it, and so did the German people. The British wanted us to starve to death. They incited the Poles to attack us. The Poles swept over our border with no notification. And thank God, the Wehrmacht—excuse me, the German Army was there to defend us. That was the Fuehrer's foresight."

Nixon, who had seen a lot of the war, turned red in the face. He stood up and shook his fist in Gertrude's face.

"That is a lie," he told her. "What makes you say a thing like that?"

"Tell us, Gertrude," Hackner cut in, "tell us how that brutal Polish Army attacked the Panzer divisions with their great weapons, their broomsticks and their straw rakes."

The conversation zoomed to a loud, clashing peak.

"Gertrude, how do you know these things you believe are true?" I asked her.

"I read them in my newspaper then. Today I read in my newspaper that the water of Berlin is polluted, that the bread ration is so many grams a day. That is true, too."

"Do you believe Roosevelt was a Jew?"

"That is a political question I cannot answer," she said. "Most German women are not consulted on politics."

"Do you believe Hitler was right in the way he treated the Jews?"

"I have known Jews," was her only answer.

In the lack of any better news, I wrote an interview with Gertrude, based on the long bull session we had in our dining room. And to my surprise, it was widely printed, particularly in England.

Within a matter of hours after we had moved into the house on Berrenstrasse, "Herr Doktor," who had been the head of the house and the owner until we arrived, asked to speak to me.

I met him in the driveway.

He was a little, graying man with a kindly face and

stood leaning against his bicycle. He spoke English that was almost flawless and without accent.

"I just wanted to tell you about my son," he said.

It seemed that his son, sixteen years old, had been pressed into the German fighting forces in the last defense of Berlin. Russian bullets knocked out one eye and seriously wounded him in other parts of the body.

"I'm going now to the little hospital where he is," the doctor said. "I go every night to lie in bed with him. My body warmth helps to keep him alive."

"What do you want of me, Doctor?" I asked.

With a little servient smile, he asked, "Maybe you could help a little in getting some drugs. He has no medicine. He will die in a matter of days."

"What do you want?"

"I have heard of your penicillin. We gave the world the sulfa drugs, but during the war you passed us with this new drug. It might save his life."

"Doctor, I'm a father, too, and German or no German, I'd like to help you, but I can't. That medicine is entirely in the hands of the army medical officer at the evacuation hospital (a few blocks away). Why don't you talk to him?"

The little doctor's shoulders drooped and I felt genuinely sorry for him.

Henry Griffin, one of the A.P.'s top combat photographers, heard some of the conversation.

"Smitty," he interrupted, "tell the guy to go to hell. That son of his probably was shooting at American troops three weeks ago."

The doctor shrugged his shoulders and started to get on his bike.

"Doctor, go over to the army hospital and explain your case."

"There will be questions," he said.

"Sure, when they know that you were the head of one of the big German drug firms, they will ask you how much sulfa you sent to Belsen and Dachau."

He looked a little pained.

"Those were government matters over which I had no control. I am not a Nazi. I'm not a Nazi now. I never have been. It was undoubtedly a mistake by some members of my generation that we did not voice our protest when the Nazi party started into power. But that is all done now. Thank you, Herr Schmidt."

With that, he got on his rickety bicycle and rode away to lie another night next to the tortured body of his bullet-torn child. I felt pretty bad about the whole exchange until that night. I sat in the doctor's library, looking at his books, most of them in German but a few in English. At the back of one shelf was a German-language biography of one of America's great industrialists.

In curiosity I leafed through the book and found a collection of pictures hidden between the pages. Most of the pictures showed the doctor in Nazi uniform, one with Hitler. And there were pictures of his son, then much younger than sixteen, strutting before his parents in the garb of the Nazi youth.

On July 26 we flew to Frankfurt with the President. General Eisenhower put on a big show for him which ended with lunch at the suburban headquarters of Major General A. G. Bolling, commander of the 84th "Railsplitters" Division. It was a handsome German home

and I met the President in what once had been the
library.

"How're things going?" I asked the President.

He shook his head and said vehemently that "they"—
obviously Stalin and Churchill—were giving him a run
for his money. The President knew he was in the Big
Leagues.

They were trying to push the little man from Missouri
around and he wouldn't take it. He pushed back. The
slick phrases of international diplomacy did not faze
him. When a polished diplomat spoke of an *aide mé-
moire,* the President spoke of a memorandum.

When Stalin went to call on Churchill, hordes of
N.V.K.D. agents and more than fifty expert Russian
riflemen covered the one-mile route of his bulletproof
sedan. Going to Churchill's quarters the same evening,
the President, Byrnes and Leahy walked down the road
from their house to the British headquarters, accompanied by two Secret Service agents.

Mr. Truman tried as hard as he could to understand
and cope intelligently with the large accumulation of intricate international problems put before the conference.
The purely military and war problems seemed easier. In
the closing days of the conference, he knew he had a
dangerous, but thoroughly effective trump card in his
hand. He didn't mention it to Stalin or Attlee, but Mr.
Truman had tucked away in a carefully guarded dispatch case a report on the successful test of the atomic
bomb.

We didn't see the President again until we were back
aboard the *Augusta* on August 2 at Plymouth, England.
The Big Three meeting ended about midnight the night

before. We had to leave Berlin in such a hurry that the reporters who accompanied the President were unable to report the Big Three communiqué which was issued some hours after our departure by plane.

Mr. Truman had just finished showing King George VI of England around the ship. The King left in the royal barge and we got under way. We met the President in the flag cabin. He seemed in good spirits, but a little tired. He was glad to be on the way home. He felt rather successful. When we asked when Russia would come into the war, he winked. That was a good sign.

As we—the wire service men and the network representative—walked out of the cabin, the President said casually that he wanted to see us early the next morning. It wouldn't be a story we could write immediately, but he thought we would be interested.

We were—it was the atomic bomb.

At 8:30 A.M. (British double summer time) on the morning of August 3 the President asked us to be seated around the green, felt-covered table in the flag cabin. He laid out a big loose-leaf notebook and began to tell us the fascinating story of the atomic bomb. The New Mexican tests had been completed—Secretary of War Henry L. Stimson flew to Potsdam to report the results. And within a matter of twenty-four or forty-eight hours, the bomb would be used for the first time over Hiroshima.

Mr. Truman's emotions about the atomic bomb seemed to be divided. He was happy and thankful that we had a weapon in our hands which would speed the end of the war. But he was apprehensive over the development of such a monstrous weapon of destruction.

He was confident that its powers to kill could be turned to the purposes of peace and wholesome human advancement. He was confident, too, that such would be the fate of the bomb if left to this nation to determine.

But as to what some other nation might do if it developed facilities to produce such a bomb, that was the worrying question. He knew that for the time being, the United States was the only nation in the world capable of manufacturing the bomb. But he did not know how long we would remain the exclusive producers.

Here was the greatest news story since the invention of gun powder. And what could we do with it? Nothing. Just sit and wait. The President expected word early the next morning that the bomb had been dropped. But when we caught him on deck next day, he shrugged his shoulders. No word yet.

The log for Saturday, August 4:

The President was up at 0500 [5 A.M.] this morning and spent some time strolling about the decks. He appeared completely rested from the strain of the long and tiring conference discussions. He had breakfast early [what the hell does the Navy regard as late?] and spent most of the forenoon studying conference reports and working on the address he planned to deliver on his return to the United States.

August 5: The President spent most of the afternoon poring over voluminous conference reports and working on his report to be delivered to the nation upon his return to Washington.

August 5 was a tense day for us. The President was worried because no word had come from the first atomic bombing. The secret was so big and terrifying that we would not discuss it with each other. I locked my note-book on the first atomic briefing in a safe.

The log for August 6:

The President received the first news of the successful bombing of Japan with the newest and most powerful weapon ever invented by man, the atomic bomb, while he was eating lunch with the crew today.

A few minutes before 1200 [noon] Captain Graham carried him a brief message . . . informing him that . . . Hiroshima had been bombed a few hours before, under perfect weather conditions and with no opposition.

The results of the bombing were reported to be even more successful than previous tests of the weapon had led us to hope for. The President was excited and pleased by this news. Turning to shake Captain Graham's hand, he said, "This is the greatest thing in history."

Ten minutes later, a second report, even more optimistic in tone, arrived from the Secretary of War. When handed this message [all this was going on in the enlisted mess] the President jumped up from his seat, called to the Secretary of State and read it to him.

He said to the Secretary, "It's time for us to get on home!" Then the President called out to the crew to listen for a moment. As the noise in the mess hall died down and the sailors listened expectantly the President announced that he had just received two messages informing him of the highly successful results of our first assault on Japan with a terrifically powerful new weapon, which used an explosive 20,000 times as powerful as a ton of TNT.

As the President left the mess hall with the exciting messages clutched in his hand, the crew cheered and clapped. The President then made his way to the wardroom where he made the same announcement to the ship's officers at lunch and again he was greeted with applause by the officers who saw in this good news a hope that the Pacific war might come to a speedier end.

Mr. Truman almost ran as he walked about the ship spreading the news. He was not actually laughing, but there was a broad, proud smile on his face. In the small dispatch which he waved at the men of the ship, he saw the quick end of the war written between the lines. He saw more than a "hope."

But he saw something else—the problems that would follow in the wake of harnessing atomic energy; problems the likes of which the world had never known.

When the President walked into the wardroom at lunch that day and shouted his good tidings, an awful load lifted from our backs. For the better part of three days we had been on the "inside" of one of the world's most terrible secrets. It was wonderful to be able to talk about it.

The next day we landed at Newport News, Virginia. And the next day Russia went to war with Japan.

Total distance for the trip: 9,346 miles.

CHAPTER EIGHTEEN

You Meet All Kinds

THE duties of a White House correspondent bring him into contact with a wide variety of persons. You run into virtually all of the big names of the world if you stay on the job long enough. And you meet a number of interesting "little" people, too.

Without attempting to be biographical at all, let me tell you some of the things that happened when I bumped into people like Winston Churchill or Madame Chiang Kai-shek.

Winston Churchill

Every time I encounter Winston Churchill he causes me trouble. I don't believe for a minute that he means to do it, primarily because I don't believe he knows me from Adam. But just the same, Churchill is bad news as far as I'm concerned.

The first time was in December, 1941. Just after Pearl Harbor he came flying to Washington to confer for about two weeks with Mr. Roosevelt on how to stand up against Germany and Japan.

He arrived in the late evening and Steve Early made the announcement at a press conference in his office.

The room was jammed. Steve was red-faced and nervous as we piled into his office and there was a snarl in his voice denoting a big story. We had waited for hours and had a fairish idea of what Steve was about to tell us.

There were two stacks of mimeographed announcements on Early's desk. One announcement was a bare, single paragraph. The other one was considerably longer. Steve turned them face down to prevent premature reading.

"Now," Steve said as the reporters quieted, "no one leaves this room until I've finished.

"The Prime Minister of Great Britain, Mr. Winston Churchill, has just arrived in Washington. He is in the White House and with the President now.

"I have two announcements all prepared. One is a brief announcement of his arrival. The other is an explanation of his visit, sort of a communiqué. Now they're both ready for you here. . . ."

Steve motioned to the two stacks of papers before him.

The casual wave of his hand toward the announcements on his desk started the riot. I reached for one pile, just to get the top copy or two. Then things began to happen.

I saw Cornell of A.P. pick up an entire stack of one announcement. So I picked up all of the ones on which I had my hand, figuring we could make a trade. But Cornell seemed in no mood to trade, so I held to three copies of the first announcement, dropped the rest on the floor and made a dive for Cornell.

About fifty other reporters had the same idea and completely smothered Doug and me. The weight of my colleagues on my none too broad shoulders forced me to the floor. As I sagged downward, I grabbed the stack of announcements in Cornell's possession. He pulled at them. So did I. And they tore across the middle, all of them.

An angry roar of rage came from the other reporters, but above the noise of the struggle came a bull-like bellow of infuriated pain.

As the battle raged in front of Early's desk, he was forced steadily into a corner where he was threatened by amputation as his desk was rammed against him.

When I heard the sound of breaking glass, I decided it was time to go, regardless of what part of the announcement I had. By butting a few older and less active correspondents in their ample paunches, I cleared a path to the office door and sprinted for the press room where I finally pieced together enough scraps of paper to collect a single copy of the long text.

When we finished dictating the story, a White House policeman said Early wanted to see me.

With some misgivings I walked into Early's office. Only a crew of drunken firemen with new axes could have produced better debris. Steve was so mad as he paced over the mulch of broken glass—from pictures, lamps and desk ornaments—that he was unable to talk coherently.

I beat it before he could find words sufficiently purple to match his mood.

We had a press conference with Churchill and the President about a week later and saw for the first time Churchill's showmanship in full display.

Churchill obviously knew he was up against another good showman, F.D.R. So, to the howling delight of the photographers Churchill hopped up in his chair beside the President and stood towering over the room, waving his long black cigar with one hand and flashing his famous *V* sign with the other.

The press conference itself was a pencil-pushing nightmare. Mr. Roosevelt quickly finished his own news and turned it over to the Prime Minister.

Churchill rose as Mr. Roosevelt introduced him to "my wolves—my beloved pack of wolves." He took his familiar stance, one foot just a little ahead of the other, and glared at the reporters.

It was a tense moment. The safety of the British Empire hung by the very thin thread of bulldogged British perseverance. The United States was in mortal danger in the Pacific.

The first question came from a British correspondent.

"Mr. Prime Minister," he said in a high, nasal inquiry, "are you of good cheer?"

The President laughed so hard that he nearly choked on his cigarette holder.

The next time Churchill made trouble for me was in South Carolina in the early summer of 1942. The three press association reporters—much to the anguish of Reuter's, the British agency—were the only correspondents to accompany him to an army demonstration at Fort Jackson, South Carolina.

After trailing Churchill all morning over dusty roads and getting ourselves thoroughly filthy, hungry and thirsty, the British would not let us aboard the train for lunch because some members of the P.M.'s "stawff" refused to eat at the same time in the same diner with some bloody journalists.

And the train was parked a great distance from even the nearest water faucet.

(I hope some of the "stawff" will be glad to learn that the Pullman porters and diner waiters—old friends of the three reporters—were so indignant that they gleefully smuggled bountiful helpings of lend-lease delicacies to us.)

The following summer I helped play host to Churchill at a luncheon given for him in Washington by all of the reporters' organizations.

As one of the hosts, I was on the committee which welcomed Churchill to a suite at the Statler Hotel for drinks before lunch in the main ballroom.

We had drinks of every kind awaiting the Prime Minister when he lumbered in with his aides. After the introductions, Churchill stared around the living room, spied a comfortable couch and sat down.

The waiter brought up a tray loaded with a variety of cocktails and straight drinks.

Churchill shook his head and looked up at his hosts.

"You Americans have a savage habit, this drinking before your meals."

Having heard for years that Churchill was a handy man with a bottle, we were aghast.

"I much prefer drinking with my meals," he said. "It would be quite nice to have a whisky with lunch."

The waiter was nervous and started to back away. As he took his first step, Churchill's pudgy arm shot out toward the tray like a well-thrown dart.

"But," he said with a grin, "perhaps . . . second thought."

And he picked up a Martini.

It went down almost at a gulp and he soon had a second. His aide, a starchy young naval officer resplendent in his crisp, high-necked white uniform, sat near Churchill, just across a cocktail table.

The Prime Minister picked up a canapé—caviar on toast. I was fascinated to watch his system. He hooked the piece of toast on his bottom teeth and scraped off all the caviar.

Then he looked around for a place to discard the toast. His aide had just put his own Martini on the cocktail table and was chatting with someone. Churchill saw the glass and plopped the toast into the half-finished drink.

A second later, the aide turned from his chat to pick up his glass. A puzzled look spread over his face and he motioned to the waiter.

"I say," said the officer, "there seems to be a bit of bread in my glass. Could I have another?"

Churchill was busy talking to several people standing by his couch and paid no attention.

The equally puzzled waiter handed the aide another Martini. And the aide took a sip, then resumed his chat. Churchill selected another canapé, this time a mammoth ripe olive.

The Prime Minister nibbled industriously at the olive for a moment, decided he didn't like it and looked around for a place to unload. And again he spotted the aide's half-finished cocktail. Plop went the olive.

I have never seen such a look of confused annoyance as on the face of the aide when he picked up his drink again to find the half-eaten, oversized olive bobbing around beside his perfectly good and untouched green olive.

Churchill gave me trouble all through the war. At the two Quebec conferences with Mr. Roosevelt he made so much news for the British and so little for the Americans.

At Yalta, I had very little to do with him, principally because I was not at Yalta, but in Algiers wanting to be in Yalta.

I saw him again at the Potsdam conference, but he didn't speak. Evidently remembered those Statler Martinis. When Clement Attlee defeated him and Churchill had to go home from Berlin, I thought we'd seen the last of him.

But lo and behold, he turned up right in our back yard in March, 1946, and we trooped out to Fulton, Missouri, with the President to hear Churchill lambaste Russia. I had to sit up all night during that trip, writing the story on his speech.

Of course, that wouldn't bother Churchill. He seems to think that sleep is something one should do in the daytime.

Wendell L. Willkie

I saw Wendell L. Willkie when he wanted a job. Not for the pay, but for a part in the war effort.

For some months before Japan attacked, the Republican party's unsuccessful Presidential candidate of 1940 indicated he would like to be the big boss of defense production. This job later went to Donald M. Nelson.

At any rate, he wanted to serve. A trip to England in 1941 and the sight of a nation at war made him more anxious than ever to be a part of the government.

After Pearl Harbor, national unity became a religion with Willkie. From banquet halls and even prize fight rings, he preached the theme of unity in the drive against the Axis.

Willkie met Churchill on his trip to England, and when the Prime Minister came to this country just after Pearl Harbor, Willkie wanted to renew the acquaintance, he wanted to be around men of action.

One night in early January, 1942, Willkie, in New York, received a call from the White House. It was W. C. Martin, Churchill's secretary, who suggested that the Prime Minister would be glad to see him. Willkie came on the run.

Soon after he reached Washington on the morning of January 13, Madame Perkins called Willkie at his hotel and asked whether he would accept a post as "umpire" or "arbitrator" to assist the President's new National War Labor Board in deliberations on more important labor disputes. Willkie without receiving any details, asked for time to think it over.

Then he hopped into a taxi and dashed for his White House appointment with Churchill. A White House attaché suggested to Willkie that he not enter through the executive offices lest the correspondents spot him. So he arrived at the North Portico and was ushered to the President's study.

Mr. Roosevelt chatted with him briefly, expressing concern over price control legislation then pending in Congress. Then the President started down the second-floor hall to Churchill's workroom, calling back over his shoulder to Willkie as he rolled along in his wheel chair a laughing inquiry whether Wendell would like to become an umpire for the labor board.

Before Willkie could answer, they were at the Prime

Minister's door and the President, after a morning greeting to Churchill, continued on to his office, leaving
Willkie and the pink-cheeked Britisher to talk over the
war.

Meanwhile, however, Steve Early met White House
correspondents for their regular morning press conference and told them of Willkie's appointment with the
President, failing to mention that the real purpose of
the Republican leader's visit was to see Churchill.

Early made public for the first time that Willkie's
name was on a list under consideration by the President
for service as "umpires" to work with the labor board.
Early explained the functions of the umpires and the
fact that the list was incomplete, that Willkie had not
been approached nor had he accepted. Early added cryp-
tically that he thought the post of umpire was "not necessarily the main purpose" of Willkie's visit to the White
House.

The newspapermen discovered quickly that the President was in his own office, but Willkie still was in the
White House. This meant only one thing though they
had not been told: Willkie was talking to Churchill.

After an hour and a half chat with Churchill, Willkie
came out of the White House, feigning surprise at seeing the group of eight or ten White House reporters in
the slushy driveway waiting for him.

"Just a courtesy call, boys," he said, smiling. The reporters snorted "Nuts," letting Willkie know they knew
the real purpose of his visit. He stumblingly admitted
that he had seen "a certain famous visitor," but reminded
the boys "there are many things all of us can't talk about
because of the war."

Willkie was at a loss for comment on Early's story about his being considered as a labor board umpire. "I just can't talk about it now," he begged off. Gossiping off-record, he said he hadn't accepted such a post, knew little about it and that the situation was very indefinite.

About an hour after Willkie left the White House, Early confronted several of the White House reporters with the sad tale that Willkie didn't want the job, wouldn't take it, thus placing Early in an embarrassing position.

"I talked too much this morning to you fellows," Early said ruefully. "Willkie doesn't want the job. Probably isn't big enough for him. Anyway, I've got to come off this limb somehow and come off it right away. Any suggestions?"

Early's newspaper friends had no immediate ideas and left him with the hot potato stinging his hands.

Several hours later, Early told the boys with obvious relief that the Willkie problem had been solved. Willkie had agreed to be an umpire and Madame Perkins had promised never to ask Willkie to take part in a case before the board. Willkie's big objection was that his newly acquired directorships might conflict with his performance as a labor board umpire.

Willkie told some of his friends in Washington after the Churchill conference that the Prime Minister had expressed amazement that Mr. Roosevelt occupied his time with such problems as labor and prices. Churchill explained to Willkie that he left such problems "to Attlee," Clement R. Attlee, British labor leader in Parliament.

(And look what happened to Attlee!)

Willkie also disclosed privately to his friends that he wanted nothing of labor relations and similar functions of a purely domestic nature. What he wanted was an actual inside view of the war. He pressed on Churchill his desire to go to Australia or Singapore and have a look-see for himself as a private citizen, not as an employee of Mr. Roosevelt. Churchill did not commit himself but promised Willkie he would do anything in his power to facilitate arrangements for such a trip once Willkie decided definitely he wanted to go into the Southwest Pacific.

Friends of the President were dubious about giving Willkie a high, responsible post in the war government, not because of his political leanings and past opposition to Mr. Roosevelt but because of his flighty antics.

The afternoon of the day Willkie conferred with Churchill, a man who knew Willkie well, said, "The goddam fool wants to go into the trenches—can you imagine that!"

Actually Willkie didn't want to go into "the trenches" or the Army. Instead he appeared to breathe the incurable desire of a much younger man to be on the scene and see for himself the terrific conflict going on in the Pacific. He wanted to go and come back and then probably go again, interspersing his trips with fine chunks of publicity in this country with his eyewitness version of the war. He still had an eye on the Presidency.

The day Willkie talked with Churchill in Washington had one more hectic angle. He had told Churchill how he still opposed much of Mr. Roosevelt's domestic policy but went along with his foreign policy one hundred per cent. The same night Willkie was to address an annual conference of mayors and in his prepared text, he literally blistered the Roosevelt administration for not centralizing American war production under a central, all-powerful head instead of leaving the production program to the sprawling machinery of O.P.M.

Advance stories on Willkie's address already had moved on press association wires for later release. Then, within an hour or so of the time Willkie was scheduled to start speaking, Mr. Roosevelt announced he would establish a War Production Board with Donald Nelson at the head and empowered to make "final" decisions on all matters of procurement and production. Nelson was given full responsibility for direction of the gigantic production program and Willkie was forced to revise his address drastically, necessitating lengthy corrections and explanations on the press association wires and in newspapers.

Adrian D. Tolley

It would be possible to work at the White House for years and not know Mr. Tolley. And I've never heard anyone refer to him as Adrian—only as Mr. Tolley.

He works for the White House social bureau. His job is to write names.

That might sound like a simple task, but not the way Mr. Tolley does it.

The little, gray-haired man is probably one of the finest penmen in the country.

The White House keeps on hand an ample supply of engraved invitations to dinners, receptions and teas. The only space left blank is the name, the date and the hour.

Mr. Tolley fills in these details by hand in such perfect script that it is virtually impossible to tell the engraving from the hand-done script.

Among Mr. Tolley's other duties are writing in the vital statistics on the hundreds of commissions issued annually by the President.

Madame Chiang Kai-shek

A woman of contrast, she can be as soft and gentle as peach fuzz one moment, and an arrogant, high-handed despot the next. Her friends say it is just a matter of understanding her, and of understanding oriental ways.

Maybe so, but I didn't understand:

In the morning—during her 1943 visit to Washington —she made an appeal for aid for China, battling the Japanese over long, weary years and continuing the fight although her population was hungry and in rags.

In the afternoon she was the honor guest at the most lavish—for its size—reception ever given in Washington. Three thousand people jammed the main ballroom of the Shoreham Hotel and drank hundreds of cases of whisky and champagne. They ate hundreds of pounds of meat, luxurious meat that Washington housewives had not seen at their markets in months. The Chinese Embassy paid the bill which certainly ran over ten thousand dollars.

Her friends explained this apparent discrepancy by saying that the hungry people of China would have been disgraced had the Generalissimo's wife been entertained in anything less than superlative style.

While she was a guest at the White House during the war, she and members of her immediate staff clapped their hands at such important people as Grace Tully, Mr. Roosevelt's private secretary, and other White House officials.

Madame Chiang and her assistants soon learned, however, that the "chop-chop" method of summoning servants in China is not the proper way to call members of the White House staff. When I heard about this, I wondered at the time whether Madame clapped her hands at her professors and schoolmates when she went to school in Georgia.

On the other side of her ledger, she presented valuable, custom-made wrist watches—three hundred dollars apiece—to each Secret Service agent who guarded her during her wartime stay in this country.

Bob Hope

This great comedian was a headliner at the White House Correspondents' Association dinner for Mr. Roosevelt in the spring of 1944.

I sat by the President that night and Hope will never know how much Mr. Roosevelt enjoyed his gentle— and sometimes not so gentle—kidding.

Mr. Roosevelt got two terrific kicks out of Hope's routine. One was when Bob told how Churchill wanted another conference with the President.

"Churchill wants to figure out how to open a second front and still keep Eleanor out of the crossfire," Hope shouted.

Then Hope pointed to the President who was seated at the head table in a big armchair sent over from the White House.

"Willkie," said Hope, "has his eye on the President's chair. But just look what Mr. Roosevelt has on it."

The President laughed so hard that he groaned.

Later, Hope went upstairs to a suite where the correspondents entertained members of the Cabinet and other officials after the dinner. Hope stayed for about thirty minutes, then left to attend another party.

I walked down the hall with him toward the elevator. Suddenly, from a broom closet or stairway off the hall, two young girls about eighteen years old leaped out at Hope.

The prettiest and most aggressive of the two gasped that she wanted Hope's autograph.

"Sure, honey, sure," Hope said amiably, scratching his name on a card offered by the girl.

As he handed it to her, she moved in close and kissed him soundly in what seemed to be a hint-and-run.

Hope stepped back a little sad and shocked.

In his most fatherly tone—and looking at her sternly, Bob said, "Now why did you want to do that?"

"Oh, Bob," said the girl soulfully, "I just couldn't help it."

Shaking his head woefully, Hope said tiredly:

"Look, baby, you've got the shape for it, but me, I'm not in shape for it. S'long."

Spencer Tracy

As a man who has seen only three movies* in his lifetime, I could not have been expected to be too bright about it when I met Spencer Tracy at the White House.

He was being shown around the place one afternoon

* "Birth of A Nation," "The Jazz Singer," and "Gone With the Wind."

by Grace Tully and she introduced him to me. He was a handsome, well-dressed man. I'd never seen a politician that looked like him, so I asked, just to make conversation, where he was from.

Grace covered up my ignorance by quickly steering Tracy to the other end of the White House lobby to meet Bill Simmons, the President's receptionist.

As Tracy walked away, I noticed that he used a very strong cologne. I found it pleasantly masculine and spicy, as the ads say.

Tracy went on to another part of the White House. I noticed Simmons fumbling around among the papers on the desk, obviously hunting for something.

"Some lady," Simmons said, "must have left her handkerchief on my desk. I can smell the perfume."

"Did you shake hands with Mr. Tracy?" I asked.

"Oh, sure," he answered, continuing his search. "Nice fellow."

"Smell your hand, Bill."

Slowly Simmons lifted his right hand to his nose.

"Well, what do you know . . ." he said with surprise. He went and washed.

CHAPTER NINETEEN

Reporting the Light Side

LIEUTENANT COMMANDER WILLIAM M. RIGDON, USN, kept the official log of most of Mr. Roosevelt's major wartime trips. His log on the Yalta trip contained some priceless anecdotes.

He reported the basic facts of the visit aboard the U.S.S. *Quincy* in Great Bitter Lake, Suez Canal, between the President and King Ibn Saud of Saudi Arabia. The King and his royal party journeyed from the Arabian city of Jidda to the rendezvous aboard the *Quincy* and back again on the American destroyer *Murphy*.

Rigdon's log showed:

En route from Jidda to Great Bitter Lake, every day just prior to prayer time, one of the higher (Arabian) officials of the party would contact the ship's navigator and request a bearing on Mecca. The chaplain (Abdul Rahman Djuez) would then lead the congregation in prayer, facing in that direction.

A direct radio circuit was set up from the *Murphy* to the Prime Minister at Mecca. Each half hour the radio operator, who was the Saudi Arabian Director of Communications, would call Mecca and using Arabic language but international procedure, would ask "O.K.?" Mecca would reply "O.K." and sign off.

The King also had in his party an official whose sole duty it was to monitor all the radio news broadcasts and report their substance to him.

The King of Arabia brought an unusual and colorful party with him to the *Quincy* meeting.

My two favorites were Abdullah Ibn Abdul Wahid, chief server of the ceremonial coffee, and Abdullah al Hadrami, the royal purse bearer. Two other important members of the party were Majid Ibn Khathaila, the court astrologer and fortuneteller, and Sirag Dhahran, the official food-taster and caterer.

The boss of the ceremonial coffee came fairly close to blowing up a good bit of the cruiser.

Carrying his coffee-making equipment, including a charcoal stove, the No. 1 coffee man and his assistant got separated from their colleagues on the *Quincy*. A polite American navy officer found them talking excitedly not far from the President's quarters.

Not knowing one word of Arabic, he tried vainly to understand their sign language.

Suddenly the officer nodded brightly and with polite courtliness ushered them into the nearest toilet, or head as they say in the Navy. The Arabs burst out immediately, plainly outraged. They stalked away in full Arabic anger.

The officer reported his apparent mistake and a search was started for Coffee Servers 1 and 2.

They were finally discovered in a small ammunition storage room which they had decided would be a fine place to light their stove. If they had been found after they got their fire going, there's no telling just how explosive the Roosevelt-Saud meeting might have been.

A part of the White House correspondent's life about which the public hears little is the endless succession of dinners he attends.

Before the war, there were only four really big dinners a year—the winter and spring dinners of the very exclusive Gridiron Club, the spring dinner of the White House Correspondents' Association and the annual affair of the National Press Club.

A lot has been added in recent years, however. The Radio Correspondents now have their own dinner, as do the White House News Photographers. The women reporters now have two dinners a year—one by the Newspaper Women's Club, and another by the Women's National Press Club.

Outside the newspaper business, there are many other functions which involve many reporters—the Friendly Sons of St. Patrick, the Alfalfa Club, the J. Russell Young School of Expression (a gag party thrown annually by Young, former White House correspondent for the Washington *Star* and now a District of Columbia commissioner). This list does not include the countless other affairs which have no connection with our business.

The President attends most of these parties, in addition to a number of other smaller-scale functions during the year. Mr. Truman makes almost all of them. The late Mr. Roosevelt confined his attendance to the Gridiron, White House Correspondents' and the Jackson Day dinners in his latter years. He went to one radio dinner before he died.

When the President goes to a dinner, the "regulars" of the White House press room usually accompany him. Since the war, this has meant wearing dinner jackets or white tie frequently. One of the few blessings of the war was the temporary abandonment of dinner clothes.

Mr. Roosevelt had a trick suit. It looked like a dinner jacket—a Tuxedo—but it really wasn't. It was a midnight blue suit with a slightly silky sheen, but no satin on the lapels. With this he wore an everyday white shirt and black bow tie. This way, if everybody dressed, he was dressed, too. If everybody came in business suits, Mr. Roosevelt also was perfectly dressed.

Mr. Roosevelt objected to the Gridiron dinners, for one reason, because he had to wear white tie, and that meant a stiff shirt. He often referred to the dignified Gridironers as "the stuffed—oops, I mean stiff shirt club."

Aside from the stiff shirts, the President also did not like the very forceful needling that a President always receives at a Gridiron dinner regardless of his political inclinations.

When Mr. Truman came into the White House and the time arrived for his first dress dinner, some of the wags around the Press Club bar wagered that the farm boy from Missouri didn't own a piece of evening wear.

They were wrong. Mr. Truman, before he went to the White House, had several formal and informal outfits for summer and winter. He looks unusually well in tails, considering the fact that most men don't unless they are at least six feet tall. Mr. Truman is very erect and that military posture makes for his dashing look in a tail coat.

To give a dinner for a President requires months of work. Settling on a date is the first big chore. Once the date is agreed upon with the White House, the hotel selected usually has to cancel many reservations to clear space for hundreds of guests, not only in the banquet hall and the private dining rooms used for pre-dinner cocktail parties, but for out-of-town guests, too.

An average dinner for the President given by the White House Correspondents' Association costs, with prices like they are now, better than six thousand dollars. A Gridiron Club dinner costs even more because the club goes in for an elaborate wine service and such delicacies as terrapin and breast of capon.

The members of the organizations split up the cost individually and if the club breaks even, everybody is happy.

Most of the work at any of the big dinners given by newspaper and related organizations goes into the show. The Gridiron show is staged by its own members who work for months writing song lyrics and rehearsing casts. Most of the other organizations bring in outside professional talent. This type of show was pioneered by the White House correspondents and their show every year usually presents an array of the biggest stars of Broadway and Hollywood.

The professionals usually donate their services as a favor to the newspapermen and for the privilege of performing before the head of the nation. The club pays their expenses which sometimes run into astronomical figures, particularly if the artists have to be flown from any distance away.

I can remember when Frank Sinatra was just a singer. That was before he became interested in politics.

It was during the fourth term campaign and Sinatra called on the President who was no mean man with a microphone himself. I thought it was something wonderfully new in the usually grim business of electioneering and reported Sinatra's visit in this dispatch for the United Press:

WASHINGTON, SEPT. 29.—(UP)—THE BOYS ARE SITTING AROUND TOOTS SHOR'S NEW YORK CHOP HOUSE AND GRILL A COUPLE OF NIGHTS AGO, SEE, AND WHO WALKS IN BUT BOB HANNEGAN, THE BIG POTATO IN DEMOCRATIC POLITICS.

THIS HANNEGAN WALTZES OVER TO A TABLE WHERE THREE GUYS SIT BEATING THEIR GUMS AND PUTTING AWAY SOME OF SHOR'S STEAKS—FRANKIE SINATRA, WHO MAKES A NICE PIECE OF CHANGE CROONING DAMES TO A FAINT, RAGS RAGLAND, WHO WORKS STEADY AS A MOVIE COMEDIAN AFTER DOING TIME IN BURLESQUE, AND TOOTS HIMSELF.

RAGLAND SAYS TO HANNEGAN, WHO IS CHAIRMAN OF THE DEMOCRATIC NATIONAL COMMITTEE, THAT IT SURE WOULD BE GREAT TO SEE PRESIDENT ROOSEVELT. RAGS AND TOOTS LIKE ROOSEVELT, SEE.

SO DOES FRANKIE. HE'S A DEMOCRAT AND BECAUSE HE'S ONLY 28, HE'S NEVER MARKED A BALLOT FOR ANYBODY ELSE. HE LEARNS TO CROON, LISTENING TO BING CROSBY RECORDS, BUT HE DOESN'T THINK MUCH OF THE POLITICS OF DER BINGLE WHO IS PLUMPING FOR TOM DEWEY.

HANNEGAN, WHO CAN GET IN AND OUT OF THE WHITE HOUSE AS EASY AS HULL OR MARSHALL OR FALA, ASKS THE BOYS HOW THEY WOULD LIKE TO COME DOWN TO WASHINGTON AND MEET MR. BIG.

SEEMS MR. ROOSEVELT IS HAVING A LITTLE TEA FOR A FEW BIG SHOTS SUCH AS HANNEGAN, ED PAULEY, THE PARTY TREASURER AND ASSORTED SENATORS AND EX-GOVERNORS PLUGGING A FOURTH TERM.

AND AS SURE AS CROSBY'S HORSES DON'T WIN RACES, FRANKIE, TOOTS AND RAGS SHOW UP AT THE WHITE HOUSE ABOUT TEA

TIME YESTERDAY. THEY GO IN THROUGH THE EAST ENTRANCE, HANGING THEIR POLO COATS RIGHT BY THE SENATORS'.

THEY WALK IN AND HANNEGAN DOES THE HONORS. FRANKIE GETS A CUP OF TEA, A LITTLE SANDWICH, AND A RIB FROM THE PRESIDENT, WHO THROWS A FAST GAG ABOUT HOW SINATRA IS THE GUY WHO REVIVED AN ART THAT'D BEEN LOST FOR 50 YEARS—THE ART OF FAINTING.

RAGLAND SWEARS SINATRA DOES A DOUBLE-SWOON. FRANKIE IS USED TO HAVING YOUNG BABES IN BOBBY SOCKS TEAR HIS SHIRTS OFF FOR THE BUTTONS, SEE, BUT HE GETS LOOSE LEGS WHEN HE MEETS A MAN WHOSE CROSSLEY RATING IS SOMETHING TO MAKE ANY GUY IN THE RADIO BUSINESS GROAN—OR CROON— WITH ENVY.

"HE SWOONED HIMSELF," IS THE WAY RAGLAND PUTS IT. "WE HAD TO PICK 'IM OFF THE FLOOR TWICE."

RAGLAND ADMITS THIS MAY BE A LITTLE OVERTELLING, BUT HONEST, HE SAYS, FRANKIE GETS QUITE A WALLOP.

"AND I TOLD HIM," SAYS RAGLAND, REFERRING TO THE PRESI-DENT, "THAT IT LOOKS LIKE DEWEY WILL BE THE NEXT GOV-ERNOR OF NEW YORK."

SINATRA GIVES WITH A BLUSH AND GOES STARRY-EYED WHEN A REPORTER WANTS THE "I-WAS-THERE" VERSION OF THE MEETING.

"IT WAS VERY NICE," HE SAYS. "HE KIDDED ME ABOUT THE ART OF HOW TO MAKE GIRLS FAINT."

"DID HE WANT ANY POINTERS?"

"NO, HE DOES VERY WELL HIMSELF."

"DID YOU SING ANYTHING?"

"NO, BUT I WISH I'D HAD THE CHANCE."

THEN SOME NEWSPAPER GUY WHO IS VERY SERIOUS COMES UP AND ASKS, "WHY, MR. SINATRA, ARE YOU IN FAVOR OF A FOURTH TERM?"

"WELL, YOU MIGHT SAY," SAYS THE VOICE, "I'M IN FAVOR OF IT."

FRANKIE LOOKS PRETTY HAPPY, SIGNS AUTOGRAPHS FOR A
FEW WHITE HOUSE GUARDS AND GETS IN A CAR WITH TOOTS AND
RAGS AND OFF THEY GO.

HANNEGAN? HE STAYS BEHIND TO TALK SOME MORE WITH
THE BOSS. BUT FOR PUBLICATION, HE AIN'T TALKING.

In early March, 1942, the war was going very bad for
the United States. A thick gloom hung over much of
Washington. The tenseness reflected itself in many ways.

There were, for example, many critics who attacked
the President's conduct of the war. Mr. Roosevelt was
trying to do his best, and some of the criticism needled
him into open irritation.

One day at a press conference, he told how a slip of
the pen by a commentator or columnist could cause him
to receive a deluge of highly critical mail. He spoke of a
recent letter, demanding that he create a joint general
staff.

The President explained a little wearily that such a
joint staff had been in existence for a long time and working in close co-operation with several meetings a day.

Annoyed by inquiries and statements of this kind, the
President started looking back into history to see if other
leaders had suffered the same kind of troubles.

(President Truman is another Chief Executive who
goes back through history for parallels when he is having pretty rough sledding.)

Mr. Roosevelt found his man in Lucius Aemilius, a
Roman consul who was selected to lead the war against
the Macedonians in 168 B.C. Mr. Roosevelt said Lucius
made an address to an assembly of Roman citizens saying:

In all public places where people congregate, and actually
[the President interjected "Would you believe it?"] in private

parties there are men who know who are leading armies into Macedonia, where the camps ought to be, what strategical positions ought to be occupied, when and by what pass Macedonia ought to be entered, where the magazines are to be formed, by what mode of land and sea transport supplies are to be brought, and when it is better to remain inactive.

The President stopped reading to the reporters for a moment to say this sounded just like Washington. He chuckled when he picked out another passage from the address:

I am not one of those who think that the generals are not to be advised; on the contrary, the man who always acts on his own initiative shows, in my judgment, more arrogance than wisdom.

If then, there is any man who in the interest of the commonwealth feels confident that he can give me good advice in the war which I am to conduct, let him not refuse to help his country, but go with me to Macedonia. I will supply him with a ship, a horse, a tent and his traveling expenses as well.

If anyone thinks this too much trouble, let him not try to act as a sea pilot whilst he is on land. The city itself affords plenty of subjects for conversations, let him confine his loquacity to these; he may rest assured that the discussions in our councils of war will satisfy us.*

It was a sad day when newspapermen started writing about each other. But as long as somebody else started it, I did so in this book without hesitation. A piece about me that caused anguish around our house was written in 1945 and carried in the Boston *Globe*. Here it is, in its entirety:

* The President said he quoted from Book XLIV of Livy, Chap. 22.

GLOBE MAN'S DAILY STORY

Jonathan Daniels, the President's assistant who is now acting as White House press secretary, held a short, to-the-point conference with correspondents a few days after assuming his new duties. A transcript of the proceedings gives this picture:

Reporter (Merriman Smith of the United Press)—Good morning, Mr. Secretary. Any news this morning?

Daniels—I have no news whatever today.

Reporter—Thank you, Mr. Secretary.

Daniels—Were you up late last night, Merriman?

Reporter—Slightly.

Daniels—Did your wife speak to you this morning?

Reporter—Slightly.

While at Warm Springs in the winter of 1944, Bill Hassett, secretary to Mr. Roosevelt, asked to be inducted into the mystic art of hush-puppies. He heard the phrase, and knowing that I was a native Georgian, came to me for details.

I explained that hush-puppies are balls of corn meal dough, flecked with raw onion, and cooked by dropping into deep fat in which fish have been previously fried. The result is a delicious but somewhat heavy bread.

Hassett demanded a sample and I prevailed on some friends in Macon, Georgia—Mrs. E. Dayton Moore and her mother—to prepare a batch of fried fish and hush-puppies for Bill. He then went to the President and asked for a day off.

"And what are you going to do, Bill?" the President asked.

"Go to Macon, Mr. President, and eat hush-puppies."

"What in God's name is that?"

"I don't quite know, sir."

Bill managed to explain in a labored way that it was a fishy sort of bread known only along the muddy river banks of the Deep South. The President in turn suggested that he would like to try some hush-puppies, too, and why couldn't Daisy, his Negro cook at Warm Springs, prepare some for the table at the Little White House.

When Hassett suggested it to Daisy, she flared up. Not over her dead body would such "peasant food" be served to the President.

And what's more the nearest Mr. Roosevelt got to a hush-puppy was a cold one Bill brought back from Macon. And Daisy was offended that it even got inside the house.

A classic story trailed Mr. Roosevelt from town to town during his 1942 "secret" tour of the nation's war plants.

It was about the foreman who got home four hours late. His irate wife wanted to know why. He explained that his shift was held over because President Roosevelt toured his plant.

Next morning he was awakened by a vicious clout over the head.

"You lying bum," shouted his wife who stood over the bed with the morning newspaper in her hand. "President Roosevelt wasn't at your plant yesterday. There's not a line in the paper about him."

As President Roosevelt had his Lucius Aemilius, President Truman has his Alfred Lord Tennyson.

En route to the Potsdam meeting of the Big Three in 1945, I talked with the President about his foreign policy, particularly a speech he had made a few weeks before in Kansas City advocating a republic of the world.

Like a shy school boy, he admitted that the idea was not original with him, neither did he think the League of Nations was original with President Wilson.

Mr. Truman fished in his coat pocket for his wallet and brought out a worn piece of paper. He said he had carried it with him constantly since 1910.

The paper contained ten lines of Tennyson's *Locksley Hall*, written before the middle of the nineteenth century.

As the Presidential train moved toward Norfolk where the Chief Executive was to sail for Germany, Mr. Truman read from the yellowed slip of paper on which he had copied the verse years before:

For I dipt into the future, far as human eye could see,
Saw the vision of the world, and all the wonder that would be;
Saw the heavens fill with commerce, argosies of magic sails,
Pilots of the purple twilight, dropping down with costly bales;
Heard the heavens fill with shouting, and there rained a ghastly dew
From the nations' airy navies grappling in the central blue;
Far along the world-wide whisper of the southwind rushing warm,
With the standards of the peoples plunging through the thunder-storm;
Till the war-drum throbbed no longer, and the battle-flags were furled
In the parliament of man, the federation of the world.

The people of Georgetown, South Carolina, were extremely nice to us during our stay there with Mr. Roosevelt in 1944. They invited the three reporters and many members of the White House staff to an endless succession of fish fries, shad suppers and plantation barbecues.

The Washington gang put their heads together toward the end of the visit and decided we should give a reciprocal party for the Georgetowners—the banker, the sheriff, the storekeepers, the Chamber of Commerce executives. In other words, the solid citizens of the town who had been so nice to us.

We decided to serve three kinds of drinks—Martinis, rum cocktails and Stingers. We sent to Washington for the brandy and crème de menthe with which to make the Stingers, and instead of sending us the white menthe, the dealer sent green.

We made Stingers anyway and when the time for the party arrived—Sunday afternoon on the riverside veranda of the little but comfortable Prince George Hotel—everything was in fine order. We had two waiters off the President's train, and also had filched the services of his Filipino car steward.

The green Stingers were in a large punch bowl. The Martinis and rum cocktails in smaller containers on either side of the bowl. There were lovely trays of canapés—mostly purloined from the President's dining car.

The first guests arrived at five o'clock right on the dot. It was one of the leading citizens of the town and his two daughters, both at least in their thirties.

I offered them drinks. The man was rather offended, explaining that he didn't drink and certainly his daughters didn't. The vision of a horrible flop flew across our thoughts.

Then Gene, the little Filipino steward who had over-heard the entire conversation, suggested politely that maybe the ladies would like some "peppermint punch."

Papa said fine; that was more like it. And Gene served the two spinsters punch cups brimming with Stingers.

I didn't have the nerve to watch the results and fled to the other end of the veranda as the guests began to arrive in volume.

A few of the men took drinks; none of the women, until Gene went through his devilish "peppermint punch" routine.

It seemed that each lady just loved peppermint punch. It was so cute. Then after the second one, all the men were so cute. I could see horrible disaster approach-ing because the leading and good ladies of Georgetown were beginning to feel a little gay.

I grabbed one of the waiters and told him to serve the rum punch to the nondrinking males under the label of a fruit cup. Quite a few tried it.

I cornered one of my colleagues.

"Look, pal," I whispered, "this thing is getting out of control. When these people find out we've been filling them with high-powered jolts of brandy and rum, there'll be hell to pay."

"Let's leave," was his simple remedy.

"No, we can't do that. Maybe if we got them to eat the canapés, it might help."

At that moment, the leading businessman of the town slapped me rather roughly on the back and asked for a private audience. My heart sank as I walked over to a corner with him.

"Smith, there's one thing I want to know," he said sternly.

"Yessir?"

"My wife says she hasn't had such a good time since we were on our honeymoon. What in the hell have you got in those drinks?"

I confessed to the brandy and crème de menthe, but described it as a ladies' drink, utterly harmless.

"Hmm," he said and walked away.

The crowd drifted out, most of them with a happy army officer who offered to take everybody to dinner. Most of them went, but some of us stayed behind to clean up the debris.

One of the most dignified of all the ladies had left singing "Down By the Old Mill Stream," and I was sincerely worried about the horrible deed.

But everybody in our gang felt better next morning when the Leading Businessman called us individually and asked us to a party at his house two days later.

"My wife and I," he explained, "are going to try some of that peppermint punch ourselves."

Norman Davis, then national chairman of the American Red Cross, came back from Hyde Park one night aboard Mr. Roosevelt's special train. Accommodations were crowded that night and Davis could not be given space in the President's private car. Instead, he was given a compartment in the car with the newspapermen.

As he boarded the train, the reporters heard Davis complain rather bitterly about having to be in the same car with the press.

Well, in those days standard travel equipment for one or two of the writing brethren included several five-inch firecrackers for practical jokes.

Davis retired early and in somewhat of an apparent huff. Then the pixies went to work. One of the reporters took two of the big firecrackers, twisted the fuses together. He lighted them, quickly slipped them into the shoe box of Davis' compartment and ran like hell.

In a few seconds there was a deafening explosion. Davis, barefooted and in a nightshirt, shot out of the compartment as though propelled by a slingshot. Gunpowder smoke swirled around him. He let out an unintelligible roar of rage, but not a soul did he see.

Finally, Davis shouted:

"All right, all right."

And went back to bed.

I don't know why so many funny things happen in Brooklyn, and not in other towns.

When Mr. Roosevelt campaigned in New York in 1944, he made a five-hour, four-borough tour which began in Brooklyn.

The crowds in Brooklyn were dense and loud.

Just as his black phaeton rolled by a modest apartment house, a corpulent lady Democrat leaned out of a fourth-floor window and let go with a loud "Yea—Frank!"

She gave the "Frank" so much emphasis that her upper plate popped out of her mouth and dropped like a bomb toward the crowded street.

A split-second later a stalwart, dignified uniformed policeman let out a yelp of pain. The teeth made a solid hit on his head, then splattered over the street.

CHAPTER TWENTY

In Time of Crisis

I T SEEMS," said President Truman to a friend, "there always is another crisis around the corner."

That may have been an epigram at the time, but the President learned later that his wisecrack was a dismal fact.

When he took office, after the first shock of Mr. Roosevelt's death was over, Mr. Truman found himself in a sunny atmosphere of enthusiasm and praise. The war was still on and he seemed to have the solid backing of the nation, even the support of people who a few weeks before were bitter enemies of the New Deal. Many of them had changed their tune. Here was a real Democrat, a relief from the dictatorial Roosevelt policies, a man who would not try to run the entire government himself. That is what they said.

The new President blinked at the news camera flash bulbs which seemed to be blazing in his face every hour. He talked with endless Congressional delegations. He pored over the newspaper editorials. Painstakingly, he checked his own ideas against what seemed to be the judgment of the Congress and the country as a whole. He sensed a popular demand for delegation of authority and decentralization of control. And he took immediate steps to carry out what seemed to be a mandate.

When he made homely, amiable Lewis B. Schwellenbach the new Secretary of Labor, the President said in effect: Okay, Lew, labor is your baby. Handle it.

And the same thing went for the rest of the new Cabinet.

Mixed up in the national enthusiasm for the new President was a certain amount of wartime unity. Labor was operating under its no-strike pledge. Rigid controls over wages and prices kept the economy on a fairly even keel. There were occasional bulges in the anti-inflation line, but for the most part the American economy was about as well-balanced as could be expected in wartime.

Then came the end of the war in Europe. It was like a bellboy knocking on the door of the honeymoon suite. The party was about over. National unity began to deteriorate. There were protests about the redeployment of troops from E.T.O. to the Pacific. There were cries for cessation of certain types of rationing, demands for lower taxes. Manufacturers became increasingly anxious about the production of munitions as they saw some of their competitors switching over to civilian production.

The noise got louder under the White House windows. "Stop the draft . . . bring home my husband . . . I must have a higher price . . . we need a pay raise . . . we want . . . we demand . . ."

Then came VJ-Day and the reconversion derby was on with the rush of an Oklahoma land race, and employer and worker alike jostled each other in the drive toward inflation.

This history is cited in general terms to understand better the transformation of Harry S. Truman, the mild-mannered Missourian peering over the threshold of a better world, into a heavy-handed Chief Executive fighting almost ruthlessly to prevent industrial collapse and national chaos.

Just after the war ended, Mr. Truman tried to drop wartime production controls, rationing and much of the wage-price control system as rapidly as possible. He soon discovered, however, that some of the people who had urged speed were then criticizing him for moving too fast. For the first time, he ran up against nationwide criticism. And he did not like it. No President ever does.

But even as the Congressional sharpshooters got out their squirrel guns and went to work on him, the President found some solace in his sympathetic and philosophical staff. He reasoned that the nation's reconversion to peace was bound to have certain painful moments, regardless of who was in the White House.

Mr. Truman's first big dose of industrial grief came in the closing weeks of 1945 with the automobile and steel strikes, each in itself threatening to disembowel the Administration's reconversion program. Here was a crisis that could not be written off as a "growing pain." It had to be solved lest the return to a productive economy come to a halt.

The solution required a major shake-up in the government's economic administration. Chester Bowles was elevated from the O.P.A. to Economic Stabilizer and Paul Porter was brought in from the Federal Communications Commission to take over the O.P.A. post. To get the auto factories and the steel mills working again, the President had to agree to an expedient "bulge" in the line against inflation, and the pay raises allowed in each industry were offset by approved price increases.

The President heaved a sigh of relief and peeked around the corner. There they came, more crises. This time, walking with his hat crammed down to his famously bushy eyebrows, it was John L. Lewis, head of the United Mine Workers. And not far behind Lewis were the Peck's Bad Boys of the railroad unions, tough and quarrelsome Alvanley Johnston of the engineers and A. F. Whitney of the trainmen.

Mr. Truman tried letting the Labor Department and the Railroad Mediation Board settle these disputes, but the only tangible results had been strike calls.

The coal strike began first and quickly generated public sentiment against Lewis and his miners. It was a strike people could see in a hurry as the nation went into a power famine. The government played a waiting game as Lewis wrangled with the mine operators, waiting for Lewis to become sufficiently worried about public reaction and trends in Congress before seizing the mines. Lewis called a brief truce in his strike, but there was no let-up at the White House. The railroad squeeze was on and again, government seizure became necessary. And again, a truce kept the railroads operating for a few additional days.

The coal situation eased somewhat as Lewis began contract negotiations with the new "employer," the government. But the railroad strike presented a different situation. Twenty unions were involved. Eighteen of them and management agreed to accept a compromise suggested by the President, but not Whitney and Johnston. And while the government, through John R. Steelman, special assistant to the President and White House labor expert, tried to keep the negotiations going, the President was taking a pasting in some of the newspapers.

On May 22, the *Wall Street Journal* said: "President Truman's timorous handling of one strike after another is winning for his administration a 'do nothing' label."

Mr. Truman found himself in his toughest spot yet on the afternoon of May 24, 1946. His office was hot and the men in it were tired, sick and tired of crises.

The nation's railroads lay idle. Lewis and the coal miners were to resume their strike within another day. The worst industrial paralysis in American history was starting to spread.

During the morning, the President met with his full Cabinet. They had discussed various means of ending the rail strike. Some of the Cabinet members advocated caution. Others favored strong-armed action. But no decision was reached.

Then, in the afternoon, the President called back to his office the Cabinet members most vitally involved in the strike, plus his top labor advisers. General Eisenhower was summoned back from a Georgia vacation.

The White House was a scene of mounting tension. The big lobby outside the President's office was littered with cigarette stubs, empty Coca-Cola bottles and crumpled newspapers. Reporters filled every chair. Latecomers lounged on the huge Philippine mahogany table in the center of the lobby.

Inside, the President listened to the clashing waves of conversation breaking over his desk. He doesn't smoke, but he watched some of his colleagues puff nervously on cigars and cigarettes. A secretary handed the President a late dispatch off the Washington City News Service ticker. Perishable foods were endangered in numerous freight yards. Runs on food stores had started.

The big question was how far to go; what type of action to take? The President's mail was full of angry protests. Members of Congress denounced Whitney and Johnston as they would have roared against national enemies. Although there was some division in the Cabinet as to the stringency of Mr. Truman's next move, it had to be his final decision.

Quietly, the President decided. He would go before the people in a radio address that night. He would appeal over the heads of Whitney and Johnston and ask the railroad men to return to work. And he would call in the Army to run the trains by four o'clock the following afternoon if the strike continued.

The conference broke up into smaller conferences about the speech. The President didn't say much as he got up from his big chair and walked from the room. He strolled leisurely over to the White House swimming pool. The President walked into his small dressing room and peeled off his clothes. He got into his swimming trunks and plopped into the pool. For more than a half hour, the President paddled around alone in the small pool. Then he got out, dressed and walked to the family dining room in the White House. He ate a brief evening meal, and returned to his office about six o'clock.

Members of his staff looked at him and immediately sensed a new tranquillity about Mr. Truman. One of them told me "it was the tranquillity of decision."

The President had thought over the railroad strike a thousand times. He had tried everything from compromise and reason to blunt language just short of threats.

But Whitney and Johnston persisted. The strike continued. Mr. Truman knew well enough that the action he was about to take could be politically lethal. But he had made up his mind. He was doing what he thought best for the country.

When he returned to the office from his early dinner, the President had with him a thick pad of penciled notes, ideas for his speech. His repose as he started work was like a tonic to his staff. Behind that repose was his complete lack of fear. It took courage for a politician to decide to use the Army to break a strike—and with the Congressional elections only a few months away.

To my way of thinking, the President found it tough to be tough. Essentially he is a friendly person. He dislikes quarrels. The idea of having to slap down any person or any faction was distasteful. But the old artillery captain came out in him. He saw what he considered his duty and he did it.

His radio speech was written like a hot news story just before edition time. Actually, the last draft of the copy he read on the air was completed only four minutes before he sat down in the Oval Room of the White House and started speaking into the microphones of four networks.

Between six o'clock and ten o'clock in the evening when the President spoke, the scene in his office and in the near-by Cabinet room resembled a busy newspaper rewrite desk with only a few minutes to make a deadline.

Bill Hassett rushed in with a copy of Bartlett's *Familiar Quotations*, hastily thumbing the pages in search of a line that had been suggested for the speech. Judge Rosenman, in his shirt sleeves, walked into the press room to borrow a dose of Bisodol, then returned to the Cabinet room, reading the rough draft of part of the speech to himself as he strolled through the lobby. The President presided over the mill of ideas that was grinding rapidly, with John W. Snyder, the Reconversion boss, and George Allen, one of the President's closest friends and an R.F.C. director, throwing in suggestions.

Charlie Ross walked in and out as parts of the draft were completed, taking the copies back to his own office where he made last minute revisions and straightened out grammatical constructions that would sound awkward over the air. As the President's "reading copy" was completed a sheet at a time, Leonard Reinsch, Mr. Truman's radio adviser, ran over the text with him. Bad phrasings were hastily penciled out and the sheet retyped. Points of emphasis were noted.

At four minutes to ten, the last sheet was rushed to the President in the Oval Room. At ten, he looked at Reinsch who brought down his arm in a sharp gesture to signal the President that he was on the air.

"Timorous" Mr. Truman started out by telling the people that the crisis caused by Johnston and Whitney— he blamed them squarely, repeatedly and personally— was comparable with Pearl Harbor.

"It is time," he said, "for plain speaking.

"The railroads must resume operation. I call upon the men who are now out on strike to return to their jobs and to operate our railroads."

The President's voice was deadly serious, sometimes sharp. When he spoke of Whitney and Johnston, he spoke in clipped sentences. There was a definite note of grim determination as his voice sounded through the loud-speakers of the nation.

"If sufficient workers to operate the trains have not returned by 4 P.M. tomorrow, as head of your government I have no alternative but to operate the trains by using every means within my power. I shall call upon the Army. . . ."

Press association teletypes throughout the country stopped when he spoke of the Army, then began chattering out new leads on the story that seemed to have no ending.

"This emergency is so acute," the President said to the people, "and the issue is so vital that I have requested the Congress to be in session tomorrow at 4 P.M. [Saturday] and I shall appear before a joint session . . . to deliver a message on this subject."

On that curt note, the President finished his speech. The announcers said, "And now ladies and gentlemen, our national anthem."

Mr. Truman's delivery that night probably was his best radio performance to date. He poured conviction and determination into the speech, and he went to bed shortly afterward with a clear conscience. He was aware that he had taken a drastic step, but he was serene in his conviction of the right and justice of his decision.

By the time the light blinked out above his bed shortly before midnight, the President was hearing from the people. Within a matter of minutes after he finished speaking, telegrams were rolling into the White House wire room. By morning thousands had arrived, and this flood of messages continued, most of them lauding the President's stand.

The President was up early Saturday morning. The railroad strike was still on. The coal miners were to resume their strike Monday. Angered by the stubbornness of Whitney and Johnston, the President summoned Steelman and told him to end immediately all government participation in the railroad negotiations.

Most of Saturday was spent working on the speech to Congress. Mr. Truman had a lot of advice from members of his government and he sifted it carefully. The President decided to write one main speech predicated on the assumption that the railroad strike would still be in force when he appeared before the House and Senate. Then the Chief Executive and his staff prepared an alternate opening of four pages to be used if the strike ended before the President went on the air.

Bolstered by the effect of the thousands of praising messages—more than he had ever received on any one issue in so short a time—the President fashioned another hard-hitting speech. More than ever, more than any other time since he had been in the White House, the President felt he had the backing of the public and the support of Congress.

He left the White House at 3:40 P.M. by auto for the House chamber. He was to speak at 4 P.M. Steelman was at the Statler Hotel where he had just witnessed the signing of a contract between the eighteen nonstriking railroad unions and the carriers. The fact that railroad labor itself was aligned 18-2 for the President's suggested solution of their dispute made him feel even more on solid ground.

There was no late news from Whitney and Johnston. During the morning they had tried to submit a new plan through Secretary of State Byrnes. It was unacceptable to the President, however, because it accepted his proposed settlement only if he would then negotiate additional wage increases for the engineers and the trainmen.

The President did not know it then, but at 3:57 P.M. Whitney and Johnston were in a room at the Statler, reluctantly signing a contract with the carriers on the President's terms—a wage increase of eighteen and a half cents an hour. Steelman was with them and it took him a few minutes to reach the Presidential party on Capitol Hill by telephone. Despite last-minute checks by Leslie L. Biffle, the Senate Secretary, and Captain Clark M. Clifford, the President's naval aide, Mr. Truman did not have word of the settlement when he started speaking.

During the brief motor trip to the Hill, the President was grave. His aides and secretaries riding with him in the long, black limousine, wanted to relieve the tension to some extent to put their Chief at complete ease before he faced the big audience in the House chamber. They were wisecracking with each other when the President asked them to stop. He did not want to walk into a joint session of Congress on such a serious occasion with a broad grin on his face born of a joke told in the car.

Mr. Truman was given an enthusiastic greeting by Congress and the applause seemed to make him a trifle impatient. He wanted to get going. After he started speaking, he was broken frequently by sharp hand clapping.

Not until he was starting on the last page of his text did Biffle hand him the small note announcing the end of the rail strike. The President had just said:

"I request the Congress immediately to authorize the President to draft into the armed forces of the United

States all workers who are on strike against their government."

Biffle edged up to the center of the rostrum and handed the note to the President. For a split second, Mr. Truman glanced at the slip of paper, then announced bluntly and without adornment that he had just been informed of the end of the railroad strike. But he returned to his text immediately without varying a syllable or indicating the slightest pleasure over his interpolation.

"These measures may appear to you to be drastic," he said: "They are. I repeat that I recommend them only as temporary emergency expedients and only in cases where workers are striking against the government."

The President took his ovation calmly, and hurried back to his car. He rode back to the White House, again confident that he had done the right thing.

The flood of telegrams to the White House reached new highs. Western Union was so clogged with the thousands of messages that they ran hours behind in delivery and had to install extra equipment in the White House to handle the traffic. There started to appear between the plaudits, however, messages of sharp censure. Whitney returned to his Cleveland headquarters and trumpeted threats of what he would do to the President; he'd spend millions of his union's dollars to lick him; the President had signed his political death warrant.

By Monday morning, the President was well aware that all was not praise for his actions. Opposition began to snowball in Congress. It undoubtedly was disappointing, if not confusing, to the President. He'd been a hero on Saturday, a heel on Monday. This was particularly apparent in the Senate. The House minutes after the President finished speaking Saturday rammed through his emergency legislation in nothing flat. But not the Senate. Republican and Democratic elements teamed up and blocked what they loudly denounced as an abortion on labor's right to strike.

By Tuesday, the President could see that the Senate would not give him what he had asked. Then Lewis got together with Secretary of Interior J. A. Krug and signed a contract with the government which ended the coal strike.

Mr. Truman peeked around the corner again. Right on schedule was another crisis—the turmoil in Congress which threatened not only to block the labor legislation he wanted, but a number of other legislative items, particularly the draft extension.

The *Wall Street Journal* said on May 28: "President Truman's strike control bill, passed by the House in thoughtless haste, is in several respects offensive to our every instinct of political safety and impossible to apply in practice. The country is consequently relying upon the Senate to nullify the President's erratic and probably unconscious plunge in the direction of dictatorship."

One day he was timorous. A few days later, a dictator. The circle seemed to have come full wheel.

(It should be pointed out that one thing the President asked was legislation providing that when the government had to seize an industry, the profits made during government possession would go to the government. That could have been one of the main reasons behind the objections to the Truman program which came from people who cannot be described as pro-labor.)

This chronicle has no end, not for a few years at least.

As soon as the coal mines and the railroads were operating again, the President took another look around the corner. Yes, sir, it was there—a maritime strike.

On June 1, 1946, he put aside his fat folder of crises for a few hours and drove over to the eastern shore of Maryland to accept an honorary degree—his eighth in a year—from little Washington College.

In the bright sun on the platform looking out over the college campus, the President's hair was white. When he took office a year before he was referred to as "gray haired."

The President looked down at the twenty-four graduates seated on the campus lawn. He said he was thankful that under the American system of government, there was sufficient diffusion of power to prevent any one man or group of men from gaining absolute control over the nation.

"Sometimes they think they have [absolute control]," he said, "but it has never turned out that way and it never will."

Including himself.

Set in Linotype Baskerville
Format by A. W. Rushmore
Manufactured by The Haddon Craftsmen
Published by HARPER & BROTHERS
New York and London